Turning Life into Fiction

ROBIN HEMLEY

Graywolf Press

Publication of this volume is made possible in part by a grant provided by the Minnesota State Arts Board, through an appropriation by the Minnesota State Legislature; a grant from the Wells Fargo Foundation Minnesota; and a grant from the National Endowment for the Arts, which believes that a great nation deserves great art. Significant support has also been provided by the Bush Foundation; Target, with support from the Target Foundation; the McKnight Foundation; and other generous contributions from foundations, corporations, and individuals. To these organizations and individuals we offer our heartfelt thanks.

MINNESOTA
STATE ARTS BOARD

NATIONAL
ENDOWMENT
FOR THE ARTS
A great nation
deserves great art.

First published by Story Press © 1994

Published by Graywolf Press
250 Third Avenue North, Suite 600
Minneapolis, Minnesota 55401
All rights reserved.

www.graywolfpress.org

Published in the United States of America

ISBN 978-1-55597-444-2

4 6 8 9 7 5

Library of Congress Control Number: 2005938150

Cover art and design: Julie Metz

For my teacher, Barry Hannah

ACKNOWLEDGMENTS

▼

I want to thank the following people for their help
in the writing of this book:

Madison Smartt Bell

Judith Ortiz Cofer

Anne Czarniecki

Philip Gerard

Philip Graham

Judy Goldman

Margie Hemley

Jack Heffron

David Jauss

Bret Lott

Ian MacMillan

Fiona McCrae

Josip Novakovich

Jerry Saviano

Steven Sherrill

David Shields

Sharon Solwitz

Peter Turchi

Steve Yarbrough

Xu Xi

CONTENTS

▼

Turning **Life** into Fiction

❡

Experience Versus the Imagination:
A Transformation

"What kind of fiction do you write?" I've been asked more than once.

"What do you mean?" I ask.

"Do you write true fiction?" I'm asked.

This question always stumps me. I stammer in bewilderment for a bit and come up with some unsatisfactory answer about how I sometimes write from my experiences. But that makes me sound like I'm a writer of true confessions.

I don't mind when people ask me if anything in my stories is autobiographical. For me, the two questions are different. The people who want to know if I write true fiction make me bristle. I think the trouble lies in that true things (things that really happened in real life to someone really real) are sometimes considered more important than things that never happened. On the other hand, people sometimes want to know what really happened because they're interested in the process of changing experience into fiction. I don't think there's anything wrong with that.

Someone once told me she didn't believe in autobiographical fiction, that if it wasn't completely imagined, one wasn't writing fiction. That's such an absurd statement I'm sure I'll remember it my whole life. Good fiction depends on the perceptions and observations of the writer, not on the source of the material.

Still, many writers distrust fiction that smacks of autobiography. They believe that autobiographical fiction represents in some way a failure of the writer's imagination, or that such writers have only "one good book" in them and, after they have finished their autobiographical effort, they will have spent their creativity and no more will be heard from them. There's

< 3 >

an air of smugness in that kind of attitude. The writer who makes such a claim is, in effect, saying, first, "Autobiographical writing is not *real* writing," and second, "I'm a real writer, and people who want to be real writers should write like me—that is, from the unlimited stores of my superior imagination!"

Such a writer might point to Harper Lee's semi-autobiographical book, *To Kill a Mockingbird,* as an example of the pitfalls of autobiographical writing. Until a couple of years ago, I wasn't sure if Lee was still alive, so I went to the library and found that she was supposedly working on a second novel. That's a long time to wait for a second novel, but so what? If *To Kill a Mockingbird* is the one good book Harper will ever publish, that's not a fate worse than death. I'd settle for writing such a book.

There might be *some* truth in the fact that writers whose first novels are autobiographical find it more difficult than other writers to write a second novel, but writers of any stripe have a difficult time following a first novel. I've heard that as many as half of all first novelists never write a second.

There's definitely a tendency for writers to write autobiographical first novels—the standard coming-of-age novel, inevitably compared by one reviewer or another to *Catcher in the Rye* if the teenage protagonist is at all disaffected with society. And what teenager isn't? I'd bet that more reviewers use the protagonist Holden Caufield as a comparison to the main character in the book they're reviewing than any other character, with perhaps the exception of Scout, the young protagonist of *To Kill a Mockingbird*. It's no wonder. Growing up is the natural territory of any young novelist, and there's absolutely nothing wrong with adding one's own version of this life transition to the pile. The overall experience of growing up might be the same for most people, but the individual details of each person's story are always unique, and that's what makes good fiction: the details.

For my part, I assiduously avoided writing a growing-up story for my first novel, *The Last Studebaker.* That, however, doesn't mean my novel was devoid of real-life experience. My novel is set in South Bend, Indiana, where I lived for a couple of years during high school. Many of the details about South Bend in the book are things I have observed firsthand.

One of the main characters in the book, a woman named Lois, is loosely based on a friend with whom I used to frequent garage sales, which is one of the central activities of the book. My real-life friend has five children; the character in the book has two, neither of whom are much like any of my friend's children. The children in the book, an eleven-year-old girl named Meg and her sixteen-year-old sister, Gail, are modeled after myself, when I was Meg's age, and my brother Jonathan, who is five years older than me. The sexes are different, but the behavior is much the same.

And that's the way it is throughout my novel. Plenty of incidents and characters are based on real life, but nearly all have been transformed. As we'll see in this book, transformation is the key to writing fiction based on real life.

Even the most autobiographical book stretches the truth from time to time, exaggerating and bending events to fit the story or the characters. And the most outlandish stories often contain some bit of real life or autobiography. The important fact to keep in mind is that a transformation is always involved. In writing fiction, a dialogue is always going on between one's personal experience and one's imagination.

Sometimes, I'll be discussing a story in a workshop, and several people will remark that a particular episode seems unbelievable.

"I just don't believe that Michael would stab Fran for saying that he had halitosis," one student will say.

"I agree completely," says another student.

The rest of the class nods.

At this point I look in the direction of the author and see that he has this smug look on his face, and I know what he's going to say next.

"But it really happened!" he says with an air of superiority, as though he's just pulled one over on us.

"It doesn't matter that it really happened," I explain as patiently as possible. "The question to ask is, 'Is it believable?' The worst defense a writer can use is the excuse, 'But it really happened!'"

The fact that something really happened does not make it good fiction. In fact, it's irrelevant, at least in terms of the story's quality. Plenty of things happen in real life that just don't seem believable on the page. On the other hand, the fact that it really happened shouldn't exclude the material from one's writing. The trick, of course, comes in molding the factual material to the specifications of one's fictional world.

With any kind of fiction, there are basically two ways to incorporate your real-life experiences. Either you write a story based on something that happened to you, or you write a largely imagined story, with snippets from your life woven into the basic fabric of the story. You might set your novel during the last ice age, and your main characters might be a family of ir-ritable mastodons. But the main mastodon, the way he chews his food with his mouth open, might clearly portray your father. In this way, every novel is based on real life. It's nearly impossible to stop our real lives from intrud-ing into our fiction, even when the story is clearly not about ourselves.

We can even see real life bleeding into the fictional world of a writer as absurdist as Samuel Beckett. In a letter to a friend, he wrote of watching old men in the park flying kites "immense distances" and "right out of sight," and how transfixed he was by the sight. "My next old man or old young man [meaning his next character in a fictional work] must be a kite flier," he wrote. At the time, Beckett was working on his novel *Murphy,* and true to his word, he included the following scene in which an old man is lying in bed, imagining himself flying a kite. Note the similarities between the wording in his letter and that of the scene:

> "Before you go," said Mr. Kelly, "you might hand me the tail of my kite. Some tassels have come adrift."
>
> Celia went to the cupboard where he kept his kite, took out the tail and loose tassels and brought them over to the bed.
>
> "As you say," said Mr. Kelly, "hark to the wind. I shall fly her out of sight tomorrow."
>
> He fumbled vaguely at the coils of the tail. Already he was in position, straining his eyes for the speck that was he, digging in his heels against the immense pull skyward. Celia kissed him and left him.
>
> "God willing," said Mr. Kelly, "right out of sight."

I think that's a marvelous scene. You don't have to know anything about the book to feel the richness of this image of an old man lying in bed, pre-tending to fly his kite. Later in the book, Celia looks for Mr. Kelly in the park where other old men are flying their kites. Beckett has transformed his real-life experience in the way all good fiction writers do: building on the initial image, stretching it, exaggerating it, seeing how far he can take it.

In an interview with Robert S. Boone, novelist Ann Beattie claims she's "never written anything directly autobiographical. But at the same time I've never written anything that didn't honestly reflect some emotional state." She also says that she never directly transfers an overheard conversation into her fiction, but molds it to the story. "What I hear in a New York City restaurant will be cast in an Iowa City bus depot."

Let me tell you a couple of autobiographical stories.

One time in elementary school, I built a time machine in my art class. I announced that I was going to send Ann Holmes, a girl I had a crush on, back in time. My art teacher made a point of telling the class it wouldn't work. I insisted it would. Half the class believed my teacher, half believed me because, I suppose, I acted so confident in my invention, which was nothing more than a large cardboard box with Styrofoam knobs. The day came when the machine was ready. I helped Ann into the box, turned a few knobs and . . . Ann went back in time. Well, of course not. After a minute, Ann's voice, from inside the box, said, "I'm still here."

"No, you're not," I said.

Ann stepped out of the box and announced, "It didn't work."

"You see?" my teacher said.

"Good job, Bemel," said one of my classmates. Bemel was my nickname. Simply a strange bastardization of Hemley. It doesn't mean anything, but for some reason it still makes me cringe to think of it.

The teacher savored her victory and asked the class what lesson they had learned. Tony Trimball, a little turncoat who had just that morning asked to be the second person I sent back in time, raised his hand. He waved it around in that annoying, urgent manner of fourth-grade boys.

"Yes, Tony?" the art teacher asked.

"Don't say things that aren't true."

Of course, I was ostracized for the rest of the day, and I didn't get many valentines that year. I was the fool, and it probably hurt me a lot at the time. Now I'm proud of my fourth-grade self, just as I'm proud of other goofy things I did at that age, like wearing my pajamas to school because I bet my mother that I could get away with it. (A gentleman's bet, we used to call it; no money involved. My mom didn't encourage gambling.) I insisted that my pajamas looked like regular clothes. And I almost *did* get away with it. The only people who noticed were my fourth-grade math teacher, Mrs. Hill, and her student assistant. During a math quiz, I noticed them looking my way and giggling. Mrs. Hill called me over to her desk and whispered, "Robin, are you wearing your pajamas?"

"No, Mrs. Hill."

"Are you sure?" she asked again, tilting her head slightly.

"Yes, Mrs. Hill."

I didn't like Mrs. Hill at the time, but now I do. She, too, could have humiliated me in front of the class, if she chose. She, unlike my art teacher, had an innate appreciation for the ridiculous, which, after all, isn't that far removed from the sublime. And you'd think the art teacher, not the math teacher, would be the one to foster my creativity.

I could say that these two stories about myself are untrue. Completely untrue. Didn't happen. Nada. No such person as Mrs. Hill. And my art teacher thought I was Picasso.

Would it matter that the stories didn't happen?

The question to ask is not, "Did it really happen?" but "Is it believable?" If it *could* have happened, if it has some relevance to what it means to be alive, that's all that matters. Believability. Authenticity. That's why "But it really happened!" is such a lame defense for a story you've written. If it doesn't seem believable, forget it. I'm not going to be moved by your story.

I do acknowledge there's such a thing as simple curiosity, so I'll tell you what's true and what's not true.

Both stories happened. Almost exactly as I told them. The key word is *almost*. The fictional part is in the details.

Mrs. Hill really was my fourth-grade teacher, and I really wore my pajamas to school, and that conversation occurred pretty much as I said it did. Of course, I couldn't vouch for every word. If I were writing a story about the pajama incident, I'd make up even more details to make the story seem believable. I'd tell you what the pajamas looked like. They must have been made out of some coarse material, not your typical satiny pj's, and the shirt probably had a collar.

And that whole thing with the art teacher happened as well. I'm pretty sure Ann Holmes was the one I sent back in time, though I'm not positive. It doesn't matter. It could have been Ann Holmes. The dialogue, of course, was made up, though something very similar was probably said.

Tony Trimball didn't exist, but Tony Turnbull did, and hopefully still does somewhere. Tony was my friend from second through fifth grade, when my family moved away.

My nickname was Bemel, and it does give me a strange twinge when I recall the hated name. So in this case, I was being true to the emotional experience of being in fourth grade. It's a hundred times more important for the story to seem emotionally honest than for the story to be honest in the conventional sense.

I don't know if someone called me Bemel when the time machine failed. But when I came to that moment in the story, my mind just flashed, "Bemel." It's not only the details but the associations that count in writing fiction. All artists, not only fiction writers, have associative minds. One event recalls another. And part of fictionalizing material often involves putting two real details (two actual events or observations from your life) side by side, even though they might have been separated in actuality by months or years. That's fiction, too: the ordering of events.

So one can be honest without being truthful. One can be believable without being factual.

But remember what I said about believability. Maybe I'm just *saying* the above stories really happened so you'll believe me. Maybe Tony Turnbull is as much a fiction as Tony Trimball. Maybe I'm an incorrigible liar and need to seek therapy.

Maybe. I'm not telling.

I'm not trying to frustrate you or show you how clever I am. I'm just trying to make a point.

Gail Godwin, in her essay "Becoming a Writer," writes about some of the formative experiences of her life and how they shaped her as a fiction writer. Near the end of her essay, she writes:

This account of my own unfolding as a writer has been the truth. But it is also full of lies, many of which I'm not aware of. But in one sense, perhaps the most important, it is all true: it could have been written by nobody but me. What I have chosen to tell, how I have chosen to tell it, and what I have chosen not to tell, express me and the kind of writer I am.

If you want to write at all, whether from real life or not, you must be willing and able to use your imagination. That means you must be willing to take risks and sometimes look the fool. You must be willing to transform experience, not simply record it. If you were a good liar, daydreamer, or troublemaker as a child, you'll probably make a good fiction writer. Daydreams, lies, and trouble. That's the stuff of fiction.

▼

CHAPTER ONE

Journals

To understand how to turn life into fiction, one must be observant. As a fiction writer, you try to convince the reader of the authenticity of the world you're creating, and that's why a journal comes in handy. Not every writer keeps a journal, and it's not necessary, but some writers find it invaluable. It's akin to an artist's sketchbook. It hones a writer's skills and makes him more observant. At parties, Victor Hugo used to stop conversations in mid-sentence, take a little notebook from his pocket, and jot down what someone had said. A year later, the conversation would appear in his latest novel.

We're not talking about diaries here, though many writers have kept diaries. The diaries of Virginia Woolf and Anaïs Nin are widely considered works of art. There *is* some crossover between the subject matter of diaries and that of journals, but I see a diary as a day-to-day recording of existence, a reckoning of sorts, a justification of one's existence through a kind of chronicling that ends, ideally, at the end of one's life. Keeping a diary is certainly a creative act, but diaries are essentially private, although Thomas Mallon, in his book about people and their diaries, *A Book of One's Own*, convincingly argues that diaries do have an audience, whether one's future self, a friend or relative, or posterity.

Some people might find it crude to see one's experience as grist for the mill, and certainly if you go through life simply trying to figure out how to use every real-life experience in your fiction, then, emotionally and spiritually, you'll lead an impoverished existence. A certain amount of distance is necessary to write successfully about real life, and if you always maintain that distance, you're not really living your life to its fullest.

But nothing is wrong with jotting down a detail here and there, an overheard conversation, a memory that comes upon you, a dream. Some writers

< 11 >

believe that if you can't remember something, it must not be important, so they see no use for a journal. Each to her own, but if I didn't have my journal with me the other day, I would have had nowhere to record the slogan I saw on a plumber's truck on the highway: "A good flush is better than a full house." Okay, it's corny, but I like a plumber with a sense of humor. Maybe I'll never use this slogan in a story. It doesn't matter. To me, there's something wonderful in simply recording this fragment of plumber wit.

Maybe someday I'll be writing a story with a plumber in it, and I'll think to myself, *What was that slogan I saw on the side of that plumber's truck that one time? Three of a kind are better than two pair? Nope, that wasn't it.* Luckily, I'll have my journal to flip through to refresh my memory. And in the process of flipping through my journals, I'll probably come across three or four other intriguing fragments or story ideas I've completely forgotten about.

Writers and Their Journals

I've kept a journal on a capricious basis since I was sixteen. For me, my journal is a supplement to my imagination. I recently heard of a novelist who cuts out magazine photos of people, pastes them on his study wall, and uses them as the basis for his character descriptions. I completely approve. Writing is hard enough, and I welcome anything that helps me along. Besides, I can't help but filter what I see through my imagination, so even my most autobiographical fiction is, in a sense, wholly imagined.

As F. Scott Fitzgerald's career was waning, he not only recorded observations and ideas in his notebooks, he also purposefully set about "stripping" his unpublished short stories for phrases and descriptions he might later use in his novels. The entries were dutifully logged by his secretaries. This stripping down of stories for later use is by no means a terrible thing to do. Most writers cull phrases or paragraphs from failed stories for later use. It's just rare for a writer to be so deliberate about it.

The Austrian writer Peter Handke uses the journal form as an end in itself in his novel *The Weight of the World*. Critic June Schlueter writes of *The Weight of the World*:

> Each entry stands as an independent fragment of experience. The
> seemingly random images, observations, memories, and thoughts

of the journals . . . are held together only by the central consciousness of the author-narrator, who remembers and creates a mélange
of outer- and inner-world experiences, mingling present and past,
real and surreal, convictions, speculations, impressions, and ideas.

I can't think of a more concise definition of a journal.

There's a certain random quality to a journal, or there should be. Ab-
sent from a journal is the deliberate, day-to-dayness of a diary. Part of the
joy of keeping a journal lies in its randomness. It's your own personal *I
Ching, or Book of Changes*. Instead of casting sticks to tell your future, you
flip pages.

Here are a few randomly chosen excerpts from Peter Handke's *The
Weight of the World*:

Alone with the glugging of the dishwasher.

"Are you disgusted with me?" "No, I knew what to expect."

F. imitated my way of laughing: a malicious laugh which I hated in
my father.

Names are ridiculous. Why couldn't I have a number instead?

The balloon vanishing over the treetops: so this is death, I thought
for a moment.

Most of the book tends toward the morose and self-serious in this way.
Nothing is wrong with that. With a title like *The Weight of the World,* you
should have some idea of what you're wading into.

Allen Ginsberg's journals are a lot more whimsical, though still quite
serious in their own way. In his journals of the early 1950s and '60s, his
musings often take on the tone of the satirist and gadfly:

Do big fat American people know their Seoul from a hole in the
ground?

I can't even commit a crime with a Clean Conscience anymore.

"You're fighting problems that are outside your control—in this business (Dentistry)—you gotta outguess the factors that are involved." Meaning: "my patients never brush their teeth properly.

"After I got thru living in Milwaukee . . . I developed a taste for Blatz."

Ginsberg even quotes from Kafka's diaries in his journals:

Feb. 25, 1912—"Hold fast to the diary from today on! Write regularly! Don't surrender! Even if no salvation should come, I want to be worthy of it every moment."

David Michael Kaplan, a short-story writer and novelist, keeps a journal as a source for ideas for his fiction. Kaplan says, "My working method is to keep a journal, and I've been keeping a journal for God knows how many years, twenty years? I've got a whole shelf full. I couldn't work without them. Whenever there's something that grabs me, what I think of as the potential seed idea for a story, around which eventually other seed ideas will coalesce like a crystal, I copy it down in the journal. They can come from anywhere—a conversation I overhear, or something that I see in passing, or they can be something that I read in the newspaper, or an anecdote that somebody tells me, that might not be much in itself, but it has something there that interests me—or it can be something that directly happened to me. Anyway, all of these things are kind of in the air, they're floating around. They're there to be grabbed, and I find that if I don't grab them, if I don't write them down in this journal that goes everywhere with me, then they disappear. You don't remember. A lot of people might say the things that you don't remember aren't worth remembering anyway. The stuff that's important, that'll become a story eventually, you'll remember. But I don't think that's actually true. From my own experience it hasn't *been* true. Things that developed and became parts of stories of mine are things that I would not have remembered otherwise."

Judith Ortiz Cofer, an author known equally for her fiction, poetry, and essays, doesn't keep a formal journal anymore, though at one time she did.

These days, she travels a lot and finds index cards more convenient and useful in her creative process. "I mainly put a bunch of index cards in my purse," she says. "It works better than an actual notebook because it allows me to shuffle them and think of something in a different structure without having the linear form that a consecutive journal gives it."

Triggers

A journal is essentially the place we store triggers—things that have caught our attention and started our imaginations rolling. Anything can be a trigger for your imagination, from seeing a license plate (a story of David Michael Kaplan's, "Anne Rey," came from a chance spotting of a vanity license plate on an L.A. freeway) to an overheard snatch of dialogue. It's not important what the trigger is. What's important is that something gets your imagination going, allowing you to make that leap from fact to fiction—and also that you write it down.

The trigger for Sue Miller's wonderful story, "Inventing the Abbotts," which originally was titled "The Lover of Women," was a chance meeting with an old boyfriend. As she explains in the 1987 edition of *The Best American Short Stories:* "In July of 1983, while I was helping my father repair his house in the mountains, I ran into a man who'd been my first sweetheart in that summer place, when I was fourteen. We sat around together for a long, black-fly-ridden New Hampshire evening, talking about the various complications and joys and wrinkles of the intervening twenty-five years or so. In the course of the evening, he told me a story of dating all three sisters in a family we both knew, of running into the mother years later, of her saying curtly to him, 'Well, I've no more daughters for you.' That line seemed expressive of so much . . . that it stayed in my mind. . . .

"I had an office that year . . . with a large grassy yard behind it. Over the time I was working on 'The Lover of Women,' this yard was the site of several parties, and the band music floating across Brattle Street into my windows seemed part of what helped me write . . . .

"Even now [the story] seems a gift: the accident of meeting my old sweetheart, the wonderful line that triggered my imagination . . . the music that wound its way into it."

The Transformation Process

It's not the material. It's how you write it. A friend once told me an anecdote that I wrote in my journal, not once but twice. I guess I forgot about the first entry.

> Scott told me a couple of children, one white, one black, who were no more than five years old, and they were running around Boston Commons with a pizza box. They ran from one person to the next, saying, "You want a slice of pizza?" Then they opened the box. Inside, there was a squirrel that had been flattened by a car. They came up and did this to someone who was standing near Scott, and Scott yelled after them, "You kids should be ashamed of yourselves!"

I used this entry in a story, "Installations" [see page 187], about an unlikely affair between a conductor on the Chicago El and a fledgling performance artist named Ivy, who sees everything, all experience, as art. I have as much trouble with people like Ivy, who see everything as art, as I have with people who want "just the facts, ma'am," and feel that art is irrelevant.

I don't want to be self-aggrandizing here, but I want to show you how I transformed the passage. I used the basic idea of the squirrel in the pizza box, stretched it, dramatized it, and altered it to fit the specifications of my story. In the following scene, my protagonist, the El conductor, has just been taken by Ivy to his first performance art exhibit, called an "installation," and he has no idea what to make of it. By the way, the description of the installation is a pretty accurate one of an actual installation I saw in Chicago while *I* was dating a fledgling performance artist, though her name wasn't Ivy and the similarities end there. I didn't, however, record the installation in my journal. It was so bizarre I knew I'd remember every detail for the rest of my life.

> We pass through a white curtain into this scene: a darkened room with a naked man and woman, thirtyish, lying like two sticks of old butter in the middle of the room. Either they're dead or mannequins. The music in the room sounds like the part in *The Wizard*

of Oz where Dorothy and her boyfriends are looking at the witch's castle, and the soldiers march around singing: "O-li-o-eyohhh-oh."

Ivy takes my hand and we approach the couple on the floor. A dozen other people saunter around as though nothing special's going on. We can't get any closer than five feet. The couple on the floor are surrounded by hundreds of apples in the shape of a cross. A ragged bat hangs above them, its ribbed wings stretching six feet. A sideways neon eight sways between the wings and glows pale blue.

This is what Ivy calls an installation. This is what I call a fun house.

Up close, I see their chests moving slightly, a small tremor from one of the woman's fingers touching the man's hand, a flickering eyelid. I study them and wonder if I've ever seen them on the El. I wonder if the woman's parents know this is what she does for a living.

"The man looks a little like the button man without his buttons."

Candles burn on their chests. Luckily the candles are in jars, or the wax would be excruciating. Still, the heat must get to them. Not that I can tell. They're not exactly your liveliest couple. I can imagine showing up at Angel's Shortstop, my neighborhood bar, with them stiff as corpses on the bar stools, the candles still stuck on their chests. Angel would serve them up a couple of Old Styles, and squint at me and say, "They friends of yours?"

Yeah, they're installations.

We take the El back to Belmont and walk over to Clark Street. Everything seems strange tonight: a man waiting in the window of a tattoo parlor, the moan coming out of a storefront church.

Ivy asks me what I think about the installations. I don't know. I haven't thought about it. What are you supposed to think about a naked man and woman with candles on their chests?

"Everything," she says. "Adam and Eve lying in suspended animation beneath death and infinity. Christ figures surrounded by the forbidden fruit."

Yeah, well, I guess.

We turn the corner of Clark and Belmont, and two kids, one

black and one white, not more than nine years old, slam into us as they tear through the parking lot of Dunkin' Donuts.

"Hey, watch where you're going," I say, touching the white one lightly on the shoulder.

"You watch where you're going, you fag," the kid tells me.

The black kid has a pizza box in his hands. He smiles and says, "You want some pizza?"

"Yeah, you want some pizza?" says the white kid.

The black kid opens up the box. Inside is a squirrel, its head smashed, its legs stretched out, its belly split open. At least a hundred cars have run over it. As flat as a pizza. A circle of dried tomato paste surrounds the carcass.

Before I can react, the kids run off shouting and laughing. They block one pedestrian after another yelling, "Hey, you want some pizza? Free pizza."

Ivy picks up a soft-drink cup from the sidewalk and throws it after them. The cup, plastic lid and straw still attached, falls to the ground three feet away.

"You brats," she screams. "Come back here."

Ivy takes off. The white kid trips. She chases the other one. I can't make out much through the distance and pedestrians. A few minutes later, she comes smiling back with the pizza box in her hands, the lid closed.

"What do you want *that* for?" I say.

"Stealing is the most sincere form of flattery," she says. "Picasso did it. Every great artist does it."

"Throw it away."

"Are you kidding?"

"Throw it away."

"Don't give me orders. I had to fight them for it."

I don't say a word. I'm tired of her. I was curious before, but now I'm just tired. I head for Angel's Shortstop and Ivy tags along. I figure it's Ivy's turn to feel out-of-place. Not many out-of-place people ever wander into Angel's. If they do, they wander back out again in a hurry. The crowd at Angel's is as tight as a VFW post.

Ignoring Ivy, I sit down on a stool at the bar. There isn't one for her, so she stands in between my stool and the next guy's, and places her pizza box on the counter. Angel gives her a look. Then she looks at me. I order a couple shots of Cuervo with Old Style chasers.

"I'll have to tap a new keg," says Angel. "How 'bout something else in the meantime?"

"How 'bout a mug of beefalo swill?" I say. "Come on, Angel. I'm talking brand loyalty."

"I'll go tap a new keg," she says. Angel is about sixty years old and has a white bubble hair-do. She comes to Chicago via the coal mines of Kentucky, and her husband's long-gone with black lung. Angel's jukebox has only the thickest country-and-western songs, with three exceptions: "A Cub Fan's Dying Prayer," Sinatra's version of "Chicago," and "Angel of the Morning." She's always pumping quarters painted with red fingernail polish into the jukebox and pushing those three tunes. I can't count the number of times I've come into the Shortstop and heard her belting, "Just call me angel of the morning, baby. Just one more kiss before you leave me, angel." She thinks of the Shortstop as a family establishment, even though I'd fall off my stool if I ever saw a family walk through the door. Maybe a family of cockroaches or sewer-bred alligators. Definitely not a family of mammals.

When Angel returns with the Old Styles, Ivy pushes hers away and says, "I don't drink alcohol."

"Angel, this is Ivy," I say. "She comes from Cody, Illinois, the beefalo capital of the Midwest. It's ten miles south of Beloit."

"Blech!" says Ivy.

"What?"

"Beloit. I grew up with the name. It sounds like a quarter being dropped in a toilet. Beloit . . . Besides, I live in Chicago now."

"Yeah, she's a performance artist," I tell Angel.

"Pleased to meet you," she says.

"You want some pizza?" Ivy says.

"No, she doesn't want any pizza," I say, and put my hand on the lid.

"Domino's?" Angel says.

"It's not pizza," I say. "It's a squirrel."

"A squirrel."

"Yeah, a dead one."

"Pepperoni," Ivy says. "You want to see it, Angel?"

"Sure, why not?"

"No, you don't want to see it," I say. My hand is still on the lid.

Ivy looks sideways at me and gives me a half smile, a dare. Her look says "What's the big deal?" She's right. After all, Angel's not my mother.

With my job and all, I'm not easy to faze, but Ivy definitely fazes me. Not only her actions, but the way she dresses. An orange scarf as big as window drapes. Black fishnet stockings and metallic silver lipstick. Usually my life is pretty dull, but around Ivy, I feel the way I do when I'm sitting on the pot and I hear the fans cheer in Wrigley Field.

"You ever had squirrel?" says Angel. "Tastes just like chicken. Of course, there ain't as much meat on a squirrel."

"Do you always believe what you see, Angel?" Ivy says.

"Almost never," says Angel, leaning toward her, a look of concentration on her face. "A fella come in here the other day selling key chains. He had a metal man and a metal woman on the key chain, and when he wiggled a lever they started doing things. He said he had a whole trunkful in his car, and did I want to sell some on a card behind the counter? I said, 'Look around, this is a family place.' He said, 'You'd be surprised. People just love them. I've seen grandmas and young girls go crazy over them.' 'Yeah, well this is a gay bar, buddy,' I said. 'That's fine,' he said. 'I can take off the woman and put on another man. I already did that with one gay establishment. I'll put on dogs. I'll put on a man and a horse. Even two Japanese girls and a rhinoceros if that's what you want. Whatever turns you on.' Some people just want to shock you. I could have called the cops, but I ignored him. Eventually, he just slithered back under his rock."

"You want some pizza?" Ivy says.

"Yeah, why not?" says Angel.

I take my hand off the lid and wait for Ivy to open up the box, but she doesn't move. What's she waiting for? I wonder if I'm going nuts. If Ivy's brainwashing me. I've known her two days, and suddenly I want to show Angel the dead squirrel in the pizza box.

"One object can have many functions," Ivy says. "Consider this pizza box. For you and me, it signifies food. For Rocky the squirrel, it's his final resting place. When you put the two together, it's repulsive. Why? Because food and death are opposites, right? No, not at all. Food and death go hand in hand, but our escapist society allows us to blithely ignore that fact. Hold the mayo, hold the lettuce, special orders don't upset us. Right, Angel? Next time you go to an open-casket funeral, don't be surprised if you see a pizza with the works lying there."

I have a strange feeling in my mouth. My tongue seems to be getting bigger. I've gone through my whole life barely noticing my tongue, and now, all of a sudden, it seems humongous. I can't figure out where to place it. I try to settle it down by my cheek. I stick it between my teeth.

Angel tucks her chin into her neck.

My tongue has swollen to the size of a blimp.

Still, I manage to say to Angel, "Ya wa thom peetha?"

"Sure, why not?" she says.

I open up the box and Angel shrinks back.

She gives me a look and I can already tell that she's canceled me out as a regular. Now, I'm just another bar story: "You remember Rick? He came in here with a squirrel in a pizza box. Yeah, it was dead."

Now, is that stealing? I don't think so. I took a bare-boned anecdote from my journal and stretched it. You, undoubtedly, would have taken the squirrel in the pizza box and done something completely different with the image. You might have focused on the two children or a character based on yourself in that situation.

The writer and teacher George Garrett did something similar with the image of a wedding cake in the middle of the road, an image that one of his students, Beverly Goodrum, came up with in a class. Based on Goodrum's story, he and radio commentator Susan Stamberg asked twenty-three writers, both well known and not (including Garrett and Goodrum), to each write a story based on this image. Of course, a central question in each story was, "What is a wedding cake doing in the middle of the road?" Their versions were broadcast on NPR and collected in an anthology titled—what else?—*The Wedding Cake in the Middle of the Road*.

It's not the material. It's what you do with it.

A lot of the craft of writing fiction is in one's ability to order the material at hand, whether autobiographical or not. The content of the story itself means nothing. The form you give it, the way you shape the material, is everything.

Still, it might be helpful to know what from the above passage really happened—where it came from. As I mentioned, the installation itself was something I actually saw, though in this case, I had no need of recording it in my journal. When I lived in Chicago, there was a neighborhood bar called Kaye's Dugout, and a woman like Angel tended bar there. I never knew much about Kaye (if that woman behind the bar was indeed Kaye), where she came from, or whether she'd ever been married. But it's true that a lot of ex-coal miners from Kentucky have, over the years, moved to Chicago, and that a number of them suffer from black lung. When I was writing about Angel, I remembered this, and so this is the history I decided to give her.

It's also true that at the corner of Clark and Belmont, you can still find a Dunkin' Donuts. I believe the storefront church is gone now, and so is the tattoo parlor. The neighborhood has been gentrified.

Another real-life episode was the encounter with the man selling the funny key chains. That, too, happened, though not at Kaye's Dugout. It was at a more upscale bar in the area. This was something I recorded in my journal. It happened in midafternoon on a hot summer day in Chicago. I'd stopped in for a beer and was sitting at the bar when I overheard the man with the key chains trying to convince the bartender to sell some of them behind the bar.

I didn't record the conversation as it happened, but I wrote it down a short while later at my apartment. Almost everything Angel said in my story is verbatim what I overheard the man tell the bartender at the bar. However, there was more to that scene than what I chose to include in my story. Only the key chain episode fit in. Here's how the journal entry reads in its entirety.

Today, the humidity was about 70 percent. I walked all over town, and by the time I got off the Southport El I was drenched, so I stopped off for a beer at Justin's, a polished wood/ceiling fan kind of bar across from the station. An acquaintance, a guy named Carl, was tending bar, so I sat up at the counter, ordered an Augsburger. Carl started chatting with me, but as he was opening the bottle, it slipped out of his hands and he dropped it on the floor, beer splattering the front of his shirt. He said, "This hasn't been my day at all, man," and went to the rest room to wash the beer off. After he returned, neither of us had much to say to each other. Instead, he started flipping channels with the remote control for the two bar TVs, one at either end.

"Donahue," he said to me.

He kept the sound off one of the TVs, and that was the one I watched. I tried imagining the sound from the Donahue program to the other TV. The guests on Donahue were an unwed couple whose baby needed a heart transplant. The other TV had a burger commercial with talking burger cartons. Or, at least I assumed they were talking, since the burger boxes were flipping up and down in imitation of conversation. I listened to Donahue for a minute, placing the voices of the couple in the burger boxes. (Maybe I was suffering from heat stroke. I can't help editorializing there. Such a weird thing to do).

After the commercial was over, I turned back to Carl, who wasn't looking at Donahue, but talking to three guys at the bar. The one closest to me had a long, stubbly face. The man in the middle was dark-skinned, Hispanic, and the guy at the end wore a green Justin's T-shirt with a dog mascot on front. This man looked large and boyish.

"So I guess I'm moving to North Carolina," I told Carl, loud enough for everyone to hear.

Carl turned toward me and said, "No kidding." He looked surprised.

For some reason, I thought I had mentioned it to him before.

"Yeah, I got a job there."

"You ever been to North Carolina?" the man with the stubble asked me. He had a hard tone in his voice, as though he was talking about prison.

"Yeah," I said.

"Oh," he said. He took a sip of his beer and said, "I've been there."

The phone rang and the man with the stubble said, "I bet that's Justin."

"Justin hates me," said the Hispanic man.

Carl looked over at the man with the stubble, who said, "He's a real obnoxious son of a bitch, but he mellows out once you get to know him," and he pointed at the Hispanic guy.

Carl went to the phone and the Hispanic man laughed and yelled after him, "Tell Justin that Mexican son of a bitch is here. Yeah, he *hates* me."

Carl picked up the phone and took it around the corner, speaking softly.

The three men at the counter looked at each other and broke out laughing.

"It *is* him," said the Hispanic man.

"Don't worry," said the guy with the stubble. "Carl can handle it. He's a good guy."

Carl hung up and started talking to the three guys again.

"Do you like working here?" I asked Carl.

"Yeah, I love it," he said. "But the hours are catching up with me. I opened this morning and closed last night."

Carl looked past me toward the door. A man in his fifties walked in wearing oily brown polyester pants.

Carl went to the middle of the bar and leaned forward.

"Can I help you?"

"Yeah, is Justin here?"

"No, he won't be in till six. Can I help you?"

"Well, I wanted to see if he'd be interested in buying some of these," and he took out a key chain from his pocket. The key chain had two metal figures attached to it, a man and a woman. The guy in the brown pants wiggled a little lever.

Carl took it from the man and wiggled the lever himself. Then he brought it to the end of the bar and showed it to the three guys there.

"Justin will love this," said the man with the stubble.

"How much you want for this?" asked the Hispanic man.

"Well, I'm asking three," said the man, who had now positioned himself between me and the other three men. "But I'll take two."

The Hispanic man who was holding the key chain laughed. The guy with the stubble whipped out his wallet and threw two dollars at the man.

"Justin'll love this, he said. "It's the perfect present for him."

"I got more in my car," said the man. "Who else wants one?"

"No, that's all," said the man with the stubble.

Then he took out another dollar bill and threw it at the man. "Here, it's worth three," he said.

"I got a whole load of them in my trunk," said the man. "It's right around the corner. I've got thousands."

"One's plenty," said the man with the stubble.

But I was thinking of giving you a bunch to sell on a card behind the bar."

The four other guys laughed and the man with the stubble said, "Not here. That wouldn't go here."

"You'd be surprised," said the man. "People just love them. I've seen women and young girls go crazy over them."

"Yeah, well this is a gay bar," said the guy with the stubble, and the other guys laughed.

"That's fine," said the man. "I can take off the woman and put on another man. I already did that for one gay bar."

"What about dogs?" said the Hispanic man. "I want one with a man and a dog."

"Fine. I can put on anything."

"Well, I want two Japanese girls and a rhinoceros," said the Hispanic man.

"I want a man and a horse," said the guy with the stubble.

"Sure, whatever you want," said the man.

"This is all we want," said the man with the stubble. "You'll have to go somewhere else."

The man laughed and started walking out. "Anything you want," he said. "Well, I'll be back tonight to see Justin."

"No, don't come back," said the man with the stubble.

"Yeah, come back," said the Hispanic man. "Justin likes your element."

After the man was gone, the guy with the stubble said, "Did you see that guy's pants? I would have given him three dollars for those pants."

I love those characters, and I love some of their lines. I like the whole scene, in fact. The personalities seem pretty distinct to me. I love that line, "Justin likes your element." Too bad I couldn't use more of the scene in my story. Note, I referred to these guys as characters, not people. They *are* people. But the journal entry isn't flesh and blood. I couldn't reproduce real people in flesh and blood, in all their complexity, even if I wanted to. With the exception of Carl, I met them once and wouldn't know them again if I saw them. I can only imagine. That, again, is the key word. Imagine. Once you set pen to paper, even in your journal, your imagination plays an important role. There's no such thing as objectivity, as any basic philosophy course will tell you. Everything is a matter of perceptions. You'd write down the above incident in a different way from the way I wrote it. The words you'd choose would be different. What you thought was important would be different. You might not even see the scene as important at all. You might forget it entirely. But as soon as you started recording it, you'd be using your imagination.

That might sound like a great rationalization. Obviously, you can't go around thinking of everyone as a character. There are limits. All I'm saying is that your journal is your sketchbook. Don't think of it as a diary. As I mentioned, I wrote all of this down after I returned home. I have a good memory, but I can't swear that every word I recorded in my journal was exactly the way it was uttered. Does it matter? I don't think so. It's your journal. You're a fiction writer, not a reporter. Nineteenth-century English poet and critic Matthew Arnold said, "Journalism is literature in a hurry." Don't be in a hurry. Play around with it. You don't have to try to be faithful to reality in your journal. You couldn't be, even if you tried.

In any case, what I used from that journal entry was only a smidgen of the scene. Notice that in my journal entry I hardly paid any attention to the third guy, the one with the Justin's T-shirt. In a story, I'd probably cut him out or give him a larger role. Everything in fiction counts, and that's not always the case in real life. In real life, there are people who sit at the end of the bar without a role to play. In fiction, a character is either necessary to the story or extraneous.

In "Installations," none of those guys was necessary. I used the key chain incident itself, and I condensed what the men at the bar said and attributed their whimsical requests to the key chain man. Then I further removed the scene from real life by filtering the dialogue through Angel's perceptions. As much as I liked some of those other passages in the journal, I had to be careful to use only what fit into my story, no more, no less.

What would have happened to the story if I'd simply lifted the entire journal entry into my story without transforming it? What would have happened if I'd included Carl, the Hispanic man, the guy with the stubble, the guy with the Justin's T-shirt, *and* the key chain? Obviously, the story would have become unfocused. We'd forget about Ivy and Rick, not to mention Angel. In a later chapter we'll discuss strategies for focusing stories like this that are based in real life.

One thing you must understand as a fiction writer: Real life matters only as a conduit for your imagination. As a fiction writer, your imagination takes precedence. As a human being, life takes precedence over your imagination, and it's best not to confuse the two.

One other journal entry found its way into the squirrel in the pizza box scene, and that was the mention of Rick's tongue suddenly seeming large. A friend once told me that an acquaintance of his had one day stopped midsentence and said, "You know, all of a sudden I'm noticing my tongue. I've gone through my whole life without noticing it, but now I can't figure out where to place it in my mouth. It keeps getting in the way." My friend laughed and said, "Maybe you should seek therapy."

When I came to the climax of the scene, when Rick finally decided to show Angel the squirrel in the pizza box, I wanted to show a change in him, a change in his perceptions, a hint that he was going through almost physical changes because of his association with Ivy. That's when I remembered the man who didn't know where to put his tongue.

Many passages in my journal are irrelevant and will never find their ways into stories. I don't even know what some of the passages mean.

At the end of the Justin's entry, there are three lines that make little sense to me:

> Maybe follows him out to car?
> Something about his move, his girlfriend.
> "Why are you trying to alienate me?" Mother asks.

I may have been thinking of a story. Judging from the strength of those lines, I wisely abandoned the idea.

Some of my journals contain these kinds of lines, indecipherable and abandoned ideas and passages. I also have grocery lists, quotes from other writers and artists, phone numbers, addresses. And, of course, I've included notes to myself on where to proceed in my novel or short stories, such as:

> Henry feels threatened by Gail, but he can't leave. He feels at home here. It *is* his home. Still, he feels compelled to redeem himself, to prove himself. Gail thinks Henry's clumsy, wimpish, impotent, un-masculine. He decides to take action. He needs to show Gail she's wrong.
>
> There used to be an element of the macho in Henry.
>
> Henry needs to be less passive.
>
> Bring back Sid.
>
> Henry and Willy have bidding war at auction. Henry suddenly gets aggressive, but the fact that he gets car might redeem himself in Gail's eyes.

Basically, stage directions. Then there are the story ideas:

> About Al at Our Place. How I thought he was brilliant and wanted to be just like him, but then we, the regulars of Our Place, decided he was really mad, and this diminished him as a human being.

This is more or less indecipherable to you and probably doesn't seem like much of an idea at all. But *I* know what I'm referring to, and in a journal that's all that counts.

I don't include anecdotes in my journals with the intention of putting them in future stories. It's not that calculated. I write something down because it grabs my attention, because I'd hate for it to be lost. For instance, there was the time a local theater critic came to one of my classes and told us about an amateur production of *Amadeus* in which everything went wrong:

> Perry Tannenbaum came to my Review Writing class today and he told us a story about reviewing a local production of *Amadeus*. Apparently, they got everything wrong. First of all, the guy playing

Salieri had never acted before. Halfway through the play, he forgot his lines and ran offstage. Then, during the scene in which *The Magic Flute* premieres, something went wrong with the sound and there was just silence as the courtiers applauded. Then, at the end of the play, as Mozart lay dying, he was supposed to have a vision of his father appearing in the door wearing his three-cornered hat while portentous music played. Instead, when they cued the sound, the light, airy music of *The Magic Flute* started playing when his father, dressed in black, appeared in the doorway and glowered.

I doubt this entry will ever find its way into a story of mine, but who knows? I wrote it down simply because it was funny. But now that I think about it, I can see it working into a story in a couple of ways. The way in which I'd incorporate the anecdote would depend entirely on whose point of view the story is told from. The haughty critic would view the episode differently from the unfortunate amateur thespian who played Salieri.

I keep a journal for a variety of reasons. Sometimes I want to chronicle, as in a diary. Sometimes I want to record a detail that otherwise would be lost forever. Sometimes I record a dream, and a couple of these dreams have actually been the kernels for some short stories I've written.

Whatever the case, it's important to write in your journal before the event or image becomes stale. We've all had dreams that have awakened us in the middle of the night, that seem so striking we want to record them. But we're tired and want to go back to sleep. We say, "Oh, I'll write it down in the morning when I wake up." Almost invariably, when we awake in the morning, the dream has disappeared. So we rationalize further. "Oh, it probably wasn't that interesting anyway." But what if it was?

Of course, what's worth noting in your journal is up to you. But I'd suggest carrying a small notebook with you at all times, one that can fit in your pocket or purse. Don't go anywhere without it and take along a pen that works. As Thoreau wrote, "The writer who postpones the recording of his thoughts uses an iron which has cooled to burn a hole with." That's a quote I wrote down in one of my journals.

Writers are spies, liars, and thieves. Some, like Jean Genet, have been real criminals; some, like Graham Greene, have actually been spies. But most are spies and thieves in a more general sense. Your journal is basically your spy notebook. Don't let it fall into enemy hands. Greene used his journals extensively to write *The Heart of the Matter* and *A Burnt-Out Case*. Later, we'll discuss ethics, but remember, you're writing fiction. There's nothing wrong with borrowing from real life. It's neither crass nor unimaginative unless one goes about it in a crass or unimaginative way. *Imagination comes in the ordering of events, not in their source.*

Weaving Journal Entries into Fiction

Writing is an associative process. And fiction writing is a kind of mosaic, a piecing together of memory and imagination. One's journal can come in handy in this way, but I don't want to give you the impression that I simply flip through my journal, filling in the blanks with fun-filled episodes from real life until I have enough pages to call it a story. It's not a matter of simply dropping overheard bits of conversation into a story. I wish it was that easy. One must attempt to weave in what one uses.

For instance, here's a bit of overheard dialogue from Fitzgerald's notebook: "He wants to make a goddess out of me and I want to be Mickey Mouse."

In the completed story, "On Your Own," which was published posthumously, the Mickey Mouse quote isn't dropped in casually. On the contrary, it's woven seamlessly into the story, which concerns a young actress named Evelyn who's returning by boat to America after a five-year absence and some success on the British stage. On the voyage, she becomes entangled with a rich young lawyer named George Ives. The story was rejected seven times by various magazines, something Fitzgerald wasn't used to. Fitzgerald thought it was his one unpublished story with that "one little drop of something . . . the extra I had."

Early in the story, after the young couple meet, they walk the deck together:

> "You were a treat," he said. "You're like Mickey Mouse."
> She took his arm and bent double over it with laughter.
> "I like being Mickey Mouse . . ."

Later, after an on-again, off-again romance (and after Evelyn discovers George is rich), they have the following exchange:

"Would you consider marrying me?"

"Yes, I'd consider marrying you."

"Of course if you married me we'd live in New York."

"Call me Mickey Mouse," she said suddenly.

"Why?"

"I don't know—it was fun when you called me Mickey Mouse."

A little silly, but then, Evelyn is a little silly. That night, she wonders what she's gotten herself into:

"He wants to make a goddess out of me and I want to be Mickey Mouse."

Finally, George's mother, a wealthy society matron, invites Evelyn to dinner. At the dinner party is a certain Colonel Cary, whom Evelyn has met before—under slightly darker circumstances. It turns out that when she was a starving young actress on Broadway and had to go for days without eating, she survived by being a "party girl." Intimidated by Colonel Cary's presence, Evelyn gets drunk on champagne, blabs everything, and lashes out at George's mother, who's properly horrified but tries to put a good face on things. Of course, George, under his mother's wing all along, tries to dump Evelyn, who, in her world-weary fashion, takes it all with philosophical aplomb.

Ah, well, maybe she'd better go back to England—and be Mickey Mouse. He didn't know anything about women, anything about love, and to her that was the unforgivable sin.

Fiction, unlike real life, demands a kind of *symmetry,* or balance. No phrase or image or overheard bit of dialogue should be wasted or thrown carelessly into a story or novel. There's an old dramatic trick here that Fitzgerald has employed. If you want a reader to pay special attention to an image, put it in not once or twice, but three times. The first time you make a reference to Mickey Mouse, the reader will hardly notice. The second time, the reader's subconscious takes note, but it barely registers on the reader's conscious mind. The third time is the charm. In this case, Mickey Mouse becomes an organic symbol of Evelyn's frivolity, as well as her vacuousness. Fitzgerald has taken this overheard dialogue and fashioned it to suit his characters and their situation.

Fitzgerald also wrote ideas for short stories in his notebooks, including the following one, based on a true story:

> There once was a moving picture magnate who was shipwrecked
> on a desert island with nothing but two dozen cans of film (Herbert
> Howe).

As far as I know, Fitzgerald never did anything with the idea. I've thought about it myself. It's intriguing, but it's sort of a one-joke story, the idea of the creator stranded with nothing but potential, and without the means to do anything about it. The fact that Fitzgerald never did anything with the idea is all the more fitting. We all have canisters of film that we'll never develop.

The point is that a journal entry is little but a raw piece of information. What you do with it later is the tricky part. For the time being, enjoy yourself. Whoop it up. Have a party in your journal. Your journal entries can be more or less formless. They can be ungrammatical. You may misspell all the words you like. They can make no sense at all. There'll be enough time later for biting your fingernails to the quick, gnashing your teeth, and beating your breast in frustration—once you decide to develop your ideas into a story or a novel.

EXERCISES

Journals aren't only repositories for overheard conversations, but places to experiment, to recall a scene from your childhood, to try out first lines. A fiction writer, or any artist, attempts to see the world in a new light, in a way that makes the ordinary seem extraordinary (or the extraordinary seem ordinary). Simply paying attention to the everyday world around you will soon yield extraordinary results.

1. Go to a park or a shopping mall or somewhere else where people congregate in large numbers. Sit on a bench with your journal and sketch the people walking by—not with pictures but words. Describe at least three people in as much detail as possible: their

gestures, what they're wearing, what they're saying. Try not to pass judgment on the people you're observing. Let the descriptions do all the talking.

2. Close your eyes. Remember a scene from your childhood. It doesn't have to be a traumatic event or something inherently dramatic. In fact, it's best to simply go with the first memory that surfaces. Remember all its details. Use the senses. If you remember making orange peel candy with your grandmother, imagine the smell of the orange rinds, the sight of the curled crisp rinds, smothered in sugar, and baking. The ones that invariably burned, but your grandmother liked those, right? Or maybe she just said she liked them so you could have the ones that came out perfect. What did they taste like? What did you and your grandmother talk about? Try to evoke the memory with as much clarity as possible. Now write it down in your journal. It doesn't have to fit into a story. It's just practice. But if it *does* fit into a story, that's fine, too. I once had a teacher who said he didn't understand when people said they had nothing to write about. All they have to do is keep their eyes open and/or remember.

3. Eavesdrop on a couple of strangers. (Don't be obvious. I don't want you to end up in jail.) Again, this is just practice, so don't worry about it. Write down what they say as close to verbatim as possible. Do you notice any difference between the conversation you've recorded and the dialogue of short stories and novels? Generally, fiction writers try to make their dialogue seem as realistic as possible. The key word is "seem." Dialogue also has to flow smoothly. In real life, people stutter, say "ah" and "um," change subjects midsentence, ramble, pay no attention at all to what the other person is saying, trail off, talk at the same time. To a certain degree, this can be imitated in one's fictional dialogue, and it can even heighten humor or tension. Film director Robert Altman has been playing with the way people really speak for nearly forty years. Look at *M*A*S*H* or *Gosford Park* and notice how often characters speak at the same time. It's intriguing. It's funny. And it's often darned annoying. If you try to

be too true (recording dialect *exactly,* printing every "um"), you risk losing your readers, making them stumble over awkward phrases and misspellings—in short, making them conscious that they are reading a story. That's the last thing you want to do. You don't want to call attention to the fact that what you've written isn't real. You want to seduce readers into believing they have entered a world as real as the one they inhabit every day. Paradoxically, that often means not being absolutely realistic with one's dialogue. A good rule of thumb: If it's going to jar readers and make them stumble, cut it out.

4. Here are a few of Fitzgerald's ideas from his notebooks. See where you can go with them. Remember, it's just practice, and it's not how he would have written them anyway. Identify which ideas have the best story potential and which seem like they won't lead anywhere. Which ones seem too limited? Too open-ended?

   Story about a man trying to live down his crazy past and encountering it everywhere.

   Play about a whole lot of old people—terrible things happen to them and they don't really care.

   The Dancer Who Found She Could Fly

   A young woman bill collector undertakes to collect a ruined man's debts. They prove to be moral as well as financial.

   Flower shop, Bishop, Malmaison, Constantine, clinics, black men, nurses.

   Words.

5. Think back within the last year or so and remember dealing with a service person—a plumber, an air duct specialist, a mechanic. Remember the details. Write them down in your journal. What was he wearing? Was he wearing a toupee? A high school ring? Did he tell you about his love of tying lures and fishing off of Cape Hatteras? Or volunteering to catch and tag sharks for

scientists? Was he a she? Life is in the details, and so is good fiction. Often when one imagines something whole cloth (that is, *without* incorporating bits of one's own observations and experience), one comes up with a stereotype or cliché. If you want to write a story about a plumber, the first images that spring to mind are sometimes the most hackneyed. Rely less on your preconceptions and more on your own experience with plumbers or service people of *any* kind.

▼

CHAPTER TWO

Finding Your Form

Perhaps everyone has a story to tell, but many never get around to telling them, and many others tell them poorly. Many people have led fascinating lives, but falter when they attempt to tell their stories. Often, this is because they focus on content rather than form. There's a difference between a memoir and a novel. A memoir is supposed to be true. A novel isn't. The difference between fact and fiction. As flip as that might sound, it's a complex distinction, and some writers blur the distinction to good effect. Others, claiming they want to write fiction, really want to write memoirs. If you base a story on an actual event, but refuse to alter it because "that's the way it really happened," you probably want to write a memoir instead of a story. I'm going to assume that you're here to write fiction transformed from fact rather than unadulterated fact. Still, I think it would be worthwhile to discuss some of the various forms and distinctions between them before moving on.

I don't want to be unfair to memoir writers, including myself, since such writing is much more involved than simply setting down an event as it happened. Who knows how it happened? Can you trust your eyes, your memory? Does your father remember it differently from you? Had you been drinking that night? Where do you begin to relate the event? The night before, when Joey called you and invited you out skinny-dipping, and you had to think of an excuse to tell your dad? Maybe you want to start in the tepid waters of the lake instead. Or maybe you want to begin that chapter of your memoir in a more reflective way. "Some people would undoubtedly say that I was a brat when I was a young'un. . . . " And what about word choice and diction? You really want to use the words "young'un" and "undoubtedly" in the same sentence? And who really cares about your skinny-dipping

< 37 >

episode in 1966? Was it so amazing that it's going to work as the centerpiece of your memoir, *Treading Water in the Sixties?*

"Okay," you say, slightly insulted. "If not a memoir, I'll make it a novel." Not so fast.

Writing a novel is no easier than writing a memoir. Fiction writers must be flexible with their lives, write about "what if" rather than "what is." Writers need distance from events to write about them as fiction, to accept that these real events might not work in the story. And it's more important for the story to work than for it to be true (in the narrow sense of that word).

Memoirs, Novels, and Romans à Clef

A memoir, as I said, is not simply a recording of events. That kind of recording, in its simplest form, is a diary (and that point is probably debatable, too). All types of writing have accepted forms and conventions. Letters, for instance, begin with "Dear" and end with "Love," "Best Wishes," "Truly," or some other appropriate word. Newspaper stories often use the inverted pyramid form. Short stories generally involve some kind of conflict, crisis, and resolution.

A memoir takes a certain amount of arrogance to write (not that I'm suggesting this is one of its conventions). One must think one's life important or interesting enough to palm off on an unsuspecting public. At least fiction writers have the pretense that their work has more to do with their characters than with themselves. Still, I doubt you'd find much difference between a memoir writer and a fiction writer in the humility department.

Or maybe memoir writers tend more toward exhibitionism, are more willing—eager, in fact—to slap their cards on the table and squawk, "Read 'em and weep." The fiction writer, cagier, plays his hand close to his vest, pretends he knows how to bluff.

If you slosh your life down on the page, beginning with "I was born in . . ." and ending with, "As I pen these immortal words, I gasp my last breaths," what you've probably got is a self-indulgent autobiography, not a memoir. A memoir usually deals with a portion of one's life—say, childhood—not the life in its entirety. Like a novel, the art is in the ordering of events, not the events themselves. Sometimes what's called a memoir and what's labeled a novel seems due more to the whims of a publisher's marketing department than to any true distinction. In such cases, perhaps the best solution is the one Frederick Exley came up with in his book, *Fan's Notes,* which he subtitled *A Fictional Memoir.*

One distinction we can make is between simple memoirs and sophisticated ones. Celebrity tell-all books will continue to be printed by the hundreds of thousands as long as there remain virgin forests worth pulping for that glorious purpose.

One of the books that precipitated the recent memoir boom is Tobias Wolff's *This Boy's Life.* The book recalls Wolff's childhood, growing up in the Pacific Northwest in the 1950s with his divorced mother, who marries a tyrannical and oafish man named Dwight. Wolff's brother, Geoffrey, has also written an excellent memoir, *The Duke of Deception,* about growing up on the opposite coast with the boys' con artist of a father.

This Boy's Life seems as much an autobiographical novel as a memoir. In fact, Wolff originally envisioned the book as a novel, but then decided against a fictional approach. I have a good memory and can recall dreams I had when I was three years old, but Wolff reaches back nearly forty years and fishes out whole conversations time and again. The fact is that all writing—whether a letter, a memoir, or a novel—requires some artifice. And the act of writing down memories changes them. They become more real. The line blurs between actual memory and reconstructed written memory so that the writer is less and less able to know for certain what *really* happened. Perhaps Wolff has a photographic memory, or whatever the audio version of that would be, but I doubt it. Most likely, events and conversations much like the ones Wolff reproduces took place. Or perhaps several remarks were said at different times, and Wolff patched them together to keep the story cohesive. Or maybe the conversations, some of them at least, never took place at all. So does that make Wolff a liar, or worse yet, a fiction writer? Well, he is a fiction writer of some note, and such impulses die hard.

Michael Caton-Jones, the director of the film version of *This Boy's Life,* says that during filming (in the town of Concrete, Washington, where Wolff grew up), people kept approaching him to give their own versions of events. But he fended all of them off. "Everybody's memory plays tricks, to be honest," he says. "I never let the truth get in the way of a good story, if I can help it." A man after my own heart.

The only character in the book that Caton-Jones found a little shadowy and wanted a better handle on, according to a *New York Times* article, was Wolff's mother, whom Wolff handled "with kid gloves." So naturally, he went to *The Duke of Deception,* where he found what he considered a more realistic portrait of her.

Here's a scene between Dwight and young Toby (or Jack, as he preferred to be called). In it, Dwight has just run over a beaver on the road on purpose and now stops to pick it up so he can sell the pelt. Notice how detailed the description is. Does it sound like a memory from forty years back? Are your memories this detailed?

> "Pick it up," Dwight told me. He opened the trunk of the car and said, "Pick it up. We'll skin the sucker out when we get home."
>
> I wanted to do what Dwight expected me to do, but I couldn't. I stood where I was and stared at the beaver.
>
> Dwight came up beside me. "That pelt's worth fifty dollars, bare minimum." He added, "Don't tell me you're afraid of the damned thing."
>
> "No sir."
>
> "Then pick it up." He watched me. "It's dead, for Christ's sake. It's just meat. Are you afraid of hamburger? Look." He bent down and gripped the tail in one hand and lifted the beaver off the ground. He tried to make this appear effortless but I could see he was surprised and strained by the beaver's weight. A stream of blood ran out of its nose, then stopped. A few drops fell on Dwight's shoes before he jerked the body away. Holding the beaver in front of him with both hands, Dwight carried it to the open trunk and let go. It landed hard. "There," he said, and wiped his hands on his pants leg.

Of course, that's an event one might remember verbatim, but this memoir is full of such events, all finely detailed. I'm not in any way trying to pull the curtain on the Wizard of Oz here. *This Boy's Life* is a remarkable book, and perhaps Wolff does remember every detail from his childhood with clarity. But as far as I'm concerned, the point is not whether every detail is completely accurate or each word recorded verbatim. The point is, is it a good story? Does it say something true about human relationships, about our tentative place in the world? Does it evoke a time and place outside of our own? If the answer to these questions is yes, I don't care whether it's called a memoir or a novel.

Making Distinctions

So what's the distinction between novels and memoirs? One good one is that not all novels deal with real life, while all memoirs ostensibly do. Plenty of science fiction and fantasy novels are out there, but no science fiction memoirs as far as I know, unless you count the works of Carlos Castaneda, published in the 1970s, which recount his professedly true adventures with a mystical Indian named Don Juan. They're not exactly science fiction, but they're pretty wild.

Many people in the past have written thinly veiled tell-all books disguised as fiction. They're called romans à clef. In the late 1970s, Truman Capote was working on one about Hollywood called *Answered Prayers,* and an excerpt was published in *Esquire.* Half of his friends disowned him because he'd told a lot of secrets about their lives. He uncovered a lot of dirt. His defense was pretty valid: His former friends told him these stories freely at parties, in the presence of others, knowing all along that he was a writer. "What did they think I was?" he asked with a mixture of hurt and acidity, "the court jester?"

Making the commitment to write a novel can be intimidating. When I was in graduate school at the Iowa Writers' Workshop, many students were afraid to say they were working on a novel. Instead, they'd say, "I'm working on something longer." And that's pretty much how I feel.

The late author Norma Klein once said that to begin her first novel, she didn't think of it as a novel. She told herself she would write ten pages a day about a certain group of people over a certain amount of time, and after three hundred pages, she would see what she had written. She also didn't allow herself to go back and correct more than five pages from the previous day's work.

As far as I'm concerned, Klein's model is a good one. After you've written two hundred or so pages, it's a novel. It might not be a good one. It might not be published. It's longer than a story or a novella, so what else can it be? A memoir?

Still, I know I'm begging the question. According to writer David Shields, novels in general tend to be more concerned with story, while memoirs tend to focus more on an exploration of identity. That's not to say that novels are *always* more concerned with story, while memoirs are *always* more concerned with an exploration of identity, just that those are the tendencies.

In Shields's case, his work has steadily crept away from fiction into the realm of nonfiction. His first novel, *Heroes,* about a Midwestern basketball player and the reporter obsessed with him, is, more or less, a story he imagined whole cloth. His next novel, *Dead Languages,* a widely praised novel about a boy who stutters, contains many elements of autobiography. As a child, Shields had a serious stuttering problem, but the story is almost entirely fiction. *A Handbook for Drowning,* a story collection, is a step closer to autobiography—a few of the pieces feel, to Shields, almost like essays even if most of the details are imagined. His next work, *Remote,* is a series of fifty-two interconnected prose meditations. It is unquestionably a work of nonfiction. To Shields, the prose pieces coalesce into a kind of oblique autobiography. In this book, the author "reads his own life as though it were an allegory, an allegory about remoteness." Despite the autobiographical nature of the book, Shields still thinks the persona that emerges on the page is essentially a fictional character. "The identity I've evoked," he explains, "the voice I've used, the tone I've maintained, the details I've chosen, are highly selective, and in many instances, frankly fictionalized. To me, these definitions get pretty murky. Memory is a dream machine. The moment you put words on paper, the fiction-making begins.

His books since *Remote* have all had this in common, essentially prose meditations with a nonfictional bent but a protagonist who is in some way David Shields and in other ways isn't. A persona, in other words. When he was writing his book *Black Planet,* an exploration of race through the eyes of a white basketball fan, David went to every home game of the Seattle Supersonics. He went to the games with different friends, but in order to streamline and simplify things, he transformed these people into one composite character. His own "character" was obsessed with the basketball player Gary Payton. In real life, is Shields obsessed with Payton? Not really, but for the purposes of the book's themes, he torqued up his own admiration into obsession. For the most part, the book was well received, but a few reviewers excoriated him for his supposedly neurotic obsession and phobia about race. But in Shields's defense, it was not his racial phobia he explored in the book, but society's racial phobia through a persona he created named David Shields. Does the fact that Shields becomes an everyman, a stand-in for society's neuroses, make the book a work of fiction? I don't think so because his concerns are largely nonfictional concerns having to do with a meditation on identity rather than a dramatic narrative as such. The essential distinction between nonfiction and fiction isn't one of fact versus lies, though typically a a fiction writer transforms events more than a nonfiction writer. The essential difference is one of form, a difference between the meditative/associative and the narrative/dramatic.

But the question remains, *How do you decide on a novel or a memoir?* To a large degree, that's an individual decision, based on who you are and what your material is. Shields tells his students to ask themselves, "What is it you're trying to get to? Are you essentially trying to tell a story, and if so, are you interested in setting that story in some kind of place? Then you are probably working on a novel. But if the real impulse is a kind of excavation of a self, a kind of meditation on the self, are you really working on a memoir or autobiography of some kind?" When Shields began working on *Remote,* he thought it was going to be a novel. "After a while, though, I realized I wasn't interested in character conflict per se. And I wasn't interested in a physical place, though I made gestures in those directions. What I was interested in was more autobiographical: the revelation of a psyche's theme via a sequence of tightly interlocking prose riffs, which became the book."

Story or plot as defined by character conflict seems to be the main distinction we can make here. Story involves a cause/effect relationship—that is, the character and her motivations are generally what fuels the story and its attendant conflict. A memoir proceeds perhaps more as memory does, in brief, episodic flashes illuminated by an overall picture of a central consciousness. Of course, memoir and fiction often bleed into each other, as we've already discussed, so these are not firm distinctions. Memoirs often contain conflict, as in Tobias Wolff's conflict with his stepfather, and fiction will often be concerned with an uncovering of the self in the context of the world surrounding the self—as in much of the work of Milan Kundera.

Let's take the discussion down a few notches and ask ourselves some questions that are perhaps more pedestrian, but no less important.

Ask yourself how wedded you are to the facts of the story. Must you stay true to the core of the initial experience? Must you convey the whole of that experience? If you can't bear changing even the name of your grade-school teacher, you might want to write a memoir, and you should find a book on memoir writing.

Why do you want to write this memoir in the first place? To get something off your chest? That might be good for you on a personal level, but that's not a good reason for anyone else reading your book.

The nature of the material itself rarely provides much help in deciding between a memoir and a novel. The most unusual story might make a terrible novel or memoir. The most ordinary story (growing up in Concrete, Washington) can be turned into a moving and artful memoir. The secret is in the ability and concerns of the writer, not in the material. Fiction writers sometimes pretend that their imagined writing is actually nonfiction or that their nonfiction is actually imagined, but these are simply tricks and subterfuges. Calling a story true if the writing isn't believable might fool most of the people most of the time, but not all of the people all of the time. Likewise, couching a nonfiction story in fictional terms won't necessarily stop you from being sued—but more on that in a later chapter.

Here's a note for beginning writers. If you haven't written much before your attempt to write your memoirs or your autobiographical novel, it would be a good idea to get some training. That you know how to write doesn't automatically mean you can write well yet. Think how absurd it would be for a cello student, after learning how to hold the bow and play the scales, to immediately audition for first cello in the New York Philharmonic. Like any craft, writing fiction or nonfiction well often takes a long apprenticeship. The first thing you should do is read as many memoirs or novels as you can, and at the same time, enroll in a local creative writing class at a university or community college. Don't tell your teacher that the only reason you're in the class is so you can write your memoirs or the great American novel. Put it aside for the time being. Write a lot. Listen to the comments of your classmates and your teacher. Take the same class again or move to the next level. I bet your conception of the book will change entirely.

Anecdotes and Short Stories

I heard an anecdote once that a woman I know swore was true. It concerned a woman in a small town in Scotland who was a social climber. She decided to have a party and invite the elite of her town so she could rub elbows with them: the doctors, the lawyers, the editor of the newspaper. One of the dishes she prepared was a salmon mousse, and right before her party began, she caught her cat on the table, chowing down on the salmon. Angrily, she whisked the cat off the table and put it outside. What could she do with the salmon but smooth over the spot the cat had eaten? Just as she was finishing the body job on the salmon, the doorbell rang and the first of her guests arrived.

The party was tremendously successful, and the woman hosting the party felt like she'd finally been accepted into the high society of her town.

As the party was breaking up, she went to the back door to let her cat in. There, lying by the doorstep, was her cat, stone dead. Horrified, she called the town doctor and told him about the salmon mousse and poor kitty. Unfortunately, there was no choice, he told her. She had to announce what had happened to her guests, and they'd all have to go to the hospital to get their stomachs pumped.

She knew this was going to be the end of her social-climbing days, but she thought it would be better to have angry guests than dead ones. So they formed a caravan, went to the hospital and, one by one, had their stomachs pumped. The hostess, humiliated, sat off in a corner of the waiting room and waited until the end to have the procedure. She avoided the gazes of her guests, and none of them spoke to her as they left the hospital. No one thanked her for a lovely evening.

She finally arrived home at about 1:00 A.M. exhausted and demoralized. Strangely, her neighbor rushed out to greet her as her car pulled in the driveway. "Oh, it's awful. I'm so sorry," the neighbor said.

"Thank you," said the woman, searching her neighbor's face for any hint of sarcasm. After all, she hadn't been invited. But the woman seemed sincere.

"Yes, the whole evening was a disaster because of it," said the woman.

"I'm truly sorry," the neighbor said. "I know how much it must have meant to you."

"It meant the world," said the woman, thinking that no one would accept another party invitation from her as long as she lived.

"How long did you have it?" the neighbor asked.

"Oh, only about two hours, and then we found out and had to go to the hospital."

The neighbor looked bewildered. "Well, I wish there was something I could have done. Your cat just ran behind the car as I was backing out of the driveway. And I was in such a rush that all I could do was place him by your back doorstep. When I returned home, I went over to explain, but you were gone. So I've been waiting for you ever since."

About two months after I heard the story and wrote it down in my journal, the late Mike Royko, a columnist for the *Chicago Tribune,* related the exact same story. Various people had told it to him, swearing it was true, that it had happened to a mother or a cousin or an aunt, and that it had taken place in Texas, Montreal, or Baltimore. There are plenty of these urban legends floating around, and half of the people who tell them will swear they happened to someone they know.

An anecdote generally ends with a kind of punch line, the recognition by the reader or listener that something remarkable or laughable has happened. Contemporary stories demand a little more character development and sophistication than your average anecdote.

Character development, in fact, is the centerpiece of most short stories, and plot is secondary. Or rather, the plot should arise organically out of character development in a short story. As Janet Burroway says in her book *Writing Fiction,* a character should want something and want it intensely. This desire or character motivation is the driving force in most short stories. The conflict arises from the character's desires being met or thwarted or ignored. Another way to put it is, *What does a character fear?* Or, *What does a character* not *want to happen?* Sometimes characters in a short story don't know what they want, and this can be part of the conflict as well. Or else they think they want one thing when they should want another. Or maybe they want a lot of things, too many things for one life to achieve. Grace Paley's story "Wants" in her collection *Enormous Changes at the Last Minute* is a beautiful example of characters' desires coming into conflict. The story is barely more than three pages long, but Paley manages to write in such a richly textured way that the story seems completely realized in that short span. The story involves a woman who's returning a couple of Edith Wharton books to the public library. Sounds mundane enough, but the books are overdue by eighteen years. She meets, on the steps of the library, her ex-husband, and the two of them have a discussion, which at first seems harmless enough, but then devolves into acrimony, at least on the husband's part. He tells her he always wanted a sailboat and accuses her of never having wanted anything. This narrow and bitter remark leaves her stunned on the steps of the library. The rest of the story deals with her ruminations concerning what she wanted, things her insensitive husband could never guess.

So what about the anecdote about the salmon mousse? Isn't that a short story? After all, it contains most of the usual elements: conflict, crisis, and resolution. The main character has a strong desire to better herself and is thwarted by the coincidence of her cat being run over by her neighbor.

Of all the anecdotes I've related so far, this one comes closest to being a story rather than an anecdote, partly because I doctored the anecdote (much as the unfortunate social climber doctored her salmon mousse), primarily by fleshing out the story, by inventing dialogue, and thus somewhat developing the character. The original anecdote, as I heard it, wouldn't take up more than a paragraph. Still, I'd say that the irony is too broad to make a successful short story. It relies too much on coincidence, on the punch line, to make it something more than a funny happening, something to relate at a party or to put in a newspaper column. A few years after I heard the salmon mousse story, it became part of a Hollywood film, *Her Alibi,* with Tom Selleck and Paulina Porizkova. Hollywood, of course, is the perfect place to recycle such urban legends. Short stories usually go beneath the surface. That's not to say short stories should be dry and dull, but what happens should never be as important as to whom it happens. In an anecdote, *what* happens usually takes precedence over any serious character development.

There are basically three ways to use an anecdote in a short story. One way is to flesh out the anecdote, develop the characters, and bring it beyond a simple punch line. I did this with a story called "Polish Luggage." It was based on an anecdote a woman told me about her father. He was an airline pilot who was incredibly racist and sexist and classist and other assorted "ists." He always complained that the "riff-raff" had taken to the skies ever since the airlines had started cutting their fares. He recognized "riff-raff" by their "Polish luggage." That's what he called shopping bags. He thought it was low-class to bring a shopping bag instead of a proper bag onto a plane.

For this and plenty of other reasons, the woman and her dad didn't get along. But when he died, all of their differences were forgotten, and she went home to his funeral.

The funeral was fairly elaborate. The mother had decided to have him cremated and then to have his ashes dropped from a plane to a hill on which she and her husband had watched the sunset on their first date.

When the family arrived at the little hangar, the funeral director took them to an office and explained what would happen when the plane was aloft. As he spoke, he opened a drawer, took out a shopping bag, and dumped the father's ashes in it. The ashes had been in a beautiful urn, and when the daughter saw what was happening to her father, that he was taking his last journey in "Polish luggage," she was both horrified and amused.

The story was told to me on a Wisconsin farm owned by a couple of my friends from Chicago, and the woman who told me the story came over that day for that purpose. This might sound strange, but my hosts knew it was a good story, and the woman who told it wasn't a writer herself. (This wasn't the only story she told me on that day. I've got two more ideas based loosely on what she told me. And don't think I'm going to tell them to you. You might steal them.)

I loved the anecdote, but in writing the story, I obviously had to go beyond the punch line. The first order of business was deciding who the main character was going to be. I decided to keep the main character the daughter of the airline pilot, though I changed her character around a great deal. Not because of ethical considerations, in this case. I changed the character of the woman to make the material my own.

That's an important part of transforming real life (a phrase, by the way, I have trouble with. What's the alternative? Fake life?) into fiction. The way you claim ownership of a story is by using your imagination, by transforming the story into something new. If you don't, the events and characters of the story wind up owning you instead of the other way around. You'll be afraid to deviate from what really happened, and the story ultimately might suffer.

To give the story a little more flesh than the original anecdote, I decided to expand the mother's idea of dumping the father's ashes on the hill from which they viewed the sunset on their first date. I decided to turn the *whole* funeral into a reconcoction of the mother and father's first date. The narrator of the story naturally thinks her mother's a little kooky for coming up with such a plan, but she reluctantly goes along with it.

The plan calls for a procession, stations of the cross fashion, from one memorable spot of their first date to another. First, we'll drive past the Chinese restaurant where they had dinner that night, though it wasn't a Chinese restaurant then, but a fancy steak house with a seventeen-piece band. After that, we'll swing by the Parthenon Theater, and finally we'll trek out to the municipal airport where Daddy's ashes will be scattered from a plane high above the hill on which he and Mother watched the sunrise the next day. There's a dual beauty here, because Daddy was an airline pilot, though he would have preferred a 747 to a Cessna. Rather than being dropped, he would have liked the jet to explode him into Valhalla with his Viking ancestors.

Another way to use an anecdote, from your experience or someone else's, is to incorporate the anecdote as part of a story's dialogue, or make it a monologue. While an anecdote might not always work as the basis for an entire story, such an anecdote can work quite nicely as a way to show something about the personality of the character who's telling it. For instance, the anecdote of the man selling the pornographic key chains was something I decided to put in Angel's mouth as a way of further explicating her character, giving the reader an idea of what she considers important in life, what she thinks is right and wrong.

The third way to use an anecdote is to incorporate it into a story as one of several events, but not necessarily the main one. That's what I decided to do with the squirrel in the pizza box. The story in which that scene appears continues for another twelve pages. That way, although the anecdote still retains its punch line, it isn't the superficial culmination of the story.

Anecdotes and Novels

Novels, as well as stories, can evolve from anecdotes. Peter Turchi, the Director of the MFA Program for Writers at Warren Wilson College, based his first novel, *The Girls Next Door,* on an anecdote his father told him when he was young. "The story he told was this: In 1956 and again in early 1960, when my mother was pregnant with me, these people rented the house right next to theirs, and it became clear that they were running a whorehouse. But nobody ever saw them. These girls were never outside. My father had a station wagon and a U-Haul that he hooked up to it with demonstration models of industrial equipment that he was selling. And he would have to hook up the trailer to the station wagon every Monday morning before he went on his rounds. And he'd be gone for a few days.

"One time he backed up the station wagon and he didn't back it up quite far enough so he tried to lift up the hitch and pull the trailer forward, but of course it was too heavy for him. The three girls happened to be outside this one time, so they all came over and they gathered around him. And together they were able to pull it up to the car. He looked up at our kitchen window and there's my mother pregnant with me, and on either side of her, her parents glaring out at him. And that was it. That was the anecdote. That was his memory of these women. I think they left a couple of weeks after that. And he didn't know them by name, and didn't have any more interesting adventures with them."

Even though this anecdote became the basis for his novel, Turchi didn't immediately see it as such. At first, the novel had nothing to do with this story and was instead far afield from his own experience. Turchi's witty explanation of the evolution of his novel idea shows how novelists often roam far from their own imaginative territory, simply to arrive at material that's closer to home.

"I was in England for my junior year in college, and on one of the breaks I spent a couple of weeks in Paris in this fairly inexpensive hotel that was actually somebody's house in the Latin Quarter. A couple lived there with their boy who was eight or nine. Every morning I'd come down for breakfast, and he'd be having his breakfast and doing his homework at the last minute. None of them spoke any English at all. And I spoke pretty poor French. I started to wonder what it would be like to grow up with your house as a hotel, kind of an Irving-esque idea, and seeing these strangers come through, not knowing what they're all about. And so I thought I would write this story or book about a boy who grew up in a family hotel in France. The problem was that I didn't know anything about Paris or France or anything about being a French boy. So I decided it might be a good idea to transport the whole notion for the story to Kansas, where this boy would grow up in a hotel. At least he'd be American. But of course, I'd never been to Kansas. I still don't know what made me think that would be a good place to set a novel. It should come as no surprise that I finally decided to set the story in Baltimore, the only place I'd lived of those three.

"Then I started thinking maybe it shouldn't be the boy's story because that's already kind of a cliché, the coming-of-age novel. Then I thought maybe it would be the story told by one of the boarders in the house, somebody who lived there regularly and watched this family, which is sort of the position I'd been in. And then he was going to watch something going on across the street. And finally, it turned out not to be the boy or a boarder, but the father. Somehow I realized in there that the story had grown awfully close to the story I remembered my father telling.

"For whatever reason, my first impulse was not to find out anything more about what really happened. In fact, I found out everything I know now about what happened in 1960, beyond what I've just related, after the novel was published. All sorts of people from the neighborhood came up to me to tell me their tales about these prostitutes, which were great. It would have been wonderful material—for a different book."

Turchi's hunch that he should rely on his own imagination rather than the real events of that time was undoubtedly the wisest choice to make. While the real material might have added a different dimension to the novel, it also might have bogged him down, or made him feel too responsible to the way things actually happened rather than the way they needed to happen in the novel. By reimagining events, he was able to make the material his own and divorce himself from pure remembrance. "I kept trying to imagine what it must have felt like to be my father back then, and in fact, the first draft of the novel included his occupation. Probably the only reason the novel is set in 1960 is because I was working from that anecdote. And it was probably pretty heavily flavored by the innocence with which he told the anecdote.

"What became important to me finally in writing the novel was not the premise, but what the main character was understanding in terms of his family. The real job of putting that novel together was trying to incorporate that rich anecdote into what I finally became much more interested in exploring in terms of character. That shuffling together, that integration, took seven years to figure out."

Stories Versus Novels

Whether you write a novel or a short story depends largely on your material and what kind of writer you are. Stories are much more like poems than they are like novels. Stories tend to be as tightly constructed as poems and are generally much more concerned with an economical use of language than novels are. In a story, a character might be described by a gesture; in a novel, by three or four pages of description and flashback. Digressions are much more possible in novels than in short stories. A scene that might make a nice side trip in a novel will most likely seem utterly unnecessary in a story if it doesn't directly relate to the main character. In a novel, different points of view can be more easily explored, while they might seem jarring in a short story. Although figurative language (metaphors, similes) is used by both novelists and short-story writers, a good short-story writer can create a jewel of a central metaphor so sharp and fine you'll marvel at the craft. No one says you must stick to one form or the other, though often writers, like Flannery O'Connor, will excel in short stories but not novels—or vice versa.

A friend once told me that he found it so difficult to create a believable character whom the reader cared about that he wouldn't let that character go after one short story. If that's how you feel about your characters, you're probably best suited for the novel form. If, however, you find yourself fascinated by the moment, by brief flashes of life, the short story might be your form.

One cautionary note, however. Writing workshops are best suited for the discussion and dissection of short stories, not novels. While some noble teachers attempt novel-writing workshops, the workshops could be harmful if not handled correctly. Novels are fragile things, and many fledgling novels have been nipped in the bud by a writing workshop. If you turn in the first thirty pages of your novel before you've written the next three hundred, your peers will inevitably treat it like a short story. What might seem like a fault in a short story (uncertainty about the direction of the story, lack of closure, unexplained happenings) can hardly be avoided in the beginning of a novel. Maybe your peers can praise the quality of your writing, but they can't give you direction. You're the one with the overall conception of the novel. Your classmates are clueless. A novel cannot be written by committee—so don't attempt it. The other pitfall of this approach is "first-chapter-itis," rewriting your first chapter over and over again to your classmates' delight but your own frustration. What you'll wind up with is a perfect first chapter with closure, direction, and explained happenings—in other words, a short story!

EXERCISES

1. Write an anecdote, something someone told you or that you observed. This should be a story you're quite familiar with, something that you've told before. Write the opening scene of

the anecdote, a page or two, then make notes on how you would transform it into a story, how you would go beyond the punch line. Who is the main character? What does that character want or fear?

2. Using the same anecdote, create a character who tells another character this tale. Describe the setting and circumstances in which this character relates the anecdote. Pay special attention to the reactions of the character being told the anecdote, and also what the telling of the anecdote shows about the speaker's personality.

3. Take a family incident from your childhood and write it exactly as you remember it, without embellishment. After you've finished, ask a relative how he or she remembers this incident. Are there any major or even minor differences in the way he or she remembers the event? Why do you think this is?

4. Use this same memory as the basis of a fictional scene, using a combination of dialogue, action, description, thoughts, and exposition. What choices will you have to make to fictionalize it? Are there details or characters you have to add or leave out in the fictional treatment?

5. Write this same scene over again from a point of view not your own. How have the details changed? How has the memory changed?

▼

CHAPTER THREE

Focusing Real Life

You now have some idea of the various forms, but another question must be answered: How do we impose order on something as messy as real life? Order, after all, is the essential difference between real life and fiction. Real life, if yours is anything like mine, tends toward chaos. Fiction has structure, order, refinement. Imposing the artificial—that's what fiction writers do to turn their stories into art. Fiction can be boisterous, even obnoxious at times. The art of writing fiction, like a good magic trick, is often in making it seem easy, effortless—in never letting the reader see all the practice you've put into it.

The temptation, which must always be resisted, is to include *everything* that happened, rather than making wise selections. Be parsimonious with your experience. Don't give it added weight simply because you're fond of the memory. If you include everything that happened, your book or story risks becoming muddled and weighted down by a voluminous chronicle of your associations. Remember, this is a piece of fiction, not a slide show of your various experiences. If you let the structure of your story or novel collapse, the reader will stop paying attention to what you've written.

Every novel or short story has a *handle*—that is, something the writer and reader can grab onto, a reference point, something that makes us feel like we're in good hands with someone who knows where he is headed. Anything can be a handle. What we're ultimately after is a *focus*. Your handle is simply your focusing element.

Novelist Elly Welt even took the concept literally. When she was working on her novel *Berlin Wild,* her husband brought her a wooden handle he'd found while walking on the beach. She hung it on the wall above her

< 55 >

writing desk. And that was what she looked at for inspiration when she was writing.

The following are some handles to help you rein in your life and tame it to the world of fiction. These can be used for either stories or novels, and none of these forms, of course, is restricted to stories that are based on real life. In succeeding chapters, we'll discuss various types of stories that come from real life, but for now it might be good to have some basic ideas of the ways in which authors structure their works of fiction.

Focusing on a Character

In *Making Shapely Fiction,* Jerome Stern defines voice as: "the writer's style as it is expressed in the character's speech and thoughts." Point of view is basically the central consciousness of the story (or chapter from a novel, as the case may be). It might seem like the simplest choice, when writing about a real event, to write from the point of view based on your own. But often, the character based on yourself is really unnecessary, and any time you have a character who isn't important to the story, you should cut her out. Writers tend to be observers. Even though we write about people in conflict, we tend to stay out of the fray ourselves, preferring instead a comfortable seat from the sidelines. The Hemingways are much rarer than the Prousts; rather than big-game hunters, writers are more often slightly hypochondriacal, neurotic imaginers who lock themselves in their rooms all day.

So, often when we write a story, whether based on real life or not, we'll include a passive narrator who has no role in the story other than serving as the reader's eyes and ears. Sometimes this works. A famous example is Nick in *The Great Gatsby,* but more often than not, the passive narrator simply gets in the way. If, however, you feel that a character based on yourself must be the narrator, make sure that he plays some active role, that the events of the story affect him in some way. (Don't misunderstand me. I'm not saying that Nick was based on Fitzgerald himself. Fitzgerald was undoubtedly more like Gatsby than Nick. Maybe that's why both characters worked so well. Fitzgerald was able to create enough distance to fashion a character *unlike* himself, viewing a character *like* himself.)

Often, the worst strategy for writing a story is to have one character telling another character or characters the story of her life. It's a rather bald device, used to good effect by Joseph Conrad and others in earlier days, but a little too familiar to capture most readers' attention these days. Of course, if you can twist this idea around and make it fresh, you might succeed.

It's usually best to cut out the listener and tell the story from the point of view of one of the principals. You also must decide whether you will write the story in first or third person or, less frequently, second person. Delmore Schwartz uses second person in "In Dreams Begin Responsibilities," his haunting story about a young man dreaming that he's watching a film of his parents on their first date. We can't assume, of course, that it's actually based on a true account of his parents' meeting. The writer always has the defense (sometimes more accurate than at other times) that there is a difference between the author and the narrator of a story. Ideally, you want every story you write to seem autobiographical, to seem authentic in its emotions as well as its physical details, so that the reader is tricked into thinking "this really happened."

First person is useful in letting a character speak for himself. In a first-person story, the distance between the reader and the character's psyche, what John Gardner calls "psychic distance," is foreshortened. And since we tend as listeners to more readily believe something told *by* someone than *about* someone, first person can often lend an aura of authenticity.

If you still are unsure of what voice is, listen to this opening of Barry Hannah's story "Water Liars":

> When I am run down and flocked around by the world, I go down to Farte Cove off the Yazoo River and take my beer to the end of the pier where the old liars are still snapping and wheezing at one another. The line-up is always different, because they're always dying out or succumbing to constipation, etc., whereupon they go back to the cabins and wait for a good day when they can come out and lie again, leaning on the rail with coats full of bran cookies. The son of the man the cove was named for is often out there. He pronounces his name Far*tay,* with a great French stress on the last syllable. Otherwise you might laugh at his history or ignore it in favor of the name as it's spelled on the sign.
>
> I'm glad it's not my name.

Don't use first person simply to get closer to a character. In third person, limited, you can get just as close to a character as with first. You also shouldn't write in first person simply because the story happened to you. In that case, you might be better off writing in third person so you can transform the story into a fictional realm. And voice isn't necessarily more prominent in first than third person, though it often is. But listen to the opening paragraph of Marjorie Sandor's story, "Victrola." The voice here is as different as can be from Barry Hannah's, but it's no less sure and strong. We still have a definite sense of the way the character thinks and speaks, though the story is told in third person. We also have the overlying consciousness of the narrator, who directs us through the child's world:

> She was stubborn from day one. For her, words like fate or destiny, words we throw around, were as real as the roots of the live oak, spreading under the sidewalk where no one can see them but the child who stands directly under the tree, imagination intact. She didn't know what life intended for her, but it was obvious to the casual observer that she meant to have one, since she eluded death and disaster so well, even when her mother, the beautiful idiot, was managing things. By the time Francisca was eight years old, she had already survived three Mazatlan epidemics and the stings of two deadly scorpions. She was also known for her tendency to have fever dreams that nobody could decipher. It was just after the second scorpion and its accompanying dream that she awoke to see her father's yellow guitar sailing through the air across their shed.

The point of view you choose will naturally mold your story and keep it from being too messy. When you change point of view, you change the story. Experiment. Explore your options. If a story based on a real event doesn't work from one point of view, try another.

Focusing on a Setting

Sometimes the setting of your story or novel can be the handle you're looking for. Think of how Tara, the antebellum Southern estate, functions in *Gone with the Wind*. It's the driving force behind most of Scarlett's actions. It's her motivation for most of what she does. When all else is crumbling around her, she still believes in her land. Other writers have used setting as the organizing principle behind a collection of stories: James Joyce's *Dubliners* and Sherwood Anderson's *Winesburg, Ohio* immediately leap to mind.

The writer Steve Yarbrough uses his hometown of Indianola, Mississippi, as his organizing principle. All the stories in his collection *Family Man* are centered in or around Indianola, and this gives the book a kind of unity, much the way a novel has a sense of cohesiveness.

Focusing on the Story

At some point in a novel or a short story, the reader needs a sense of direction. Some readers will give a novel a hundred pages to get going, some will allow only fifty, but if you ramble from one episode to another, your reader might not stick with you for long at all. An episode is an event within a series of events. If these events do not seem connected by a cause/effect relationship, we say the story or novel seems episodic or rambling. Short stories are sometimes criticized for being too episodic—there's no thread pulling the reader along. Sometimes episodic stories can work as long as something else holds the story together, such as a theme or a strong voice.

Scenes are the same as episodes, except they're more purposeful. Scenes are constructed. Episodes just happen. Our memories tend to be episodic. We remember in associative flashes. A scene is an episode consciously molded into the confines of a story. When we speak of a scene in a movie, a novel, or a play, we talk about an episode confined to one time and place. If the time or place shifts, we've gone on to a new scene.

We remember the time our older brother tied a string to one of our back molars and tried to yank it out by tying the other end of the string to the bathroom door and slamming it. Maybe that memory leads to another episode: our older brother lining our G.I. Joes against the wall of our house and blowing them apart with his BB gun. Now we remember how every Sunday morning our brother woke us up at six and forced us to help deliver the bulky Sunday edition of the paper. For this, he paid us a nickel or half a candy bar—our choice.

All these events happened at different times in our lives. The tooth-pulling incident took place when we were five. The BB-gun execution took place when we were nine. The paper-route exploitation took place when we were seven. No problem, as far as that's concerned. For the purposes of fiction, you can always collapse events together. No one but your mother and your older brother will care that these events didn't happen at the same time. Remember, you're writing a story, not a family history.

But let's further examine these events. How are they connected? They all show certain aspects of sibling rivalry, an older brother bullying a younger one. Are we leaving anything out? Of course. We're almost certainly leaving out the fact that the younger brother was no angel either, and that he probably tormented his older brother, too—though how he did this escapes us at the moment.

So will this make a good basis for a story? Not in its present form. Right now, it's just three episodes, all of which make the same point about the brothers and their relationship. It's true that sometimes you want to repeat themes in your writing, to reinforce them in your reader's mind, but episodes should not seem repetitive; they should build, one upon the other, to enlarge our understanding of the characters in the story.

Brainstorming

To fit these autobiographical episodes into a story or a novel, we must enlarge the story first. A simple story about two brothers who don't get along might make a good anecdote, but it's nothing new. What's the angle? What's the spin? What makes this story different from all other stories about sibling rivalry? What makes it unique?

When I'm stuck like this, I brainstorm—that is, I think of more associations from my life. I write them in my journal. I make notes. Eventually, I find the story.

Okay, these episodes occurred between my older brother and me in the 1960s when we were growing up. Is there anything else I remember about him and our relationship from that time? There was the time his friend from New York, Danny, came to visit us in Athens, Ohio, where we'd moved from New York. He and Danny decided to build a bomb. I wanted to build a bomb with them, but they told me I was too young. So they went off on their own and I stayed home and built my own bomb, starting with a Windex bottle and pouring everything I could imagine from under the sink into it. Then I found some matches in one of my father's jackets and went into the field behind our house and lit the shoelace fuse that I'd soaked in

Windex. Flames shot out of the bottle, and the field near our house caught fire. I remember how surprised I was, not that I thought it wouldn't work, but I wasn't prepared for the consequences. I was in my tennis shoes and I began stamping the flames furiously. Somehow, I managed to get them all out, though my tennis shoes melted in the process and my feet were burned.

Good episode, but still an episode. I think we're getting closer, but we still haven't found the glue to hold these episodes together.

Okay, another episode. The memory of my mother and father fighting and how my older brother, sister (who was eighteen and old enough at the time to buy alcohol) and I walked into town and she bought them a bottle of champagne so they'd stop. I think it worked. I remember feeling special as I walked into town with my older siblings—how we were acting as a kind of united front.

Now we're getting close to seeing this as a whole story and not as a series of episodes. The key is that we've started getting close to the feelings of the characters, rather than simply reporting events. It is who the characters are—what motivates them, what makes them change—that are the crucial elements of fiction, not the events themselves. That idea or theme of consequences—of children not knowing the consequences of their actions and adults not caring sometimes about the consequences of their actions— appeals to me as does the feeling I had of acting in unity with my brother and sister.

The sister here, for the purposes of our story, probably isn't necessary, so let's get rid of her. I like the idea of making bombs. It seems unique, a new spin on sibling rivalry: competing bomb factories! We probably should keep the time frame the sixties, which after all, was a good time for making bombs. And what enlarges the story beyond the sibling rivalry? The conflict between the parents. The two conflicts will be parallel in our story.

As I said, I like the idea of consequences—the consequences of both adult actions and the actions of children. Now let's decide whose point of view the story should be in. We've got the choice of an older brother, say, about thirteen; a younger brother, eight; and the parents. Each would tell a different story.

I would choose the older brother for several reasons. By taking the story out of my own experience, I would give my imagination more freedom and

I wouldn't feel compelled to record my experiences as they really happened. It might also give me a better insight into my older brother. I also like the in-between age of thirteen—one foot in childhood, the other in adulthood.

Blocking Scenes

But we still need to focus. One way to do this is to block the scenes—write notes on the various scenes as you envision them, before you begin writing the story. This process can be frustrating and time consuming, but it's one of the best ways to clear your head and find some focus to your material.

The scenes won't necessarily stay the same as you conceive of them. Your conception of a story almost always changes as you get further into it, and you must allow this to happen. Don't try to force your story in one direction simply because that's the way you originally envisioned it. With Peter Turchi's novel *The Girls Next Door,* his dilemma was to figure out how to take the initial anecdote of his family living next door to a house of prostitution and transform an essentially passive, voyeuristic story into one in which characters were interacting.

"There are some important differences between the appeal of an anecdote and the necessary complexity of a novel," Turchi says. "For one thing, I realized it wouldn't be enough for this character to simply observe these people from the distance of the driveway for 250 pages. There was going to have to be some real interaction. So I tried to imagine the various relationships this person could have with those people and at the same time maintain a certain curious distance. Almost all of the scenes are fabricated. Novelist and short-story writer Ron Hansen gave me some advice at the Bread Loaf Writers Conference. I had a character who was interested in baseball because the whole time I was growing up in Baltimore, the Orioles were often in the World Series. The character was also fascinated by these characters across the driveway. So Hansen told me these prostitutes have got to play baseball. My first response was 'What a ludicrous suggestion,' but I went home and in the next month wrote a scene in which the prostitutes have a softball game and a picnic. It worked. What it really showed me was that the premise had to be set in motion. It wasn't enough to have the possibility of something interesting happen, but it had to start paying off in different ways. Sometimes it's tempting to try to avoid the greatest confron-

TURNING LIFE INTO FICTION   <63>

tations. I still think it's good advice to try to discover the most obvious, the most dramatic confrontation, and seeing if it will work."

So let's look for the most dramatic possibilities in our hypothetical story. One other point before we block it out and try to make our discoveries: Often the final image of my story will pop into my head before I've started to write the story. I might not even know what the image means. And that's fine. As I told you earlier, fiction is a discovery process. You don't necessarily know everything about your characters when you begin to write your story. You learn about them as you go along. In this case, I see the field on fire and the younger brother surrounded by flames, trying vainly to put them out.

Fire and bombs. We've come a long way from simple sibling rivalry. Something is pretty wrong with this family. What is it? Remember, stories involve conflict, and even though the story might be modeled on your family members, you may have to change them for the sake of the story in ways that make you uncomfortable. But, at this point you need to be careful. Simply overlaying a larger, more powerful conflict on your story could ring a little false—say, if you make the real conflict in the story incest or divorce. If you're not careful, the subject might overwhelm the story, and the reader might feel like she has stepped into a talk show rather than a short story. Let's stick with this theme of family warfare and see where it leads.

There are a couple of other facts I've held back from you. (When you find yourself doing that, you know those are the ones you shouldn't hold back. What's most powerful is often what you most want to hide.)

First, I was definitely my mother's favorite, and my older brother was my father's. This wasn't any big secret in our family. My father accused my mother of spoiling me, and he was right. My mother always took my side in a fight with my brother, and my father always took my brother's side. The year I was eight and my brother was thirteen, my father died. Of course, that changed the family dynamics forever. Also, my brother lost his ally.

Now I think we're getting somewhere. This seems to me to be the central conflict and a way to unify all the disparate episodes—how they all relate to warfare and how my father was the first casualty. Part of learning how to write autobiographical fiction is learning how to dig deeper and deeper, to try to understand why a particular event or time stands out for you—and it's not always for the reasons you think.

Here are some notes I wrote just now:

Bombs—central image

Bottles—champagne bottle, Windex bottle.

These bottle images are something I'll probably keep in mind throughout the story. Maybe the beginning of a central metaphor.
Now I see a definite thread here.

Scene One—I'd probably start the story with the older brother blowing up the younger brother's G.I. Joes, maybe getting yelled at by
his mother, and establishing the fact that the father has died. The
older brother expects a visit from a friend from the good old days
when they lived in New York. Maybe here I'd also introduce the
bottle of champagne. One of the brothers has saved it because he
likes the bottle.

Scene Two—Maybe the next scene would show some kind of retalia-
tion on the younger brother's part. The mother, predictably, takes
the younger brother's side, perhaps even subtly or not so subtly
blames the older brother for his father's death. The older brother
plans revenge or running away; secretly he calls his best friend from
New York. The next day, the two brothers deliver papers together in
relative calm. The younger brother, being young and dumb, doesn't
realize that payment of half a candy bar or a nickel is not a very
good deal.

Scene Three—Danny's visit. Bombs.

Note how sketchy those notes are, especially the last ones. Not having
written the story yet, I can't know precisely where it will lead, nor all the
connections and revelations I will make along the way. Right now, I want
to play around with the idea of destruction and the various conflicts, both
external and internal. I wonder, for instance, if the older brother believes he
killed his father, and I wonder how self-destructive his actions are.
The story might work. It might not. If I've done my job right and have

some idea of cause/effect and understand the relationships among the various characters, my story will fit together into a series of unified scenes. If not, the story will seem episodic. That's the risk you take any time you set down to work on a story or novel. Not every story works, especially those created from the hash of memory. But at least I have some direction now.

Time Frames

One of the most common ways to impose a structure on your story or novel is through a *time frame*. Louisa May Alcott did this with *Little Women*. They story was semi-autobiographical, based on her childhood in the 1840s. The character of Jo was modeled on her. But Alcott structured her story by making everything happen in a year. She also changed the time, setting the story in the 1860s rather than the 1840s. Alcott's real father, Bronson Alcott, was a complex man, one of the leaders of the transcendentalists. Instead of dealing with his character, Alcott got rid of him. She sent him off to war.

You can choose whatever time frame you want. There are short stories that take place over a year or a lifetime, and there are novels that cover only one day, but the novel is really the medium for exploring the effects of time on a character or situation. And short stories generally deal with briefer time spans—one moment, one situation and its effects. There are no hard-and-fast rules about this. These are just tendencies of the forms. Some writers like to play around with time, stretching it as far as it can go. Nicholson Baker's novel *The Mezzanine* takes place in a thirty-second escalator ride. James Joyce's novel *Ulysses* takes place in one day. Back in Shakespeare's time, the convention was that a play's time frame could not exceed twenty-four hours. Shakespeare was considered a radical for breaking with this tradition.

Focusing on Metaphor, Symbol, or Theme

Another strategy for reining in your novel or short story is to weave in a central metaphor. An example of an autobiographical novel with a central metaphor is *The Bell Jar* by Sylvia Plath. Another is the play *The Glass Menagerie* by Tennessee Williams. Laura's menagerie functions beautifully as a metaphor of the girl's own fragility, just as the bell jar functions as a symbol of Plath's claustrophobia.

A metaphor should come organically from the story itself; it should never simply be inserted into a story. Writers, good writers, don't say, "I think I need a bird metaphor in this here story." By consciously inserting a metaphor into a story, you will probably wind up with a metaphor that's been used time and again, to the point of being a cliché. And your metaphor will seem obvious if it's simply inserted here and there.

By "organic," I mean that the metaphor should not be forced, but should arise naturally from the characters or situation. The trick is to trust your intuition, at least during the first draft. If your character says, "He wants me to be a goddess and I want to be Mickey Mouse," see where that image leads. Develop it. Echo it later in the story. Have it crop up in a different context. *You don't always need to know what a phrase or a gesture or a description* means *as you're writing it.* Trust your unconscious. Writing is a discovery process, and part of the fun of writing is learning why you just wrote what you did.

Perhaps that sounds outlandish to some, but it's the way most writers work. Flannery O'Connor started her story "Good Country People" with a dialogue between two women based on O'Connor's mother and a neighbor. Halfway down the page, O'Connor gave the first woman a daughter. Then she decided to give the daughter a wooden leg. She didn't know why she had a wooden leg or what it would mean, but she allowed the image to develop. And by the end of the story, the wooden leg functions beautifully as an organic symbol, if not a central metaphor. A bible salesman, who turns out to be a con artist, winds up stealing the wooden leg from the daughter, who up to that point has considered herself too intelligent and worldly to be taken in by anyone—especially by this salesman, whom she considers to be just another country bumpkin. In synopsis, the story sounds outlandish, and it is, in a brilliant way. Still, it works, and by the end of this story you believe that this bible salesman would indeed have a thing for the daughter's wooden leg and want to make off with it.

That's the idea of *symmetry* again. A good writer doesn't abandon an image or idea but sees where it will lead. Nothing happens for no good reason. If your character has a wooden leg because you want her to, but nothing is made of the leg in the story, take it out. If it doesn't serve a purpose, it doesn't belong.

A theme is the central idea of the story or novel. Often, there's more than one theme, and the themes are interconnected. Writers sometimes organize their work around a particular theme. In "Good Country People," such a theme is the difference between *professing* to be good or intelligent, and actually *being* good or intelligent. The trick is to avoid letting your theme overwhelm your characters. Don't have your characters act in a certain way simply because it fits your theme, rounds out your metaphor, or shows what a brilliant symbolist you are. There's nothing worse than pretentious prose full of symbols, themes, and metaphors galore, but little in the way of believable characters.

Journeys

The oldest form in fiction, according to Jerome Stern in *Making Shapely Fiction,* is the *journey.* A journey has a natural structure to it. There's the beginning, and then there's the end. One of my favorite journey stories, and one of the oldest, is the story of Jonah. This is really a short short story, almost minimalist, about the prophet Jonah's foolhardy attempts to go against God's will. It has all the elements of any good short story: conflict, character motivation, and revelation. Jonah, a prophet, is commanded by God to go to Nineveh and preach to the city's inhabitants so that they may be saved. But Jonah, who considers the people of Nineveh his enemy, doesn't want them to be saved, so he runs in the other direction, sets out to sea, gets caught in a storm, is thrown overboard, and is swallowed by a whale. Finally, he gets the message. "If I'd known it meant that much to you . . ." he tells God, or something to that effect, and he finally sets out for Nineveh. He preaches to the inhabitants and, lo and behold, they all repent, and the city is saved. Everyone is joyous except for Jonah, who goes outside the city gates, sits beneath the shade of a gourd, and thinks black thoughts. God, seeing this, decides to make the gourd, wither and die. That's the last straw for Jonah, who gets up and asks God why he had to go and do such a low-down thing as taking away his shade. This is the climax of the story, the point at which things change—and a story inevitably involves change. God basically says, "Look, you didn't create this gourd. And you didn't create the city of Nineveh. I did, so it's only for me to decide what lives and what dies." The story ends on an anticlimactic note: "And should not I pity Nineveh, that great city in which there are more than a hundred and twenty thousand persons who do not know their right hand from their left, and also much cattle?" Cattle? Kind of undercuts the story's power.

Some of the great classics of American literature have been journey stories. In *As I Lay Dying,* Faulkner chronicles one family's journey to bury its mother. In *The Grapes of Wrath,* Steinbeck depicts the Joads in their struggle to reach the promised land of California from their dustbowl home in Depression-era Oklahoma. In all of these journeys there's plenty of conflict, plenty of roadblocks thrown in the way of the characters on their journeys. And the roadblocks aren't only physical, but spiritual and emotional as well. By the end of these journeys, we know and deeply care about the fates of these characters.

The Big Event

A good way to organize a story or a novel is to structure it within an event: a game, a hunt, a wedding, a funeral. But you need to be careful with this form. Stay away from stasis, or lack of movement. Try to push the boundaries of whatever activity you've chosen to write about. If your characters are attending a wedding or funeral, try to see this event in a new light. Don't fall back on the standard clichés that surround such an event.

Almost everyone tries out one of these stories at some point or another. But they usually begin with something like this:

> Grandma Pickins wasn't the best woman in the world, thought
> Jolene, sitting by herself in the front row of Thunderbolt Baptist
> Church in Floyd's Knobs, Mississippi. But she wasn't the worst
> woman in the world, neither. Suddenly, her reverie was broken by
> the sight of Mabel Lee Mopes, her head bowed reverently in the
> opposite pew. Why that hussy, thought Jolene. How dare she show
> her face in here. Soon, Jolene was lost in reverie again . . .

And so on, until the reader loses himself or herself in reverie, too, and decides to go on to something more fun to do.

Jerome Stern calls this type of story, in which the main action is confined to a small space, a "bathtub story." In *Making Shapely Fiction* he writes, "While in that space the character thinks, remembers, worries, plans, whatever. Before long, readers realize that the character is not going to do anything."

I once read a story collection in which the characters kept falling asleep.

In each story, page after page would be devoted to a central character getting drowsy, nodding off, and slowly losing consciousness. The book had the same effect on me.

Of course, you can successfully turn around such an event as a wedding and make it lively and new. If you recall my story from chapter two, "Polish Luggage," I ignored my own advice and wrote about a funeral. There's no subject matter that's taboo. It's a matter of casting the subject in new light. But certain stories are notorious among creative-writing teachers, "dead grandmother stories" being at the top of the list.

Games can be great organizers for stories, too. One of the best I know of is Charles Dickinson's story, "Risk," [see page 208] based on the board game of world conquest. Dickinson's story is a tour de force in which he juggles the points of view of a group of friends who meet regularly to play this game. If you've ever played Risk, you'll remember how brutal it can be—almost as bad as croquet. But, as in any good story, the real conflict is beneath the surface, in the characters' secret lives that they reveal to the reader, but not to one another as each tries to take over the world. The game, as well as its name and all that the word *risk* implies, becomes a central metaphor of the organic variety we previously discussed. Here is the story's second paragraph:

> Frank is the first to arrive. Then Nolan. Frank wore dirty clothes
> that afternoon when he took the laundry down to the big machines
> in the basement of his apartment building; with the load in the
> washer, soap measured, and coins slotted, he added the clothes he
> was wearing and made the long walk back upstairs to his apartment
> naked. He paused to read the fine print on the fire extinguisher.
> Noises in the building set birds loose in his heart. Frank takes the
> red armies when they gather to play the game of world conquest.

What's especially remarkable about this story is the way in which Dickinson takes a static event like playing a board game and makes it seem anything but static. You can do the same with a game of chess, checkers, mah-jongg, croquet, marbles, whatever. The trick is to know your characters and their internal conflicts. Whether the conflict spills over into the orderliness of the game or remains internalized but reflected in the game is up to you.

A fishing expedition or a hunt can be a good focus for a story as well. Think of Hemingway's "The Short Happy Life of Francis Macomber" or Norman Maclean's *A River Runs Through It* or Faulkner's "The Bear" from *Go Down Moses*. But what you need to keep in mind, especially if you base your hunting story on a real-life experience (or any other stories based on real-life events), is that a lot of other people have been through these experiences before. You're not the first person who's used a deer hunt as the basis for a coming-of-age story. You're not the first person who's noticed that people can be hypocritical at funerals and weddings. You don't want your story to seem clichéd and boring. You want it to seem original and lively, much like the Charles Dickinson paragraph above. The trick is in making your characters seem real, and one of the best ways to do that is to base them, at least in part, on real people you've known or observed—which is something we'll discuss in the next chapter.

EXERCISES

1. We've all been to carnivals and fairs. Write a memory of a fair or carnival in as much detail as you can. Now make that the setting for the opening of a short story. But don't base the main character on yourself. If other memories of other carnivals flood in, be sure to include them.

2. Think about someone you've known well, someone from your family perhaps: a brother, sister, mother, father. First, write as many memories and associations of this person as possible. Mark the memories that seem especially resonant to you—ones that seem either most moving or that best show the personality of your subject. Now, brainstorm a bit and cast these memories in a fictional context. Block out scenes. Make associations. Write an outline for a story based on these memories. Be sure to stay focused.

3. Go somewhere with your journal and observe some people. Go to a mall, a park, a grocery store. Write down a description of these people. Now introduce a character in conflict with these

people, or a character who in some ways gets involved with these people—much as Peter Turchi got his prostitutes playing softball.

4. Organize the opening of a story around a game that you remember playing or observing someone else play; your grandmother playing Twister, you playing Scrabble, your younger brother playing croquet. Explore the relationships of your characters as they play this game.

5. Base a short short story of no more than a thousand words on a memory. Organize the story around a time frame: a day, a year, an hour, a minute. You may, if you want, use some of the ready-made structures we've discussed above: a game, a journey. A time frame or a central metaphor might emerge in relation to your characters. You'll notice that some memories will fit your imposed structure and some won't. Jettison the ones that don't fit and mold your memories to fit your structure. It's more important for the story to work than for the memories to be accurate.

▼

CHAPTER FOUR

Real People

We rarely write about other people simply as they're presented to us, mostly because we don't know all the facts of their lives, and so we have to make some of them up. There's nothing wrong with that. In many cases, knowing too little about someone is preferable to knowing too much. If you write a story based on a family member, for instance, or a friend, your feelings of affection and friendship for that person can easily get in the way of your story or novel. In other words, you'll leave things out—maybe the best parts of the story, maybe the details that intrigued you about this person in the first place—to protect your friend's privacy. That might be the ethical thing to do—an issue we'll explore more in depth in a later chapter—but it might also kill your story.

Transformations

Usually, there's a middle ground between imagining a character whole cloth and writing something completely biographical about someone you know. You must remember that you're writing fiction, not biography. Fiction, by its nature, involves transformation. If you want to write about Uncle Lou, go ahead, but don't make him Uncle Lou. First of all, think about what makes him so intriguing to you. The central ingredient, of course, is what you'll most likely want to keep. Let's say Uncle Lou believes in ghosts. This is something that's always fascinated you about him. This belief in ghosts sprang from an early childhood experience, when Uncle Lou was allegedly visited in the middle of the night by the ghost of his father. Other than this belief in ghosts, Uncle Lou seems rather plain and unexceptional to you. He's a balding, overweight bachelor. His politics are on the conservative

< 73 >

side. He's a quiet man who eats dinner every night with his widowed sister, your aunt Elena—she does all the cooking and cleaning. While she's in the kitchen fixing dinner, he's out in the living room reading the *Wall Street Journal*. During dinner, he hardly talks to Aunt Elena, and afterward, he departs with hardly a word.

Now you have two characters from your life, and this somewhat strange relationship between them—the kernel of a story. And what about Aunt Elena? Does she believe in ghosts, too? Or does she think Uncle Lou is just a little daffy?

Obviously, there are problems here if you want to write about these people. You may be a little reluctant to change too much about the characters and the situation. At the same time, you don't want to offend Aunt Elena or Uncle Lou. You don't want them to be able to recognize themselves. So you have two choices. Either you can wait until your uncle and aunt pass away to write about them, or you can change them. You can change their ages. But no, what interests you about them is that they're both older, a little lonely, a little dependent on each other, and also obsessed with something that might or might not have occurred when Lou was a little boy: the sighting of his dead father. Okay, so change their sexes. Make Aunt Elena the one who saw the ghost. Do they have to be brother and sister? How about husband and wife? Must it be their dead father? What about their mother or a stranger? Can you change the outward appearance of Uncle Lou? Depicting him as balding might offend him more than the way you portray his belief in ghosts. That's what happened to a friend of mine who wrote of a mutual friend in a story. He was cast as a short-order cook, a complete fabrication, but in every other way my friend captured his personality perfectly, from his wise-cracking sense of humor to his receding hairline. The mention of the receding hairline was, of course, what upset him.

The fact is, you can rarely tell what will or won't offend someone in a story you've written about them. The best you can do is to change whatever you can bear to change about them. Make your uncle Lou a short-order cook. Make Aunt Elena the owner of the diner. Or change the locale. Above all, don't mess with male pattern baldness.

All of this is done not simply to protect Uncle Lou and Aunt Elena's privacy, but for your sake as well. In a way, you must stop thinking of them as your real-life relatives for the story to be successful. You must cut loose from your ties to these people or else your story will seem stilted and you'll be afraid to take risks. The more you transform these people into combinations of your imagination and who they really are, the more liberated you'll feel in writing your story. Remember, just because you *base* a character on Aunt Elena doesn't mean you're restricted to the facts.

Mixing and Matching

Another way to transform your characters is by making them into *composites*—that is, a mix of your uncle Lou and perhaps other real people you know, people who have a certain Lou-ness about them. This way, Uncle Lou will not simply be Uncle Lou, but also perhaps your friend's father, and maybe a pinch of some stranger you once saw in passing and wrote about in your journal. By making a composite character, you actually enrich the character. Real observed detail only enhances a story.

Judith Ortiz Cofer's story "Nada" [see page 224] was triggered by a remark by a friend of hers whose husband had left her. The woman remarked that afterwards she felt like giving everything away and almost did. "This is a woman who collects for pleasure," Cofer says. "Antiques, knickknacks, books. Her house is a museum to her eclectic interests and joy of life. I had gone to her house and had commented on how much she had. 'But I had to start from scratch,' she said. 'When my husband left me, I wanted to give away everything, including the children and the dogs. I didn't want anything that reminded me of my pain. And I gave away everything but the children and the dogs. It was only when I started to heal again that I started to collect.'" This remark is what triggered Cofer's powerful exploration of the depth of a woman's anguish when she's left with *nada.* And yet, it wasn't simply that.

There was another trigger for this story that Cofer doesn't usually reveal because she likes it when people make the discovery on their own. She had been teaching Hemingway's famous story, "A Clean Well-Lighted Place," for the "umpteenth time." In the story, one of the waiters does a famous riff on the Lord's Prayer, substituting the word "nada" for nearly every word that gives the prayer meaning. Cofer wondered if her character, a woman of the *barrio* who knew nothing of existential dread, could suffer "soul anguish" in the way that Hemingway's waiter does. And so, the story became part challenge, part tribute to Hemingway—Cofer even named her main character in the story, "Ernestina."

"Not too many people get it," she says, "because there is just NO connection between a Puerto Rican woman and Ernest Hemingway in anyone's mind."

This story is not autobiographical, but it contains certain autobiographical details that Cofer was able to mix and match and transform for her own
purposes. "What I do is I use my memories of certain people I knew in the
barrio," she says. "There was always the old lady who claimed she could
communicate with the dead. There was always the sex kitten, the spoiled
new bride, the tough divorcée with their own particular Puerto Rican slant."
When writing this story, she posed the question, What if I had not left the
barrio? What if I had stayed there? What kind of woman would I have become? "So I looked at all these characters and I thought I would not have
become Doña Ernestina. I will not be defeated in this way. I wouldn't be the
cutie-pie. I decided to make myself the tough one . . . not myself, but the
persona. It isn't me because I didn't grow up there and I became an American
woman of a different sort. I take the people I know and conflate them into
characters and of course, that gives you endless possible combinations."

This process of mixing and matching is exactly what fiction writers do,
whether the story is based on real life or not. This kind of transformation
is central to the fiction process. And when you write about someone real,
this mixing and matching isn't merely good for self-protection; it deepens
your understanding of the character by involving your imaginative process.
It makes the character your own.

One might argue that simply mashing together aspects of different
people's personalities is not an act of the imagination at all, but that's a
foolish notion. The test of one's imagination is not simply in one's ability
to invent details and characters out of thin air, but also in how one orders
and overlays real events and people, how one transforms real life into something completely new.

For example, the episode of the ghost I mentioned earlier is something
that a student and her sister told me once about their father. When he was a
boy, he had an uncle who would sometimes stay with the family. The uncle
kept a bottle of whiskey hidden in the boy's dresser, and late at night he'd
sneak in and take a swig, and the boy would watch him. Then one night, the
uncle came into the room and just looked down at the boy in his bed, but
didn't take any whiskey or say anything. The next day the boy learned that

his uncle had died that night in a car accident. But the story goes on. Every night for a month, the uncle visited the boy, just staring down at him. The family still owns that house, and the father of my student refuses to spend the night there.

The other details I mentioned, about the elderly man whose sister cooks for him every night—that's the relationship between my uncle Morty and my grandmother Ida, both of whom are no longer alive. Every night he'd come over and she'd cook dinner for him, and then he'd leave with hardly a word. Of course, there's nothing terribly revealing or troubling or even all that interesting in the situation, and if I'd wanted to write about Morty and Ida and their nightly ritual when they were alive, I would have done so without any compunction whatsoever. It's only when I overlaid something else on top of these people—the ghost sighting—that the story started becoming somewhat intriguing.

Remember that all of these people are or were real, but probably none of them would have recognized themselves in the context in which I placed them. I took my real relatives and added details from the life of a complete stranger, a man I've never met.

Of course, maybe I'm fooling you again. Maybe I have no Uncle Morty or Grandmother Ida. Maybe I never had a student whose father saw a ghost. The truth of it shouldn't matter to you. Is it interesting? Is it believable? Those are the only issues that count.

Writing without Composites

Sometimes a writer will bravely, or foolishly, decide to write about a family member or friend without transforming that person much, if at all. It's difficult enough to write in the first place. It's murder when you also have to worry about how Aunt Elena will take it when she inevitably sees the story you've written, based on her life. I'm assuming a negative reaction here, but I've found that people are rarely as upset about being included in your stories as you think they'll be. Often, your aunt Elena won't recognize herself, or, if she does, she'll ignore those aspects of herself that might have been portrayed negatively.

When Thomas Wolfe first wrote *Look Homeward Angel,* his hometown of Asheville ostracized him because he wrote about them and told their secrets. He couldn't even show his face in Asheville. A few years after the book was published and he was a world-famous author, the only people who were mad at him were those he didn't include in the book.

Another Asheville native, Gail Godwin, wrote an early novel, *The Old Woman,* in which her younger sister and her mother were cast as characters, though somewhat transformed. In her essay "Becoming a Writer," Godwin recalls that her sister complained, "She'd better never put me in a novel again. I don't like being frozen in print for the rest of my life, forever wearing those silly panties and short skirts; and I'm *not* big like that, she's made me into some sort of Amazon freak." Godwin's mother was more understanding, saying obviously the character based on her was too stupid and passive to be an accurate reflection. The young Godwin responded that the character *was* supposed to be her mother. "Well, there was something left out then," her mother said.

Novelist Bret Lott hardly transformed his family at all in his novel *Jewel,* a story based on his grandmother's life. The story is about a woman who finally has to break the spirit and the will of her husband, and to sacrifice much of the childhood of her five other children for the sixth one, a Down's syndrome child. When the book was published, he went to his grandmother's house. She was happy to see him, of course, then took him out on the patio behind the house and sat him down at the picnic table and said, "Well, it's a beautiful book, but I just want to tell you I wasn't as hard on your grandfather as you made me out to be." Lott was taken aback. "I said, 'Grandma, it's a novel,' which is always the novelist's excuse, so I was able to weasel my way out of this. Because it was so known in our family that I was writing this book about her and the family, I don't think that she saw a difference between the book and the true family story, which is a dangerous thing—especially since in the novel I used everyone's name. Those are the true names of everyone. I got permission from everyone to do that, but I couldn't do any better than the real names: Jewel, Leston, Wilman, Burton, Billie Jean, Ann, Brenda Kay. So in her mind, the delineation between fiction and the truth was very blurry. But the other side of the story is that every sibling, every one of her children, all those people involved have said to me at one time or another, 'You got that exactly right.' She, in fact, did break the spirit of her husband, my grandfather. This was a truth she did not necessarily want to face."

With Lott's first novel, *The Man Who Owned Vermont,* he had to face the disapproval of his father: "*The Man Who Owned Vermont* is about an R.C. Cola salesman. My dad's life was R.C. Cola. He was an R.C. Cola man from 1951 to 1982. When you read that novel, it's a pretty disparaging account of what it's like to be a soda pop salesman. The character doesn't believe in doing what he does, so the whole thing's a sham. There's a line in there about how his whole life has been about selling something that no one in their right mind would want. Chemicals and carbonated water and caramel coloring. Who really needs this? My dad has said on many occasions, 'I know you think that selling soda pop was a waste.' I told him it's not true. All I could say was, 'Dad, it's a novel.'"

Getting Permission

Sometimes, you've got to give yourself permission to write about your aunt Elenas, your Jewels, your moms and dads. If you want to write a story about a relative or close friend, but feel some hesitation, ask yourself why. Are you sure that your friend or relative will recognize herself? If so, can you change anything about her to make her less recognizable? If not, maybe you should just go to the person you want to write about and ask for her permission. If she says no, you'll have to respect her wishes or perhaps lose her favor. But part of her response will depend on how you phrase the question. If you act sheepish about it and make it seem like a horrible thing, you can expect a defensive, negative reaction. If you explain a little bit about the story, that it's fiction, and that her life is fascinating to you and worthy of exploration, her reaction will probably be positive. But there's no guarantee. Nor is there any hard-and-fast rule about getting people's permission, but we'll get into ethical and legal questions later.

Remember that there's a certain amount of courage involved in writing, and if you always stay with material that's safe and won't get you into any trouble (even if the trouble is only with your own conflicting emotions about uncovering material that's close to home), your writing might ultimately seem limited and dull. Good writing takes risks and sometimes unsettles the writer as well as the reader. Fiction does not necessarily reflect the world as it should be, but as it is, and that means chronicling conflict. In real life, most of us avoid conflict. But conflict is a crucial element of all fiction, as it is an element of life. Imperfect beings that we are, we thrive on conflict, whether it's the base, reptilian conflict of a car blowing up at the end of a chase scene in a movie, or the more subtle, psychological conflict of a contemporary short story.

Fiction often deals with people making moral choices, and sometimes making the wrong ones. If you write about the world as it is, and not as you'd like it to be, you will definitely offend someone, and not necessarily your aunt Elena. As Flannery O'Connor put it, storytelling is "an attempt to make someone who doesn't want to listen, listen, and who doesn't want to see, see. We can't change what we see to suit the reader, but we must convey it as whole as possible into his unspacious quarters for his divided and suspicious consideration."

It is important, however, to avoid being too solipsistic in one's writing, thinking that people exist simply as fodder for your brilliant novels and stories. Donald Barthelme explores this notion in his story "The Author," which deals with a mother blithely uncovering the family skeletons of her grown children in her novels. She portrays one of her sons, a doctor, hanging out with a bunch of survivalists in Miami. She also reveals her daughter Virginia's car accident in which Virginia's blood-alcohol ratio was .18 percent. Another son threatens to sue her for writing of his habit of purchasing "U.S. Army morphine syrettes from disaffected Medical Corps master sergeants." The narrator, a former museum-curator-at-large, has been let go because of his mother's uncovering of his theft of several "inconsequential" Native American medicine bundles from the museum. When he confronts his mother, asks her why and how she can do what she does, she answers him coolly, "Because you're mine."

Acting the Part

No matter whom you base your characters on, you must think of yourself as much as an actor as a writer. You need to get into the role and learn your part. That's why details are so important, the small details that make up someone's life. One of the best ways to understand characters and motivation is to take an acting class. Of course, most good writers come to their understanding of things such as motivation intuitively; just as many have never read Freud but intuitively understand the concepts of displacement and projection.

A writer, just like an actor, needs to believe the character she is writing about. If you aren't convinced your character is real (whether based on your uncle Lou or your friend's uncle Shorty or made up whole cloth), your reader certainly won't believe either.

I'm not saying that the Uncle Shorty in your story should be a photocopy of the real Uncle Shorty. But you should be able to answer any question, no matter how seemingly insignificant, about your character. If asked, "What do the curtains in Shorty's bedroom look like?" you should be able to answer, "There aren't any curtains in his bedroom," or whatever you think best fits his character. It's not necessary that all of these details make it into your story. It's important that you know your character well enough to supply these details. Above all, you want your characters, no matter whom they're based on, to seem as though they lived and breathed before the opening paragraph of your story. You want them to have a sense of history.

Finding the Right Details

Whether a character in your story or novel is wholly imagined, partly imagined, or a true-to-life representation of someone doesn't matter at all. What matters is the character's believability to the reader. Being believable is not the same as being realistic. Plenty of writers pull off having outlandish characters and plots and settings in their stories because they make their characters and the worlds they live in believable through *salient details*—that is, physical, sensory details that make the character stand out in the reader's mind. We experience life through our senses, so it stands to reason that if we try to recreate life through the writing of fiction, using sensory details will help create an illusion of real-life experience.

When you write about a character, you must choose the details that will fix him in the reader's mind. Simply writing a sentence like "Uncle Lou was a big man," does not make him a memorable character. How big was he? "The only pants Uncle Lou ever felt comfortable in were secondhand maternity slacks." Now there's a sentence that shows a couple of things about Uncle Lou. It shows perhaps a kind of absurd frugality on his part, as well as giving one a pretty fair idea of how big he is.

When you write about a real person, especially someone you know quite well, a flood of details usually will hit you, many more than you can possibly use in your story. Write as many of those details down in your journal as possible, but select the few that will firmly anchor the character in our minds. If the remarkable thing about Uncle Lou was his shoe size (maybe he wore a size fifteen), make that the detail that types him. Maybe several things made your uncle remarkable—not only his foot size, but he had an enormous beard, never washed his hair, and wore a greasy Cleveland Indians baseball cap. Perhaps you can get away with using all those details, but you might have to toss one or two of them to make him less of a caricature. Which ones would you choose to drop? You'd choose different ones from the ones I'd choose. But the more specific a detail, the more memorable it will be to the reader, and that's a good rule of thumb to use when deciding which details to include in your fiction and which to get rid of.

Likewise, you don't have to give us all these details at once. In fact, if you do, they'll blur, and we'll have as indistinct an impression of your character as if you'd given us no details at all. As a writer of fiction, you must learn to slowly dispense information about your characters, not all in a rush, never to be mentioned again. If, for instance, you decide to keep the greasy baseball cap, it should have some role in the story. Same with the foot size. Not only should it give us some sense of who your character is, but, if possible, make it part of your story's plot. Otherwise, the baseball cap becomes a red herring, a false clue, a detail that serves no purpose other than the author's whim.

Type Versus Stereotype

Type is different from stereotype. Certain things are typical of people without necessarily being stereotypical. A plumber, for instance, will usually have typical tools of the trade: a plumber's snake, a truck or van, a jumpsuit of some kind for crawling around basements, a flashlight. So what's a stereotype of a plumber? Probably the first two or three images that come to mind are negative, since stereotypes are usually unfair and demeaning— overcharging or falling-down pants. That's not to say that such stereotypes are completely false and nonexistent in real life, just that they're stale, overused, and unfair. That's what a stereotype is, an unoriginal image of a person or group or people, most often used in a derogatory fashion.

Just because you've met someone who fits a stereotype doesn't mean that he'll be less of a stereotype when you place him in a story. In a piece of fiction, *avoid stereotypes*. The reason should seem obvious. Besides the fact that denigrating other people is not the nicest thing in the world, why bother to reinforce old stereotypes, to write about things that have been said a thousand times before? Fictional characters must seem complex for us to believe they're flesh and blood. Real live flesh-and-blood characters don't have to seem complex at all. If you have a friend with a pickup with fat tires, a gun rack, a bumper sticker that reads, "American by birth, Southern by the grace of God," and a blue-tick hound dog named Otis who rides in back, you might say, "Wow, what a stereotype, but he's still my bud." But if you put your bud in a story, I might say, "Sorry, too much of a stereotype. Make him more realistic." And you say, "How? If I make him more realistic, I'll be fictionalizing him." And I'll say, "Exactly!"

Historical Figures and Celebrities

Sometimes writers of fiction use historical figures or celebrities in their stories. Barry Hannah, while by no means a writer of historical fiction, has made forays into the area. In his acclaimed short-story collection, *Airships,* three stories deal with Jeb Stuart, the Confederate general. "Jeb Stuart attracted me because he was so unlike me," Hannah says. "He was a twenty-nine-year-old general. He was a Presbyterian who didn't smoke or drink. He was very dashing, the last of the cavalry heroes. He just about embodies everything good about the South that I know of, and about the cavalier era.

"When I wrote about Jeb after I'd read a good deal about him, I was interested in those around him, the effect that a hero has on those close to him. So I used what I knew about him but I also made up my own cast of folks to put around him. There's one gay guy. I don't think a gay Confederate had ever been written about."

Like any kind of fiction, you must have the confidence to use your imagination, to transform the historical figure or current celebrity—to make the character your own. You're mucking around in history and that can be a daunting challenge to a timid writer. But if you attempt such a story, remember that it's fiction you're writing, not history. And, depending on what your goals are in the story, you don't necessarily have to stick to the facts of your subject's life. If your aims are absurdist, you can write a story about how Judy Garland, at the decline of her career, took up sumo wrestling. Obviously, that's nowhere near the truth of her life. But a number of writers have written stories like that to great effect. These stories tend to be more cultural metaphors than actual explorations of someone's life. That's not to say that the two are mutually exclusive. Barry Hannah's stories about Jeb

Stuart have as much to do metaphorically with the cultures of the old and new South as they do with the actual life of Jeb Stuart.

"The reason you can use your imagination," says Hannah, "is that most history is not in the books. Their day-to-day life is not in the books. You only get a gloss. It's not that my guess is as good as any, because I try to be educated about the era. But it is up for grabs about what a guy is like in any given hour. People are not always postured and heroic. And they say dreadful things, even the best people. But they sure don't make speeches. And they have to get up and put their pants on. That part of history is never in the books. And I like to give a sense of it."

The main thing to remember when writing this kind of fiction is to do your research. Know something about the era. Know something about the person. Go to the library and look at microfilm of newspaper articles about the person you're writing about. Look on the Internet. But be careful here. A lot of dubious "facts" are posted on the Internet, and you need to distinguish fact from fancy. The best rule of thumb on the Internet: Consider the source. Read biographies about the person, not just one, but two or three. Biographers don't necessarily agree with one another, so you can usually get a couple of different perspectives by reading more than one, and then you can decide which is the most accurate—or you can invent your own perspective. To some degree, you must create your own perspective, or else the story will simply be warmed-over biography.

The way you introduce your famous character in such a story or novel is perhaps of more importance than in any other kind of fiction. If you're not careful, you can easily alienate the reader. If you simply rely on stereotypes of your famous character, or introduce him in a sensational manner, you can be sure that your reader will not be convinced. Consider this opening:

Napolean sat at his dresser, hand in his jacket, admiring himself in the mirror.

This is a silly opening, starting out in the most obvious fashion. On the other hand, better not to keep your reader unaware of your famous subject's identity too long. Your reader's reaction might be a groan when she discovers after thirty pages who your subject is.

Einstein's Dreams, a novel by Alan Lightman, recreates in an almost impressionistic form Einstein's discovery of the nature of time. Here is the way it opens:

> In some distant arcade, a clock tower calls out six times and then stops. The young man slumps at his desk. He has come to the office at dawn, after another upheaval. His hair is uncombed and his trousers are too big. In his hand, he holds twenty crumpled pages, his new theory of time, which he will mail today to the German journal of physics.

Several things make this opening convincing. Obviously, we know the subject by the title of the book, and in that first paragraph he's not mentioned by name. He doesn't need to be mentioned by name, because Einstein is a universally famous figure, and the reader brings a certain amount of knowledge to the story already. The theory of time is a dead giveaway, as is the slight physical descriptions of the young man's appearance, especially the uncombed hair. The reader instantly recalls the famous photo of an older Einstein with his hair going in all directions at once. The more famous your subject, the less you have to dwell on the obvious facts about that person.

Also notice that the author casts his story in the present tense. This strategy gives us a sense of immediacy. It's as though we're watching a movie unfold in slow motion with both sound and sight involved: the distant tolling of the clock, the visual image of the man slumped over his desk. Casting the paragraph in third person, objective, also adds to the sense of a cool authority giving us this information, the facts, as they were, without any interpretation—or so it would seem. It would be hard to come up with a better strategy for introducing such a famous man to us. And it's all done through salient details and a subtle handling of the information we must know about this character.

EXERCISES

1. Choose a profession. Make a list of stereotypes of that profession. Then make a list of things that are typical to that profession. Now write a scene including some, though not all, of your typical list and none of your stereotypical list. To make the character seem

more real, model him on someone you've actually known or observed in that profession or a similar one.

2. Recall someone you know well—a friend, a relative—preferably someone who's a bit eccentric, someone with strong personality traits. Identify two or three of those personality traits and list them at the top of the page. Now create a scene that shows these personality traits in your friend or relative—but never mention these personality traits. Try to convey them with dialogue, action, and salient detail. So, if your uncle Lou is childlike, forgetful, and generous, show him as such in the scene. But try to avoid easy stereotypes of generosity, forgetfulness, etc.

3. Write a scene using this same character, but transform her into a new character. Change one or two of her personality traits. Combine her with another friend or relative. Change her name, age, gender. Use your imagination so that what you end up with is *based* on your friend or relative, but is not that person at all anymore.

4. Write a scene from the point of view of someone famous whose life you know fairly well. Don't dwell so much in the scene on what made him famous, but on what made him ordinary, on the particulars of his life.

5. Interview a relative. Ask her to recall a particular year. Just pick one arbitrarily, say, 1975. Ask your relative to recall that year in as much detail as possible: what was going on in the world, what was going on in the country, in the state, in the city, on the block, in the family, with herself. As you narrow your questions, a stronger and stronger portrait will begin to emerge. After you've finished the interview, write a scene with your relative in it, set in the year you focused on in the interview. Pick and choose the salient details to make both your relative and the world of 1975 come alive. Is this the beginning of a story?

CHAPTER FIVE

▼

Real Stories

Even if you're ostensibly writing something autobiographical, you're still an actor taking on a role, and the hardest role to play is yourself. John Barth has a story that skewers the whole notion of autobiographical fiction, called "Life-Story." It's an infuriating little story about a man writing a story called "Life-Story," all about a man who's writing a story called "Life-Story," and so on ad infinitum. The disappearing-mirrors trick. It's a story about a man who can't even get enough distance from his first line to write a story.

What we're saying here is that if you base something on real life, you must resign yourself to the fact that you won't be able to tell the whole truth and nothing but the truth. Writing from real life is a constant dialogue between one's memory and one's imagination. You must give your imagination room to roam if you want to write fiction from real life successfully. You must be flexible with your life, which is easier said than done. In her essay, "Becoming a Writer," Gail Godwin writes: "Fact and fiction: fiction and fact. At what point does regurgitated autobiography graduate into memory shaped by art? How do you know when to stop telling it as it is, or was, and make it into what it ought to be—or what would make a better story?" In this chapter, we'll explore different types of fiction derived from fact, and strategies for turning real-life experiences into fiction.

Ever since Hemingway, some writers have latched onto the silly notion that you must experience life before you can write about it. That's not true, at least not in the narrow sense of experience. Flannery O'Connor said we have enough to write about for the rest of our lives if we survive childhood. It's not important whether you've actually fished for wahoo off the coast of North Carolina or saw a blue-footed Booby in St. Augustine. What you need is enough depth and range in your character and imagination to

< 87 >

make us believe in the experience of the story. That's the only experience that counts: the reader's experience of the story, whether he believes you or not, whether you've created a virtual reality much more advanced than any computer will ever be capable of.

Many beginning fiction writers seem to want to be journalists. Most journalists will swear that they're after the truth when the fact is that many journalists seem to be pretty good at fictionalizing, whether they mean to or not. Ask anyone who has ever been interviewed. Or the next time there's a disaster, flip the channels and see how wildly the accounts can differ. Any basic philosophy class will teach you that truth is in the perceptions of the viewer. So why do you care anyway what really happened in your life? Does the fact that it happened make it more important? Does it make it a better story? Fiction writers are after a different kind of truth from journalists, though no less important, and perhaps ultimately more honest. Fiction writers are after what Faulkner called "the eternal verities," certainly a high-falutin' term, but fine for him. After all, he was Faulkner. You, on the other hand, probably shouldn't go around saying that you want to write eternal verities, or people might slap you.

Ironically enough, in our quest for verities, we must often lie. Ask the successful liar what her main ingredient is, and she will probably tell you that you must believe the lie you're telling. You must convince yourself it's true, be earnest about it, or else the listener certainly won't believe you. Lying, like life, is in the details. What really happened is irrelevant. You must look at your life as almost a great patchwork. In an article in the *New York Times Book Review* about author Henry Roth, Leonard Michaels states that Roth "begins with small factual events, then imagines their emotional consequences, and finally gives them an imaginative expression that may be far from the original events." In a letter to the *New York Times Book Review,* author Susan Fromberg Schaeffer puts it quite eloquently when she writes that "fiction is a record of that conflagration that occurs when reality collides with imagination." *There's* a quote worth taping above your writing desk.

Sherwood Anderson gives us a glimpse of this conflagration in "Death in the Woods" [see page 233], the story of an old, unloved woman, who's been abused by one man after another until she collapses and freezes to death one day on her long walk from town to her farm. Her abuse starts early in her life. She is orphaned and spends her youth in servitude to a cruel farmer. Later, her husband and son treat her miserably. Her death in the woods is attended only by a pack of wild dogs who skitter and yap around her as she slips into death. They then tear the clothes from her body.

Toward the end of his story, the narrator suddenly intrudes and tells how, as a young boy, he and his brother accompanied a group of men to recover the body of an old woman frozen in the snow. And then, remarkably, he tells us how this later worked itself into his story:

> I remember only the picture there in the forest, the men standing about, the naked girlish-looking figure, face down in the snow, the tracks made by the running dogs and the clear cold winter sky above . . .
>
> The scene in the forest had become for me, without my knowing it, the foundation for the real story I am now trying to tell. The fragments, you see, had to be picked up slowly, long afterward.
>
> Things happened. When I was a young man I worked on the farm of a German. The hired girl was afraid of her employer. The farmer's wife hated her.
>
> I saw things at that place. Once later, I had a half-uncanny, mystical adventure with dogs in an Illinois forest on a clear, moon-lit winter night. . . . The whole thing, the story of the old woman's death, was to me as I grew older like music heard from far off. The notes had to be picked up slowly one at a time. Something had to be understood.

All you really need to know about writing stories based on your life is encapsulated in the above passage. The notes have to be picked up slowly one at a time. Something has to be understood.

Generating Ideas

After a reading, I'm sometimes asked, "Where do your ideas come from?" Ideas come from any number of sources, from dreams to snatches of overheard conversation to family stories. Another variation on this question is, "How do you keep generating ideas?" The answer to that one is easy: "By staying alive." The more you write, the more you naturally generate ideas. A teacher once told me that all you had to do to get story material is to look around, to keep your eyes open. That might sound easy, but it's not. Usually we're stuck in our everyday routines and notice very little about the world around us, or, if we notice it, it's in a familiar, unsurprised way. The writer, on the other hand, must try to notice what's new in the familiar, to look upon the world as if encountering it for the first time. That's why children are so naturally imaginative. They don't know the world's boundaries. They don't have expectations. If you have expectations, if you know that the tree in front of your house is only the same old tree you see every day, you probably won't have any new ideas. On the other hand, ask yourself some questions about the tree. What exactly is the view that the tree obscures? Does it block the view of your neighbor's kitchen window? Who are your neighbors? Who planted the tree?

For most writers, ideas are not the problem. It's the follow-through. Some people say that nothing interesting has ever happened to them, so they have nothing to write about. But I don't buy that. Even if you've stayed in one place your entire life, on the same street, in the same house—that doesn't necessarily mean your life is trivial and boring. Perhaps you take it for granted. You've stopped paying attention. And if you want to write, you must pay attention.

If it's been awhile since you've written a story, or if you've never written a story before, your imagination might be a little rusty, or your self-confidence might be low. In that case, go back to your journal. Brainstorm. List the names of five people you haven't seen in five years or more. Why haven't you seen them? List five lies you've told. What were their consequences? List five lies you wished you'd told. What do all of these exercises have in common? They all have a kernel of conflict within them, at least potentially, and conflict is a central ingredient of any story. You don't have to use these exercises. Anything that sparks your memory, that sparks your interest, will do.

Flexibility

If you want to write a story about a family vacation you took in 1976, think of all the other vacations you took as a family, even ones you took alone. Glue them in your mind. Use only what's helpful from one memory and then discard the rest. And now that we're on the subject, is it important that the story take place in 1976? Is there anything to justify the time other than that really was the year you and the kids or your parents or whoever decided to take that trip to Yellowstone? If that's the only reason, back up. You're not thinking like a fiction writer.

But the year is crucial to the story, you say. It couldn't take place in any other year. The story is called "Bicentennial," and it involves two brothers in a sailboat who are on their way to try to view the tall ships as they come into New York's harbor on the Fourth of July. Furthermore, the story is about the younger brother's preoccupation with his own independence and the older one's more wistful feelings about the bonds to his family. That sounds a tad heavy-handed to me, but it's your story. If you want to set it in 1976 and believe you can justify it, go to it.

Flexibility is perhaps the most important ingredient for a successful story based on real life. It's not so much a strategy as it is a state of mind. If you are unwilling or unable to change events in a story because "they really happened," you don't want to write fiction. If you are unwilling to revise your story, the prognosis is likewise bleak. Always remember that you're writing fiction, whether based on fact or not, and look for the story that didn't happen within the story that did.

Getting Distance

Not *everything* that happens to you can or needs to be fictionalized. It's unhealthy and a little creepy for one to think of everything that happens as possible fodder for one's fiction. That kind of attitude can lead to some pretty serious self-absorption. Unfortunately, we've all met writers or artists who seem to view themselves as little gods who breathe more rarefied air than the rest of us mortals. After a traumatic event, the last thing one should be thinking about is one's fiction.

Some people think of writing as therapeutic. Maybe on some level it is, but if you need therapy, see a therapist. Writing, if anything, will make you more neurotic.

If you write about a traumatic event, you generally need distance. If your parents died in a plane crash yesterday, do you really think you're ready to begin writing a short story about the event today? Is a year too soon? Three years? Why are you writing the story in the first place? To honor your parents? To help you through your grief? Or because it would make a good story? The third reason is the only correct answer. Perhaps that might sound cold to you but remember, we're talking about fiction. A story is not powerful simply because it happened to or is important to the writer. But perhaps we need to make a distinction here between private writing and public writing. Privately, you can write whatever you want, in whatever form, and for whatever reason. But once you bring that story into the world, once you seek an audience for it, the audience is under no obligation to be kind or sympathetic, or to like what you have written. Imagine how you would feel if you showed your story to an acquaintance, and she said, "Boy, what wicked characters. I'm so relieved the parents died in that plane crash. They deserved it!"

You need distance as well to judge whether your parents' death in a fiery plane crash would make a good story. Chances are it won't. It's tragic and horrible, but those elements alone don't make a good story. One problem is that people who are trying to deal with traumatic events feel a kind of ownership of the material, which can make a writer inflexible. Nothing can be written in stone. Everything must be subject to revision, and a sure sign that you're too close to your subject is the feeling that you want to be true to the subject, that you don't want to change a word. "I think thematically it would work better if the parents died in a speedboat accident," your acquaintance says. If you refuse to consider the suggestion only on the grounds that it didn't happen that way, go back to the chapter on memoirs.

One achieves distance through the passage of time, but there are some strategies to help you along. If you write about a place you've lived in, leaving it sometimes gives you the best perspective. Change the gender of the main character. Or the age. Change the point of view. Change anything that will make the character *not you*. It's important that you don't think of your main character as yourself. The character can be based on you, but you must make a distinction. Otherwise, you might be unwilling to allow things to happen to the character that you wouldn't want happening to yourself, or allow your character to behave in a way you wouldn't normally behave. And the point of writing a story is not to impress everyone with what a good or heroic person you are.

Indirection

Often, stories deal best with the aftermath of trauma rather than the unfolding of it. Instead of ending your story with a horrific car accident, try beginning your story with it, as Robley Wilson Jr. skillfully does in his short story "Favorites," which opens with the death of a man's wife in a car accident.

> On a Saturday afternoon in September his wife was killed in a car accident. As the state police explained it to him, she had finished her grocery shopping and was pulling out onto the highway in front of the shopping center when a young man in a pickup truck slammed into her car. The impact was just behind the driver's door, she died instantly, never knew what hit her—things people say in such circumstances, things the police told him. The young man wasn't hurt; he was drunk and stoned, and charges against him were pending. Very sorry. The car was written off as a total loss.

After he gets the trauma out of the way, Wilson is able to focus on his main character, the husband. Instead of focusing on the large event, Wilson chooses something much smaller and seemingly inconsequential. It seems that the woman's last words to her husband were, "I made your favorite dessert." The story deals with the man's consumption of his wife's final treat for him. That's called *indirection,* approaching the trauma sideways rather than head-on. The way he delicately eats this dessert over a period of several days is a powerful and ingenious way of showing the man's grief and love for his wife.

This method works especially well with short stories. By definition, short stories are short and tend to be somewhat fragile in their construction. The main problem is that your writing will seem melodramatic if you try to pack an emotional wallop in an unsophisticated way. If you focus solely on the traumatic event as it's unfolding, say, a car accident you were in as a child, this event might likely overwhelm your characters, and the story will become merely seamy rather than emotionally powerful.

Life *can* be melodramatic, and there's nothing wrong with extreme shows of emotion if, say, you watch your parents' plane burst into flame high above the field where they were practicing loopty-loops in front of your eyes. But fiction isn't real life. It's artifice, and what works in real life doesn't always work in fiction.

Some people might be horrified by what they consider the "matter-of-fact" tone of a story such as "Favorites." Look at that first paragraph again. There *is* a certain distance and irony to the words, especially phrases like, "Very sorry," but that doesn't mean that the story is bloodless and un-emotional. When you reach the final paragraph of this story, it's hard to read aloud without your voice cracking a bit.

> One night only a single piece of his wife's dessert remained. He cut it in half. The following night he cut the half in half. Then he must have realized what he was doing, for on the third night he ate all that was left of the dessert—luscious, irreplaceable treat—and set the empty pan to soak in the kitchen sink.

Another distinction I'd like to draw here is one between cheap senti-mentality and true sentiment. Sentimentality pulls at your heart strings in an obnoxious clichéd manner: images of orphans crying in the rain or puppy dogs wandering the streets in search of a loving home. True, these occurrences are heartbreaking in real life, but not terribly original in fiction. Leave them to the six o'clock news. Conversely, the emotional punch of a truly good story will sneak up on you. It'll be unpredictable and twice as powerful because you didn't know it was there waiting for you.

The paradox is that sometimes the more you leave out, the more you hold back, and the more tension is created in the reader's mind while she waits for that release of emotion or catharsis. If you have a constant cathar-sis on the page, characters screaming as blood gushes out of their wounds at the scene of a horrible accident, the reader will soon become bored and numbed by the steady shrill tone of your prose, just as we are numbed by the six o'clock news. A constant release of emotional energy works against the natural form of the short story—the rising action or building of tension leading to the climax.

This doesn't mean you should avoid trauma. Just avoid having charac-ters react to the trauma in a predictable way. You want your reader to think, "Why aren't you reacting like a normal human being? Where are your tears!?" just as the director of a horror film wants the audience to think, "No, don't go up those stairs, stupid!"

The Head-On Approach

Most writers will, at some point, put a sentence down on paper that makes them uncomfortable, that seems to reveal too much. Faulkner, in accepting his Nobel Prize, spoke of "the human heart in conflict with itself, which alone can make good writing because only that is worth writing about, worth the agony and the sweat." The worst kind of writing, and much of it is published, even celebrated, is fiction that takes no risks, that makes the reader comfortable about the world he lives in—fiction that reinforces our easy assumptions of the world. Good fiction often deals with moral ambivalence, not easy answers; with unfortunate or ambiguous choices resulting not in clear-cut victories or happy Hollywood endings, but haunting, sometimes troubling resolutions.

Some writers tackle the most painful subjects in a straightforward way and throw indirection out the window. This is more a personality issue than one of craft. One writer who writes on the edge, who often goes for the jugular rather than the comforts of indirection, is Sharon Solwitz. Solwitz is able to write about life's most dramatic moments without teetering into melodrama. And she's able to write about subjects that are painfully close to her. She says of her work, "When I first started, I used to take something that was interesting from the past that I had distance on. So I wrote a lot of stories about when I was a teenager or kid. That's a kind of a natural distance you have. But now, often lately, when I'm feeling kind of tense about something, when I feel an issue is unresolved, I take the issue that's right in front of me. And I write it."

Even in those early stories, she still went for the material that was most likely to deal with her own secrets and fears. For those wishing to write this way, she suggests starting with a line that gives you goose bumps. She adds, however, that "the most unendurable pieces of writing are by writers who try to work out their problems on paper without the benefit of craft. A character whines for ten pages about her need for love, and we want to close the book just as we'd want to switch seats on the bus to avoid such a relentlessly confessional new acquaintance.

"But there's something to be said for the thrill of dealing with red-hot conflict, transforming it. Much of it will be rant and rave, but sometimes the metamorphosis will happen right then and there, and you'll know it."

An example of this unusual ability is her story, "If You Step on a Crack" [see page 245] based on a real-life experience. When Solwitz found a lump in her breast, and it was biopsied, she was, of course, terrified. So she wrote a story that mirrored her situation. Both Solwitz and her protagonist are married. Both live a couple of hundred feet from Wrigley Field in Chicago.

Both have problems with baseball fans relieving themselves in the alley below their house.

Solwitz writes in a cool, often witty style that creates distance without sacrificing any of the emotion of the moment. Instead of starting with the trauma of "Is the tumor malignant or not?" Solwitz deflects the trauma a bit by beginning with the lighter problem of drunken fans.

> Her first and only husband sat on the couch in front of the pregame interview. From four doors south across Waveland Avenue the lights of Wrigley Field cast their salmon glow on his long-sleeved shirt. Three stories down, the steps of Cub and Cardinal fans crunched along the alley, overlaid by spates of mild, ritualized jeering. Blue and red caps bobbed toward the bleacher entrance. "Come let's cheer them on to ignominy," said Andy, to whom she had been married longer than any of her friends to their husbands. He held out his hand.
>
> She had been watching a golden-haired boy of twenty or so take a whiz in the alley. "What fun," she said, to either, to both.

After a page or so, she introduces the greater twin dilemmas of her possible breast cancer and her husband's seeming indifference. This is a wise strategy, whether dealing with a recent or long-past trauma. You don't have to let the reader know everything about the situation and the crisis in the story right away. There's a certain amount of timing involved in divulging important information about a character. You don't want to wait too long to tell the reader, like the last line of the story. "Oh, by the way. I'm a dromedary. You've been reading the words of a camel all along. Ha ha!" Then your story resorts to cheap gimmicks. Moreover, you don't have to tell everything about the conflict of the story in the first paragraph. Slowly divulging such information, especially if it's somewhat traumatic, can, if your timing is right, lend even more tension to the story.

In the story, the protagonist doesn't learn the results of her test. Another good strategy on Solwitz's part. Whether she has breast cancer is not the issue of the story. It might be why some readers are reading, but that's not the same thing. The central conflict is between the protagonist and her husband. As in any story, what's most important are the characters and what we learn about them, and by inference, human nature as a result of this traumatic situation. If the power of your story relies only on a dramatic question (does she have cancer?) rather than on the characters, your story probably will be melodramatic rather than having true emotional intensity, as Solwitz achieves in her story.

"It could have been a terrible cliché," says Solwitz. "A woman is afraid of breast cancer. She has a biopsy. Outcome: Either she has it or she doesn't. She's disfigured or she isn't. She lives or dies. I imagine I could have gotten the reader involved because of the unfortunate universality of the experience. But I knew even as I was conceiving it that the yes or no answer, she lives or dies—neither would ultimately satisfy. We're all helpless in the face of good news or bad news and the writer can't fix that.

"Transformation involved moving away from the cliché of the tension of the possibly terrible outcome. The not-knowing became only a psychological setting turned into the background. Foregrounded was first her relationship with her husband—he refused to participate in her fears about the biopsy—and next her attempts to come to terms with her own mortality. These conflicts derived from the uncertainty of death and disfigurement, but the next day's good or bad fortune was not the point. The story would end before the operation. My character would find for a moment the place in her mind in which tomorrow's events would cease to matter."

Regardless of how close you are to your material, you still need the ability and will to transform the real events as Solwitz did. She naturally distanced herself from the trauma of the possible breast cancer by placing it in the background of the story, making it merely a catalyst for other psychological concerns.

Still, Solwitz needed to transform the story even further to keep it from being simply a static psychological portrait. As she points out, "For most stories to be interesting something has to happen, and most often that something must be an act performed by the protagonist. Otherwise we're left with the victim story. In my story my character, who happens to live by a ball park and so do I, starts yelling at a guy who takes a whiz just under her window. In the end, overwrought by etc. etc., she insults the manhood of another fellow who's urinating on her building, and he comes back in his car and starts ramming one of the posts that holds up her house. That has happened to our house, but only accidentally. Then, in an act of solidarity, to save their home, she and her husband throw their television set out the window onto his car. That event was entirely imaginary. It came as a result of following closely the logic of the story. The Cubs are playing that night. Her husband's a fan and more involved it seems with the game on TV than with her panic. She has some odd superstition that if the Cubs lose it means they'll find cancer tomorrow. The use of the TV as a weapon against the guy who wants to demolish her house is plausible psychologically because we've been watching her grow more and more hysterical. It also means that her husband has relinquished his attitude of indifference (in the form of his interest in the ball game) and she of her superstition. While the game goes on outside the window, she and her husband listen on the radio and make love, transcending for the moment at least, the vagaries of mortality."

Basing a story on an actual traumatic event takes a certain quality that not everyone possesses—the ability to see oneself as an abstraction, as yet another character within a larger story. I'm not sure this is a completely positive attribute, perhaps it's even slightly sociopathic. Often, we hear about teenagers, children really, who are able to kill someone without remorse because they don't view the other as completely real. Perhaps writers suffer from this same kind of solipsism and arrested development.

Of course, I'm only half serious here, and in fact, I prefer to view such writers in an opposite light. I'd rather view the writer who faces her own life head-on as courageous rather than cold-blooded.

Family Stories

The best stories sometimes are the stories you already own, the stories that are part of your life, family stories. Remember Aunt Imelda, who was a gangster's moll during Prohibition? She never married, became a grade-school art teacher in Teaneck, New Jersey, and always seemed crabby when you were a kid. She seemed like the last person you'd imagine hanging out with gangsters. Think there's a story there? Or the time Aunt Imelda and your grandmother were sitting in the dinette drinking coffee and eating lady fingers while you were in your grandmother's bedroom going through a box of old letters. (Your grandmother said you could have the old stamps on the envelopes.) A check slid out, and you looked at it. It was for fifty dollars, and it was made out to your grandmother from Aunt Imelda. It was dated 1934 and was uncancelled! You ran out to the dinette to tell your grandmother of her good fortune, but when you showed it to the two women, they exchanged dark looks, and your grandmother scolded you for taking things that didn't belong to you.

There's definitely a story *there*.

Novelist Bret Lott says family stories "are the stories that have been around forever. You don't go to your family and say, 'Hey, anybody know any good stories I can write about?' The stories that were inside my novel *Jewel* were stories that I had heard growing up. I was never thinking, 'Oh gosh, I'm going to be a novelist. Keep telling me these stories. I want to write about them someday.'

"Many people might look at my family as boring. My dad was a salesman. My mom was a homemaker. It depends how closely you're willing to look. Every family has stories."

When we write about our families, we often base our stories on events that happened to us as well as the other members of our family. In these cases, the writer has as much "ownership" of the event as anyone else. But to use a word like "ownership" is misleading. You can't copyright experience.

As with any other life-based fiction, just because you base a story on Aunt Imelda's life doesn't mean you're restricted to the facts. But, at the same time, whoever your aunt Imelda is, you must know who she is inside out.

When you research a family story, you may learn something you weren't prepared to learn, and yet, if you're open-minded, these unexpected revelations can become integral to your book or story. With Bret Lott, he learned something unexpected about his grandmother on a visit just prior to beginning *Jewel:* "Before I started to write the book, I wanted to spend one final time with my grandma. You hear stories about your family. They're huge stories, but if you're going to write the story of your family, you also need to know the mundane, boring details of life. So I spent several days just talking to her at her house. I had a notebook and I was asking her seemingly stupid questions like 'In Mississippi in the 1940s, what did you eat in the wintertime? What was the first car you had? What was your favorite dress?' Detail-oriented questions that would lend authenticity to the story. Then all of a sudden, my grandmother stopped and said, 'Oh, I've got to tell you this story.' She told about how she had six children and one day her husband Leston said, 'Let's all go out for a picnic on the lake.' They went out there and they rented a canoe and they took the kids out and let the kids ride around in the canoe and then he said, 'Hey, let's you and me go for a canoe ride.'

They climbed into the canoe and he paddled out to the far end of the lake into the ... 'bullrushes,' was the word she kept saying. 'He jammed it right up in the bullrushes.' Then they made love out there in the canoe. I was sitting in my grandma's kitchen with little lace doilies around, and pictures of the grandkids on the refrigerator, and I was thinking, Grandma, don't tell me this! I don't want to see you and Grandpa ... So I kind of shrugged it off and thought Oooh yeee! But once I got into the book, once I committed myself to telling the truth of the story, the truth of the novel (there's a difference between my character Jewel and my grandmother), once I got into the life of Jewel, I thought this was something that had to be accounted for. It revealed much about her character, not that she wanted sex, but that it wove its way into the idea of her submitting to him so that she could finally exert her will over him."

Family stories can be difficult to write, in part because of the emotions such material stirs in the author, in part because of the problems such a story might cause if family members read it. Not every family member will be as forthcoming as Bret Lott's grandmother.

If you want to write a family story, the best place to start off might be with your family legends or your black sheep. Who were the strong characters, the ones who were legendarily brave or legendarily cowardly? Who are the ones the family still talks about fifty years after their passing? In my family's case, it's my great-grandmother Hannah, a woman who died years before I was born, but whom I heard about all through my childhood. She was born on a farm in Lithuania. Her mother died in childbirth, and supposedly Hannah was suckled by a she-goat! She fled the farm when her stepmother and father wanted to marry her off to some rich fellow, and she made her way to England, where she had a brother. She worked in a sweatshop, then joined the Yiddish theater and traveled around Europe. She met my great-grandfather in Holland, where he was a shoemaker and supposedly made shoes for the royal family. (Legends, like fiction, don't necessarily have to be true—who knows the truth in all this?) They fell in love, married, had a child, then moved to America. According to my mother, Hannah was, in her youth, a red-haired beauty and was always very vain, but a great storyteller. She was also the first person in our family to fly in an airplane. This was in the 1930s, and she was already elderly and had a heart condition. Everyone begged her not to go, but she insisted. She wanted to fly from New York to Cleveland, where another brother was getting married. She bought a white flying outfit for the occasion. The trip was turbulent but Hannah was calm, and upon landing she was mobbed by reporters—she turned out to be the oldest person at that time to fly in a plane. In those days, you didn't have to actually fly a plane to become famous for flying. Amelia Earhart initially became famous for simply being the first female *passenger* on a trans-Atlantic flight.

This is a bare-boned portrait of my great-grandmother Hannah. I still lack the details and the focus of the story. If you want to write such a story, recall someone in your own family and try to evoke everything you remember about this person. Write down these memories, and then ask yourself questions. Which of these stories most intrigues you? That's a good place to start. Where's the conflict? When will the story be set, now or in the past? If you set the story in the present, avoid the stock situation of a grandpa or grandma telling a story of the olden days to the young'uns on the porch— unless you do something new with the form. That kind of story is older and more tired than grandpa himself.

Of course, if you can twist this idea around and make it fresh, you might succeed, as Richard Spillman does in a powerful story called "The Old Man Tells His Story and Gets It Wrong." With a title like that, you can tell it isn't going to be your average grandpa-in-the-rocker tale. In this story, the protagonist is an old man who tells his grandson an old war tale that he's told a million times. But as he tells it, something goes wrong. The story starts to get away from him, to go in unfamiliar directions and take on a life of its own. Instead of ending as the victor this time, he's cast as the victim.

> Fiercely, then, the wounds began to hurt, and the pain brought back his sight. He lay among the white and yellow flowers staring up at the treetops, which seemed to be on fire. The soldiers were arguing in accents he remembered from his childhood, pointing to him and to the town. One was wiping his bayonet with a fistful of grass. An enemy officer stepped out from the trees and snapped an order.

This might sound like *The Twilight Zone,* but it's not. Spillman justifies all this brilliantly by letting us know quite strongly that this anecdote gone haywire is a symptom of a deep and profound physical and psychological change happening to the old man.

It's best to simply set the story in the past and cut out any character based on yourself—that is, the listener. But you must do certain things to make this direct method work well. Often, such a story involves some kind of research (a topic we'll deal with more extensively in a later chapter), such as interviewing any and all relatives who knew your great-grandmother Hannah and the times in which she lived.

You also should ask yourself if the time frame is important. Is this a story that could only have happened in Depression-era Mississippi, or is it timeless? Is it a story that could take place now? If your answer is yes to the second question, you don't need to set it in the past. Setting the story in the present might ultimately free you in your handling of the material, might make the story less biography and more fiction.

Point of view is important here as well. Often, a point of view will automatically suggest itself. You might think, *There's no other logical choice but to tell this story from the point of view of Hannah.* It depends on where the heart of your story is, where the emotional impact lies, and whose character goes through the most profound change. But if one point of view doesn't work, try another. Try multiple viewpoints if you like, but only if it strengthens the reader's understanding of the characters involved. Often, multiple viewpoints, if handled clumsily, have the opposite effect—confusing the reader and giving him a shallow understanding of several characters rather than a deep understanding of one.

You also must be open-minded and willing to change actual events to imagined ones. In my case, I might focus on Hannah's airplane ride, but the relationship I'd see as most important would be with the brother in Cleveland who's getting married. I'd probably make their relationship somewhat ambiguous, even troubled. I'd combine him with the brother in England. I'd ask myself why and how he left the farm in Lithuania first. Is Hannah going to Cleveland now to celebrate her brother or celebrate her own fierce determination and stubbornness? And I don't know if she'd even make it. You see, I'd be willing to kill off my own great-grandmother for the sake of a good story.

Childhood Stories

Childhood is not the sole domain of younger writers, but younger writers often look toward childhood for their source material for the simple reason that they remember it vividly, with all its attendant frustrations and misunderstandings. Childhood is the perfect brew pot for fiction. Of course, childhood stories are not necessarily autobiographical. Still, while I've never done a scientific study on the matter, I'd bet that autobiography plays a more significant role in this type of story than in any other kind.

One common characteristic of stories told from a child's point of view (which isn't always the case in a childhood story) is an overlay of *dramatic irony*. This kind of irony is unintentional on the part of the main character, as opposed to a more intentional kind of irony like *sarcasm*. Children are naïve, often not able to comprehend what's going on around them, and the crafty writer is able to exploit this naïveté. An example might be something like this:

> Mom says that after I take my bath we've got to keep the bathroom door closed or I'll catch a giraffe. I start crying when she rubs me with the towel. I want to catch a giraffe! "Where's the giraffe?" I say.
> "Outside," she says.
> By the time she's done, the giraffe is gone.

Many childhood stories share the ironic overlay of the naïve main character. Through the misconceptions of the child character, they make perceptive comments on the crazy world of adults. Likewise, the collision between the child's world and the adult world often produces a welling of emotion in the reader that would not be possible if told from an adult's point of view. Isaak Babel's "The Story of My Dovecot," for example, is about a boy in Russia at the turn of the twentieth century who keeps doves as pets. However, on the day he buys two new doves (as a reward for doing well on his school exams), he's caught in the midst of a pogrom. The character has no understanding of what's going on around him or why, and that makes the story all the more tragic:

> He dealt me a flying blow with the hand that was clutching the bird. Kate's wadded back seemed to turn upside down, and I fell to the ground in my new overcoat.
> "Their spawn must be wiped out," said Kate, straightening up over the bonnets. "I can't a-bear their spawn, nor their stinking menfolk."
> She said more things about our spawn, but I heard nothing of it.

I lay on the ground, and the guts of the crushed bird trickled down from my temple. They flowed down my cheek, winding this way and that, splashing, blinding me. The tender pigeon-guts slid down over my forehead, and I closed my solitary unstopped-up eye so as not to see the world that spread out before me. This world was tiny, and it was awful. A stone lay just before my eyes, a little stone so chipped as to resemble the face of an old woman with a large jaw. A piece of string lay not far away, and a bunch of feathers that still breathed. My world was tiny, and it was awful. I closed my eyes so as not to see it, and pressed myself tight into the ground that lay beneath me in soothing dumbness. This trampled earth in no way resembled real life, waiting for exams in real life.

But it does unfortunately resemble real life.

These stories also are all coming-of-age stories. Such stories focus on a young narrator, naïve by definition, who begins the story wet around the ears, understanding little of the world, and ends up through his experiences making the rite of passage from childhood into adulthood. See, for instance, James Joyce's classic story, "Araby," about the self-delusions and disappointments of a young boy's infatuation with an older girl.

It's hard to write a childhood story that isn't a coming-of-age story. Almost all stories involve some kind of character change, and one of the most profound changes of life is the transition from child to adult. This presents the greatest challenge in writing childhood stories: Since they are almost invariably coming-of-age stories and since so many are written, how can we write one that's different from the rest? It's a challenge but it's by no means impossible. Success rests in the telling of the story, how fresh the perceptions of the narrator are, how unusual the story is, and, most important, whether the ending can avoid feeling pat, inevitable in its coming-of-ageness.

However, editors, by and large, have a bias against child narrators. This bias is not universal, but it exists primarily because magazines are inundated with such stories. Be aware of this bias, but don't let it dissuade you from writing a story based on your childhood experiences. It's just an extra hurdle to jump.

I was always doing things as a kid that I've been trying to fit into my fiction ever since. Like the time I organized a pickpocket ring at Atlantic

Beach Day Camp in New York. One time, someone brought some rabbits to class in first grade, and the teacher said we could have a rabbit if we got a note from our parents. I knew that my mother wouldn't allow me to have a rabbit, so I went home and forged a note that read:

> Robin can hav rabbi
> sined Mom

Another time I invited my first-grade teacher for dinner because I had a crush on her. She said she'd be delighted, and asked me what time to show up.

"Nine," I said. Nine was actually my bedtime. I suppose I imagined my mother saying, "Well, we've already eaten, but this is Robin's bedtime. So if you want to sleep over you can."

When I arrived home that evening, I forgot all about my teacher. She showed up at nine sharp and rang the doorbell.

"Robin, go see who that is," said my mother.

"No," I said.

"Come on," she said. "Go see who it is. Tell them I'll be down in a minute."

I went downstairs, looked through the window, and saw my teacher dressed up with a fur collar and her hair made up. She saw me and waved. I waved back and ran upstairs.

"Who is it?" my mother asked.

"Nobody."

My mother shook her head and walked downstairs to see for herself. I tagged behind her saying, "She wants to eat. Don't let her in."

I've twice tried to include this anecdote in a story. The first time the editor who saw it suggested I cut it out. It was funny, she said, but it had little bearing on the story as a whole. So I cut it. Recently, I put the same anecdote in another story and another editor had the same problem with it. This time, however, I didn't cut the anecdote. In this story, I think it does have bearing on the story as a whole. Who knows? I might be wrong. Perhaps I'm too fond of the episode, and before the story makes it into my next collection of stories, I'm going to give it a hard look and decide whether to axe it again or not. I can always save it for yet another story.

The way I related the above anecdote is important, too. There are count-less ways to describe an actual event, whether from childhood or not, de-pending on who the writer is, or even the mood of the writer as he sits down to put pen to paper, or neurons to computer screen, as the case may be. I've told that story so many times I've almost got it memorized. Still, is that the way things actually happened? No. That sequence of events happened, but it's still fictionalized. Words shape the way we view an event, and they can never truly transfer the full experience to the reader, no matter how accu-rate the writer tries to be. Accuracy, in this context, at least, should not even be the writer's aim.

If you use something from your childhood in a story, an anecdote like the one above, or if you base an entire story on your childhood, there are a few things to look out for:

1. Don't romanticize childhood. While children are naïve, they're not necessarily innocent. Children can be much more brutal and frank than adults, and often adults' golden memories of child-hood are little more than wishful thinking.

2. Avoid precious-kid talk. Often, what seems cute or funny in real life might fall completely flat in a short story, seeming too heavy-handed.

3. Inevitably, someone will criticize your story, especially if it's written in the first person, on the grounds that "a child wouldn't sound like that." If you *were* completely accurate, you wouldn't have much of a story there. It would be about eight lines, writ-ten on wide-ruled paper with a fat pencil. Have you ever heard a child tell a story? In *Mollie Is Three, Growing Up In School,* by Vivian Gussin Paley, the author recorded much of the play-acting and storytelling of her class of three-year-olds.

Most first stories . . . lie somewhere between the compulsory and the accidental. They refer to scenes that are not overwhelming but need to be played out again. Mollie's first story, for example, dealt with the bad guys she heard about in school.

"About a bad guy and a horse. The robbers and the horse. He takes things away from the girl."

Here are some other first stories dictated by this year's three-year-olds:

"Batman goes whoosh. In the Batmobile" (Barney).

"The gorilla gets out of the cage" (William).

"The mommy walks and eats and takes a nappie" (Stuart).

"Me finds a train. And the train stopped. And the trains sleeped" (Edward).

"Five kitty cats run away. Superman pows them away" (Sybil).

As we discussed earlier, a short story, or a novel for that matter, is artifice. You want the story to seem real, to suspend the reader's disbelief, but if the story is any good, it will never be a completely accurate account. A completely accurate account would ricochet from one subject to another with hardly any logical progression. That's how children's minds work. They are highly associative creatures.

Your way out is to either write the story in first person, past tense, or in third person. With first person, past tense, there's almost an invisible narrator behind the child narrator. In other words, it's assumed that the narrator is looking back from an adult vantage point and telling the story, though it's not necessary to know exactly how old the adult narrator is. With third person, you have that same kind of removal between the child and the narrator. But even if you want to write a story from a child's point of view in first person, present tense, go ahead. Just steel yourself for the inevitable criticism.

Of course, not all of that criticism is invalid. You wouldn't normally have a five-year-old talking about, for instance, dysfunction in the contemporary American family—unless, of course, you used the narrator's advanced vocabulary in an ironic way as Frank O'Connor does in his story, "My Oedipus Complex." The story is about a five-year-old boy who has his mother all to himself while his father is away in the army during World War I. His father makes rare appearances like Santa Claus, which suits the boy just fine, until one day, the war ends.

One morning, I got into the big bed, and there, sure enough, was Father in his usual Santa Claus manner, but later, instead of a uniform, he put on his best blue suit, and Mother was as pleased as anything. I saw nothing to be pleased about, because, out of uniform, Father was altogether less interesting, but she only beamed, and explained that our prayers had been answered, and off we went to Mass to thank God for having brought Father safely home.

The irony of it! That very day when he came in to dinner he took off his boots and put on his slippers, donned the dirty old cap he wore about the house to save him from colds, crossed his legs, and began to talk gravely to Mother, who looked anxious. Naturally, I disliked her looking anxious, because it destroyed her good looks, so I interrupted him.

"Just a moment, Larry!" she said gently.

This was only what she said when we had boring visitors, so I attached no importance to it and went on talking.

Young writers sometimes have a difficult time finding subject matter from real life, and that's why childhood is often a good source for their stories. Not long ago, a student of mine, Courtney, wrote a pastiche of loosely connected anecdotes that she undoubtedly knocked out the night before the story was due. When we talked about the story in class, the other students felt disconnected from the narrative because it lacked any sense of structure. But there was one scene they all responded to, a scene about the parents of the narrator being chili cook-off fanatics and dragging their two kids to chili cook-offs around the country. "That's my parents," the author piped in. "They're crazy about chili. That's all they think about. My dad was the Texas chili cook-off champion last year."

Now we were interested and asked Courtney about the world of chili cook-offs. Among other things, we learned about cow bingo, a game played at many chili cook-offs in which a huge bingo card is chalked in the grass, people bet on a number, and then a cow is made to wander over the card. Wherever the animal drops a cow pie, that's the number that wins.

Soon Courtney embarked upon an epic tale of two fanatical chili cooks and their somewhat disenchanted daughter and son. The story ended up being twenty-seven pages long, and this is an intro to creative-writing class in which most students think that they've written a novel if they go beyond five pages. Admittedly, the story needed some cutting, but Courtney was engaged with the material. "I can't believe it," she lamented to me one day.

"I went away to school to get away from chili cook-offs, and now I'm writing about them."

Tell-It-Like-It-Is Stories

On occasion, a writer will write a story pretty much as it happened in real life, but this is a rarity. There are no rules or directions for writing such a story, only that, again, you should be sure you don't confuse a good anecdote for a good story. But sometimes an occurrence in life will imitate the arc of a story and all you have to do is write it down and change a few details here and there.

Sometimes you'll know the tell-it-like-it-is story when it happens to you. It won't happen often, but all of a sudden you'll find yourself in a situation that you know immediately is a story. It's a strange feeling when it happens. Regardless of your religious beliefs, you'll think about fate, kismet, karma, whatever. But beware. The ironies of life can be much more heavy-handed than those in fiction.

Josip Novakovich was able to write a story pretty much as it happened, about the death of his father. It's a story called "Apple" [see page 259], first published in *Ploughshares*. He says that the material was difficult for him, that before this story he was able to write about all else in his life but this event. And when he was finally able to write the story, he wasn't sure whether to call it memoir or fiction, but decided on fiction. He had, after all, changed some of the details and shifted a couple of events around in time. But, as mentioned earlier, even memoirists often do this.

> It was January 6th, and snow stormed outdoors, slantedly. When
> I looked through the window, I had the feeling that the household
> floated into heaven sideways. The big patches of snow resembled
> the down of a huge, slain celestial bird, whose one wing covered
> our whole valley, and the spasmodic wing must have been flapping,
> because it was windy. As soon as the snow touched the ground, it
> melted.

In real life, Novakovich's father died in February, and it wasn't snowing, but snow, he says, felt right for the story. This doesn't matter. A few details may be changed, but the core of the experience is essentially honest, and that's what's important. As proof of that fact, when his older brother read the story, he took it as a family document, a testament, and locked it in a vault with other important family papers.

Since writing "Apple," Novakovich has written an essay with his father in it, but in this he focuses more on the man's religious fervor toward the end of his life, and the death plays a background role.

So is this cheating in some way, calling something fiction that's factually based? Not at all. But some writers act sheepish about writing this kind of story, and they are reluctant to admit this is what they've done, as though we might think less of them, as though they're somehow lazy for writing something so factual. That's nonsense, of course. The details you choose, the words you choose, the ordering of events—all of these take an act of the imagination and some skill as a writer. In some ways, writing such a story is more difficult than writing a story whole cloth from your imagination. Even in the most factually based stories, you need to know what memories to leave out and what to build up or exaggerate. If you're absolutely true in every respect to what happened, you'll probably wind up with a disjointed jumble with vague and flat images. The story must ultimately seem of a piece, to achieve what Edgar Allan Poe called *unity of effect.* This unity of effect is perhaps more difficult to achieve in a completely or nearly auto-biographical story, because a memory that seems crucial to the writer might completely baffle the reader and seem extraneous to the story. It takes prac-tice to be able to decide which of these memories *really* fit in and which seem important only because the writer wants them to be important, because they happened. The best measure of your success or failure in writing such an autobiographical piece is the cool eye of an honest critic. If someone you respect suggests that something autobiographical doesn't fit your story, listen to her and make those cuts, as painful as they might be.

Madison Smartt Bell was just out of college when he wrote "The Lie Detector" and "The Forgotten Bridge," two stories in his celebrated collec-tion *Zero db and Other Stories.* Both stories are told from the first person by a narrator of whom we know very little, except that he's a young white male trying his best to survive in and around New York City. "The Forgotten Bridge" takes place in a run-down tenement in the Williamsburg section of Brooklyn and deals with the narrator's friendships with the other people in the building, most notably a young Hispanic man called Pollo and his friend Angel. Friendship is perhaps too strong a word—more like a guarded acquaintanceship, at least on the narrator's part. "The Lie Detector," a story that was reprinted in *The Best American Short Stories*, deals with the same narrator, maybe six months or so earlier in his life. In this story, he's being evicted from his apartment in Hoboken because his landlord has sold the building. The landlord refuses to return his rent deposit, and in the meantime, his new landlord and/or the super of the building (the narrator isn't sure which one) tries to shake him down for an extra hundred dollars. On top of this, the narrator is practically starving and searching for any kind of work he can find. At one point, he must take a lie-detector test to secure a job.

Bell says that both stories were fairly accurate accounts of his life at the time, and except for changing the names, the characters were all real people. "The Lie Detector" was too long, he felt, so he cut about ten pages as he was drafting it. Regardless, even if everything happened in these stories exactly as they're laid out, they're still fictional stories. The narration is purposely distant and oblique:

> I took the form to a chair and looked it over, and it was asking a
> lot of questions I really couldn't afford to answer. I hadn't expected
> anything like it. I had expected to be asked about drug addiction
> and felony convictions, two problems I happened not to have, and
> here were all these questions about problems that I did have. But I
> was up there already so I decided to try it. I filled out the form with
> what I wished was the truth and waited for them to call me. I sat
> there hoping that polygraph tests really are as unreliable as statistics
> say they are.

Makes you curious, doesn't it? It's supposed to. That's *indirection*. We never learn what those problems are, what the narrator hopes won't be uncovered about himself. Why? If the narrator doesn't want the lie detector to uncover these problems, he's certainly not going to tell us about them. That, in itself, gives the narration some of its ironic tension and makes it fiction—no matter *how* fact-based the story is.

We learn only through inference about the narrator's feelings and beliefs, and though he's supposedly telling us about the lives of other people, by the end of each story, we have a fairly clear portrait of his own moral state, in part because of what he says, in part because of what he leaves out. This method of indirection will automatically pull you back from a story that really happened to you, will give you the requisite distance to create a fictional treatment of real events. That can hardly be stressed enough. When you write a story of this kind, allow your narrator to withhold certain information. Allow him to be a little cagey, a little less than forthcoming about his own weaknesses and gray areas—just as long as the reader sees through such subterfuge. Of course, these weaknesses might well be your own weaknesses, but remember what Faulkner said about the human heart in conflict with itself. Remember also that you have the perfect defense. It's only a story, you can always say.

Jobs and Other True Experiences

I admit I've done some things in my life just for the experience, so that I might write about them later. But the truth is, most of what I consciously experienced so I could write about it later didn't pan out. I never wrote about these experiences, and I probably never will (at least as fiction). One summer I was a gravedigger's apprentice. I wasn't a very good gravedigger's apprentice, and I didn't last long, but that's what I did the summer I was eighteen. The foreman was a guy named Wilbur who wore a back brace and who said he was going to retire soon. He said the cemetery was going to give him his own plot when he retired, which, he said, was better than some businessman's watch because it would last longer. My older brother, Jonathan, worked with me, and Wilbur called him Big Jon and me Little Jon because he didn't think Robin was a proper name for a boy to have. It seems that the seminal experience in Wilbur's life had been his time during World War II in Gibraltar, because just about all he talked about while Jonny and I toiled in the sun were those "hot-blooded Gibraltar gals."

Even at eighteen, I wanted to be a writer, though I was probably more interested in being a writer than in actually writing. Still, as Wilbur talked, I kept thinking, *This is going to make a great story.* It didn't, or at least it hasn't yet. I don't think this is due to any kind of moral quandary. It's not because of my mercenary approach to the experience, the fact that I wanted to write about Wilbur and the whole graveyard crowd from the outset. No, it's probably more simply that I haven't gotten around to writing the story yet. I've lived through a number of experiences during which I thought, *I'll prob-*

ably write about this someday, and I did. Or even more likely, the answer is that what struck me as fascinating material at the age of eighteen no longer seems all that striking now that I'm older.

One summer during graduate school in Iowa, a friend asked me if I'd like to pick up some extra money as a bartender. He said a friend of his was opening a bar and needed some help. It turned out this bar was Iowa City's first and only strip joint (actually, it was right over the city line), called Taboo's.

I jumped at the chance, not because I was an aficionado of strip joints, but because it seemed like a strange thing to do. *At the very least,* I thought, *it'll make a good story.* From a gravedigger's apprentice to bartender in a strip joint. I'm not sure that was a step up.

In any case, Taboo's was a strange place in more than one way. It was located in the clubhouse on a golf course, so the decor was not your typical strip-joint fare. It had a big old hearth on one side of the room and a mantel lined with trophies of gold men swinging clubs. In the middle of the room was the platform on which the strippers did their acts.

The strippers were pretty interesting, too. The most popular one was a woman named Brandy (they all seemed to be named after alcoholic beverages) who did a rug act that people came from far and wide to see. There was also a minister's daughter (you see, if I wrote that in a story, you'd think, "Right, a minister's daughter") whose name I forget. Her boyfriend had never seen her strip and used to drop her off and then pick her up when she was finished. She danced very stiffly, as though removing layer after layer of flannel underwear. There was also a woman we nicknamed Miss Dubuque (she'd won some title like that) who absolutely loathed the audience. She danced with complete hatred in her eyes. She didn't even try to hide it, which did not make her the most popular stripper, and I don't think I ever saw a man dare stick any folding money in her G-string.

The most pathetic of all the dancers was a woman who had at one time been a stripper in Las Vegas and had owned $7,000 worth of costumes. Three weeks before she came to work at Taboo's, she and her husband had ceremoniously burned all her old costumes, thinking she'd never have to strip again. But a week later, her husband was unexpectedly laid off from his job. So now she'd gone back to her degrading work at Taboo's. The woman also had a large hysterectomy scar. I talked to her a lot at the bar and felt sorry for her, knowing she wasn't going to last long, knowing she didn't want to last long. When she danced, the men in the bar looked away, scars being something they were trying to escape from in their own lives.

It wasn't long after that I quit, realizing that what I thought of as story material was much more important than that.

But my favorite time at Taboo's was ladies' night. On this night, male strippers danced at the club, and they were much better and seemed to enjoy themselves more than the women who danced. The men dressed up in campy costumes like sailor uniforms and tails and tuxes and seemed to glory in the attention from the overwhelmingly female clientele, mostly young women who worked at the phone company. These women, in their adulation of the male strippers, acted twice as abandoned as the male clientele on a normal night. The women hooted and danced, but the men just looked slack-jawed and slobbered over themselves between gulps of beer. So I enjoyed ladies' night. I also enjoyed it because sometimes a hapless man, unaware that it was ladies' night, would wander in from the racetrack, farm, or university, and a look of horror would overcome him when he glanced at the stage. But he'd paid his cover, so he'd belly up to the bar, clutch it till his knuckles turned white, and refuse to look over his shoulder at the stage, afraid he might turn into a pillar of salt or someone might think he actually *liked* to see guys take their clothes off! The irony, of course, was that the female strippers were not available to him and his kind, but if he'd been a little less homophobic, he might have had some luck with the hooting operators there for ladies' night. Or maybe not.

So, if I wrote a story about this, where would I go with it? If I told it from a point of view based on my own, I'd say it would make a pretty obvious coming-of-age story. Or I could focus on the woman with the hysterectomy. She's much more interesting to me than I am. Still, you have to avoid the obvious ironies. Don't end such a story with the poor woman dancing on the stage and the men looking away from her scar. Avoid writing your typical down-on-your-luck-isn't-life-tragic, aren't-men-pigs story. For that matter, avoid writing *anything* typical. The successful fiction writer is not the one who reinforces our old notions of life. Actually, that's not completely true. Many monetarily successful fiction writers reinforce stale ideas and recycle plots and characters. But if you're aiming for those old eternal verities, you need to show us the world in a new light. You need to recast those verities through the rich and varied details that you have experienced and observed.

And, as we've discussed earlier, the characters, not the events, should take center stage in your story. Find out which character intrigues you the most and try writing the story about him or her. Depending on the point of view, what happens in the story will change considerably. What if you told the story from Miss Dubuque's point of view? Kind of lame, I think.

> The pigs, Miss Dubuque thinks, as she twists and turns and moans
> on the floor. You think you're in control, but I am in control, not
> you. Swine!

If you tell it from the point of view based on me, here's what it might look like:

> My friend, Will, asked me if I'd like to pick up some extra money
> that summer. I said, "Sure, doing what?"
>   "Bartending," he replied with a sheepish grin.
>   "Dang!" I said. "When do I begin?" Little did I expect where I
> would be tending bar!

Yawn.

Or you could tell it from the minister's daughter's point of view, but that seems so pointed, no one would believe you. "But it really happened," you'd say. So what?

How about her boyfriend's point of view? Maybe, but I keep coming back to that woman with the hysterectomy. Obviously, if you're unsubtle and approach the story like a mongrel with a bone in its mouth, you could destroy this one, too, by making the irony as heavy-handed as the previous examples. But there's still something emotionally interesting about this woman to me. In the words of Sherwood Anderson, "Something must be understood."

Still, if I were to write this story, I might take it out of the strip joint, at least partly, and focus on some other, less sensationalistic aspect of the woman's life. This is a strategy writers often use when dealing with autobiographical material. The notes fit together slowly, picked up from different stages of life. I might combine this tale of the Iowa City stripper with another story from my life. For instance, a friend once told me of visiting a farm in Iowa, a farm that was run by a young couple she had just met. They proudly walked her through the fields and showed her their livestock and produce. Originally, they had lived somewhere urban and were relatively new to this life. What my friend remembered most, however, was the kitchen, in which hung full strings of peppers and garlic and fresh herbs. The next day, this couple was killed in an auto accident, and my friend was haunted by the image of their kitchen, so well stocked with all these vegetables and herbs. That image, for some reason, has stayed with me, too.

What if you combined the story of the stripper with the hysterectomy and the tale of the young farm couple? Certainly, a farming stripper with a hysterectomy would be a slightly different take on things. Phrased like that, it sounds ridiculous. But if you're going to write, you must take risks, and the biggest risk is that you may look like a fool. For the sake of argument, can you see anything that might connect the two anecdotes—in terms of character, theme, plot? Again, that's what writers do when patching together episodes from life. They make *associations*. Often these associations are thematic. Sometimes we're not sure *what* they are or why our minds have made these strange connections between events separated by time and distance. Your job in the story is to find out exactly how they're connected. That might seem like an odd strategy. How can you write a story if you don't know what it's about? Writing is a discovery process, as much for the writer as for the reader.

How about this? I keep going back to the notion that this woman and her husband had burned her costumes just weeks before she was forced back to work as a stripper. At that moment, they must have thought they had life beat, or maybe it was a rash gesture, something defiant in the face of defeat. And the hysterectomy, of course, meant that she couldn't have any children, yet here they were surrounded by the fecundity of their farm. To me, there's something worth exploring there.

Sometimes this strategy of combining two seemingly unrelated incidents doesn't pan out. The main danger is a lack of focus, but if you've already completely figured out what your story is about before you've begun, your insights probably won't be that startling.

In any case, a true-experience story can be limiting if you stick to the real events of what happened to you. Ask yourself what the point is of relating your true experience. Because it was bizarre? Because it was a wacky job training spider monkeys to dance the hula at Mondo Monkey World in Ft. Lauderdale the summer you turned seventeen? Remember what we've said about anecdotes. One reason that such stories often don't work is because they hinge on the anecdotal. What should concern you first and foremost are the nuances of character in your story. And that character might not be you at all.

Stories from the Newspaper

As we've discussed, the fact that you've lived through something can actually get in your way, can make it difficult for you to tackle the material. That's why you need distance and why it's often much easier to write about someone else. Newspapers are full of potential story material.

Some years ago, Dan Rather was accosted on the streets of New York by thugs who pushed him to the ground, kicked him, and shouted, "What is the frequency, Kenneth?" The story made all the papers, but of course, no one, least of all Dan Rather, knew what his attackers were talking about. The story was a little absurd and intriguing, but only intriguing because of the dramatic questions involved: Who is Kenneth? What is this talk of frequencies? It was also intriguing because it happened to Dan Rather. If it had happened to you or me, no one would have been interested—or not many people, at least. I asked my writing students to do an in-class exercise with this incident as the basis for a scene, and predictably, the scenes they came up with weren't all that interesting. It was my miscalculation. I hadn't thought the assignment through. After all, where could one go with such a silly idea? The results were one-note stories in which Dan Rather turned out to be a Russian spy. Often, the mystery of an event is much more interesting than any solution one can come up with.

A couple of years later, a Russian circus was stranded outside of Atlanta, Georgia, when their Arab backers deserted them. They spent weeks in a motel: the acrobats, the sword swallowers, the clowns. Something about that news story seemed evocative to me. I could see an entire novel about a Russian circus stranded in the American South. I suppose the reason this seems so intriguing is that the situation has larger societal implications than, say, the Dan Rather story. I'm not quite sure what those implications are, but that's, in part, what I'd try to discover if I were going to write a novel about this situation. Also, I have lived in the South, not too far from Atlanta, so there's probably some chord in me the story touches. That's an important point. Even if the story has nothing to do with you on an obvious level, it most likely has something important to do with you on a subconscious level, or else you wouldn't be interested in the idea in the first place.

A lot of other people, millions perhaps, saw that Russian circus story. How many of those millions were writers? Let's say two thousand. And of those two thousand, how many thought the idea might make an interesting short story or novel? Maybe fifty. And of those fifty, how many do you think will actually start writing the story or novel? When this book was first published, I would have said (and did) that the answer is: none. But I've revised that opinion. Writers ARE captivated by the same material. Take, for instance, the true story of the first celebrated conjoined twins, Chang and Eng, from Siam (now Thailand). In the nineteenth century, they were renowned celebrities after whom the term "Siamese twins" was coined. Both the writers Darin Straus and Mark Slouka thought the subject matter was a good one and so, unbeknownst to each other, they each wrote novels about the twins. Straus's novel, *Chang and Eng,* appeared first in 2000 to much acclaim. Most writers might despair that they had been scooped, but a novel, after all, is a personal vision of the author's imagination. Who's to say that your imaginative telling of the Chang and Eng story wouldn't be just as powerful as Straus's. When Mark Slouka's novel, *God's Fool,* appeared in 2002, it also received deserved critical acclaim. Would Slouka rather his novel appeared first? Undoubtedly, but the fact that the same material interests more than one writer shouldn't stop you from writing about it in your own way. While I was writing a nonfiction book about a purported anthropological hoax in the Philippines, *Invented Eden: The Elusive, Disputed History of the Tasaday,* Jessica Hagedorn was writing a novel based on the same material. We were aware of each other's project and stayed out of each other's hair while we wrote. Our books came out within six months of each other, and the two of us made several appearances together to promote our very different versions of the story, one fictional, one nonfictional.

Regardless of the source, you must mold and shape the story, mixing it with your imagination and perhaps events from your own life. Ask yourself what interests you about the material. Maybe you won't completely know the answer to that question, but it should be more than, "Gee, it's terrible when things like that happen." We already know that from the news story.

What often attracts us to a bizarre story in a newspaper is the "what," the odd circumstances of the story. A short story should focus more on the "why" and "who," as *elucidated* by the "what." In other words, the action or events in the story should show us something *about* the characters and their motivations. A car chase in a movie might be exciting because we respond viscerally to visual stimulation. We don't necessarily have to know who the chasers and chasees are. Our adrenaline will naturally start pumping. That's not the case in a short story or novel. Simply describing action devoid of character, no matter how intriguing the action is, will leave readers in the dark unless we know and care about the characters.

Joyce Carol Oates based her story "Where Are You Going, Where Have You Been?" on a newspaper account of a serial rapist/murderer who was roaming the Midwest at the time. But she didn't tell the story from his point of view. She told it from the point of view of one of his victims. The violence is all implied, all off-stage. It's the threat of violence, the inevitability of it, that creates and sustains tension in the story. In the end, as the soon-to-be victim is riding with the murderer in his car, it's not necessary for Oates to go any further in the story. She doesn't have to describe the violence in detail. Our imaginations can create the scenario. And by implying the violence rather than showing it, she makes the story all the more haunting, one that lingers for years.

Almost any newspaper story can be transformed into a piece of fiction. The main strategy is to focus. And you focus on character, even in stories that deal ostensibly with the largest, most gripping and complex issues in the newspaper today: serial killers, televangelism, Elvis! You must focus on a believable character because if you focus instead on the issue itself, what you've written is an essay, not a story. The issue will overwhelm the characters. Your stories should not have a message in the sense that a sermon has a message: AIDS is terrible and AIDS discrimination is shameful and discrimination against the homeless is shameful, too. Short stories and novels, like real life, are far more ambiguous than sermons. The distinction between right and wrong, good and evil, is often blurred. You don't need to write a story with a message because most often these messages are ones we hear and acknowledge day after day. We all know that AIDS and homelessness are tragic. We don't need a short story or novel to reinforce that. The first responsibility of a writer is to create believable characters, and the issues, or themes, should arise organically from who the characters are, not from some preconceived notion of what issue you want the story to deal with.

On the other hand, it's quite all right to write a story with a character in it who has AIDS or who is homeless, as long as the story is first and foremost about the character, and AIDS or homelessness is just an aspect of his personality—like the way he parts his hair to the right or has a pet cat. Maybe AIDS and homelessness would have more bearing on the character's personality than a hair part or a pet, but the point is that AIDS and homelessness should not be emblems or symbols, thus transforming the character into a mere symbol or stereotype rather than a complex character.

There *are* artists who handle big issues well. On June 14, 1993, Anna Deveare Smith opened a successful one-woman show, "Twilight: Los Angeles, 1992," based on the Los Angeles riots. Smith did extensive research for her play, interviewing 175 people who were intimately involved with the riots. The critics agreed the play was brilliant. Part of its brilliance undoubtedly derives from Smith's own ability to transform herself into the various roles, from a Korean family to former Los Angeles police chief Daryl Gates to Rodney King's aunt. She uses their words verbatim, captured over nine months with her tape recorder, to bring about these transformations. Notice, though, that while the subject is ostensibly the Los Angeles riots, Smith focuses on character more than event—24 characters in this case, culled from the more than 175 people she interviewed. In her own words, she looks for those "characteristic moments" from her subjects, the moment "when people actually take control of their interview."

That's what any good writer looks for, those characteristic moments when the essence of who the character is seems to be revealed through speech or gesture. In these cases, the characters seem to take control of your story or novel. They speak faster than you can record what they're saying. That's when you know your writing works.

Some people might not consider what Smith has done as a creative achievement at all. As stated earlier, some writers believe that any creative work based on real life represents "a failure of the imagination." Actually, the case is quite the opposite. Any time you can transform real life—and we've seen how difficult that can be—it represents a triumph of the imagination.

But what about the case of Anna Deveare Smith? What's creative about taking the words verbatim out of the mouths of her subjects and saying them onstage? You can say someone's words verbatim, but you're still interpreting them, though perhaps subtly, through gesture and intonation. Smith taped more than 175 interviews and culled these down to 24. She looked for "characteristic moments." If you were doing the production, perhaps you'd find different characteristic moments, or maybe you wouldn't see any at all. In short, Smith ordered real life. And that's something that takes a great deal of imagination and understanding.

A lot of newspaper stories are either amusing or cute or shocking. Not human interest stories, but alien interest. Primate interest. People doing the kinds of outrageous things that work fine in real life, but when you transfer them to a fictional setting people say, "Uh-uh. Won't work. I'm not buying." Go figure.

Here's one that appeared some years back, a story that got a lot of play in the national media. Twenty evangelical Texans, ages one to sixty-three, stripped off all their clothing because they thought their clothes were possessed by the Devil, piled into a 1990 Pontiac Grand Am, and took off through Texas and Louisiana until they finally slammed into a tree. They were more or less fine, but still naked, when the local sheriff disgorged them from the Grand Am. As police officer Doyle Nealy (make a note of that name; it's a good one) observed: "It was just a religious type of thing."

While this kind of newspaper story isn't my kind of material, there *are* writers who use such material as the kernels for their work and end up with stories that are funny and profound. Much depends on the individual writer's sensibilities, and that's why you can't make ironclad rules for writers.

Newspaper stories rarely give you an in-depth portrait of a person, so if you use a newspaper account as the basis of a story, your job is to invent, to expand on our knowledge of the characters, to make them believable. As we discussed in the previous chapter, you do this through salient detail and by trying to come to some understanding of their desires, the motivations for their actions. All actions have motivations, even ones that seem "crazy." Never write a character whose motivations are unclear to you. If they're unclear to you, they'll be unclear to the reader. That doesn't mean you have to know a character's motivations from the outset. Just as you can come to discover what your story is "about," you can also come to discover who your characters are and what makes them tick. In any case, you want your readers to understand your characters, to feel what they feel, to ultimately be moved by what happens to them. If you don't know why something happens, you can't expect your reader to fully share the experience of your character.

If you find a story that interests you in the newspaper, ask yourself what is in the story that intrigues you so much. Is it the situation, or the characters? Is it both? Let's say you're intrigued by the story about the car of naked evangelical Texans. The situation is interesting, but so are the people. Why would they act in a way that seems bizarre to most of us? It's unlikely that you can write a convincing story shifting from one point of view to the other, so you must choose a central point of view. It could be the preacher. It could be one of the cops. Or perhaps another, less visible (no pun intended) member of the group. I would go for the latter because the preacher seems a little too obvious, too likely to veer into stereotype. And the cop's point of view would be too limited. So you must decide who among that tangled mob would make a good protagonist. The preacher's daughter? Again, too obvious, too much of a stereotype. A child? Maybe, but perhaps too limited again. Often, the first characters who leap to mind in a situation like this will be stereotypes. It wouldn't be easy, but you should probably invent someone who is none of these stereotypes, maybe someone based on an acquaintance of yours, someone you've known in the past who might just wind up nude with nineteen others in a 1990 Grand Am. Or maybe even better, base it on someone you wouldn't expect at *all* to be there. Maybe your mother or father. Make it the story of how she or he wound up in this unlikely situation. In that way you'd mix your memory, your imagination, and an objective newspaper account to create something completely new, and something that would really interest us—we'd want to know as much as you how your mother ended up there!

It's usually a little easier to comprehend the motivations of people in newspaper accounts. A story in the *New York Times* concerned the skeletons of four Eskimos that the American Museum of Natural History was shipping to Greenland. Apparently, in 1896, explorer Robert E. Peary enticed several Greenland Eskimos to travel to New York with him to be put on display. On October 11, 1897, the *New York Times* reported, "The unfortunate little savages have caught cold or warmth, they do not know which, but assuming it was the latter their sole endeavor yesterday was to keep cool. Their efforts in this direction were a source of amusement to several scores of visitors."

The present-day *Times* reporter, in a tone radically different from his patronizing and cruel predecessor, chronicles this shameful time when we put people on display like animals. Of course, most of the Eskimos died of disease, and the last surviving adult was shipped back to Greenland. That left one child, a boy named Minik, who was blithely handed over for adoption to William Wallace, the superintendent of the museum's building. As the article notes, it was a strange choice because it was this man who actually bleached the bones of the boy's father and the other dead Eskimos and then handed them over to the museum.

In 1907, an article in the *New York World* appeared, headlined "Give Me My Father's Body," and related Minik's anguish and his frustrated attempts to make the museum relinquish his father's skeleton. By that time, Peary had ceased to have any interest in the boy and was concerned with other, more important things, such as receiving from Teddy Roosevelt a gold medal for his exploration.

In 1909, Minik was sent to Manhattan College to study engineering. That same year, he acquired a press agent, was reported as suicidal, and then disappeared. Peary, for his part, was racing to find the North Pole when another article appeared in the *Times* about Minik, in which his press agent claimed that Minik didn't feel any particular warmth for Peary and might in some way scheme to defeat his attempt to find the Pole, though God knows how he would have done that. Still, the explorer's wife took the report seriously enough and decided the best thing to do was to ship Minik off to Greenland. So, once he resurfaced, he was offered a one-way ticket home, an offer he didn't refuse. But before boarding the ship, he gave reporters one more statement:

> You're a race of scientific criminals. I know I'll never get my father's bones out of the American Museum of Natural History. I am glad enough to get away before they grab my brains and stuff them into a jar.

But Minik was wrong. They *had* grabbed his brains. He didn't fare well in Greenland. He didn't know how to hunt or fish, and he didn't speak the language. Slowly, painfully, he learned, but he finally gave up and returned to the United States in 1916. Soon, he wound up as a lumberjack in New Hampshire, a loner who stayed in a shack he built himself. Then, in 1918, he contracted the flu that was epidemic at the time and died at the age of twenty-nine. Now he's buried in a cemetery in Pittsburg, New Hampshire, while his father's bones have finally been shipped back to Greenland for a traditional burial in the Arctic permafrost.

Does this story strike you as potentially fruitful? Minik is a complex and tragic character, one deserving of a novel. A novel such as this would be as much a portrait of the era in which he lived as a portrait of Minik. So who would be the main characters of this book? They're right there in front of us, hard to improve. There's Minik, of course, but also the vain Peary and Minik's adoptive father, who was fired by the museum for taking kickbacks and who might have spurred Minik in his quest out of his own bitterness toward the museum.

If the real story is hard to improve, why bother with a fictional treatment? There have been several nonfiction books about Minik. Maybe that's enough. Maybe not. Novels can do things and go places that a nonfictional treatment, constrained by fact and reasonable conjecture, must avoid. A novelist can, through her imagination and a substantial amount of research, take on the various roles in the drama. She can effectively become Minik and Peary and Minik's adoptive father, or a reasonable facsimile of any one of them. A novelist can delve beneath the surface into the subconscious of the individual as well as the age, can tell the story between the lines of the nonfictional account. In effect, by reimagining the thoughts and sights of these characters, the novelist gets at a powerful emotional truth that is rarely achieved in any other genre.

Are there any types of newspaper stories that *can't* be transformed into short stories? Not really. All it takes is imagination and curiosity—reading between the lines, discovering the motivations of your characters. If, however, you write the story simply as it appears in the paper, without transforming it, without trying to discover the ambiguities and the mysteries of character and situation, your story will not succeed no matter how interesting the initial idea is. For instance, there's the newspaper story about the beautician who won a $15.7 million Lotto jackpot in September and didn't tell a soul she had the winning ticket. She waited until Christmas, when she gave it to her husband in a card with the inscription, "This is the best I can do this year. I love you." Now that's a great anecdote, a wonderful and touching true-life happening, but will it make a good short story as it stands? Almost certainly not. As life it's fine. But as fiction? Let's say you tell the story from the husband's point of view. His wife has been acting kind of strange lately. He suspects that she's been cheating on him. On Christmas Day she hands him a card. No new drill press like he's been hinting around about for months. Boy, is he disappointed. He opens the card and . . . hey, what's this? A lottery ticket flutters to the floor.

That kind of story simply relies on the surprise ending and as such doesn't show us anything substantial or interesting about these people. If you tell the story from the woman's point of view, it's much the same—maybe even more predictable and sentimental. A good story is neither wholly predictable nor wholly surprising. A good story doesn't rely on simple outcomes. Remember what Sharon Solwitz said about her story, how she ended her story before the protagonist discovers what the results are of her biopsy.

If you write the story about the woman who keeps the lottery ticket a secret till Christmas, think about who she and her husband are, where the conflict is, and ways to transform the actual events—in that order. You might even have to discard the very thing that attracted you to the anecdote in the first place—the woman's selflessness, her love for her husband. I'm not saying you must do this, but be open to anything that will make the story a good one, that will keep allowing you to make discoveries about your characters and where the story is going. Maybe in your story she winds up *not* giving it to him. Who knows? Or maybe, as in Solwitz's story, the ticket itself will become irrelevant by the end of the story, for good or ill. The central conflict will be something else.

Sketch the plot. Write biographies of the principal characters. Write a possible outcome. Flip the outcome on its head and try it that way. Experiment. Be open-minded. Transform and transform again. Discover the story within the story. Surprise yourself first. Then you can worry about surprising the reader.

Dreams and Discoveries

Dreams are part of your life, too. You spend a third of your life asleep, right? So you might as well get something out of it. We often work out problems in our dreams, and even if you're one of those people who claims they don't dream, you should still understand that your subconscious plays a role in your writing. In fact, writing is in some ways a conscious form of dreaming, sitting around the front of a screen or piece of paper and sometimes molding the images, sometimes letting the images form around you out of nothing. Often in a story or a novel you don't know where you're going, much as in a dream, and that sense of mystery is one of the pleasurable things about both writing and dreaming. Many writers use their dreams as jumping-off points for their stories.

Several of my own stories have come from dreams, and I make a habit of recording my dreams in my journal when I remember them. One dream I had involved my digging a hole in someone's backyard. I jotted that down, and a couple of years later I was flipping through my notes when I found the mention of the dream and thought it might make a good starting point for a story. The story is called, surprisingly, "Digging a Hole," and it involves a man digging a hole in his ex-wife's backyard. The dramatic question is, of course, why anyone would do such a thing.

Here's how I started the story:

> When Abby, my ex-wife, finally noticed me in her backyard, I was already two feet down. She opened the back door of her house and hurried out.
> "Lawrence, what are you doing here!" she said, and positioned herself to my side, so I couldn't swing any more dirt from the hole.

In that opening, I tried not only to set up the dramatic question, but also, by introducing Abby as the man's ex-wife, I give a sense that there's history between the characters, perhaps unresolved conflicts. And, of course, there are—the story is about the internal conflicts of these two characters as reflected in their outward actions.

When I first started this story, I didn't know why the guy was digging the hole, either. I was just as baffled as Abby. I didn't even know who these two people were, and so, as I went along, I had to invent their history. Halfway through the story, I discovered they had lost a child, and this had destroyed their marriage. A similar thing had happened to relatives of mine, but I transformed the circumstances in my story so that, in their particulars, the tragedies were different, only similar in the emotions they brought up. On top of that, I added two characters from my journals, a little girl with a GAF viewmaster and her little brother, riding around nude on a Big Wheel tricycle. I'd encountered this pair back when I was eighteen. When I came to the point where I decided I needed some real live children besides the dead one, I went flipping through my journals and found them. They fit perfectly.

I tell you all this simply to show all the different sources of one story. First, I started with a dream, added a family story, and even brought my journals into play.

Dreams almost always involve metaphor, simile, and symbol. Writing a dream story is almost the opposite of writing other kinds of stories. The dream is already your real life transformed, an interpretation of sorts, so your task is to retransform it into real life—to make it seem real. Again, you do this through salient detail. Nobel Prize laureate Gabriel García Márquez says that the more bizarre a story is, the more detail it should be given so as to make the world come alive, to make it seem real beyond a doubt.

When I was eleven, I had a dream that my mother wrote a short story about a lizard that did yoga. Strange dream, right? When I awoke, I told my mother she had to write a story about a lizard that did yoga. My mother, always a good sport, laughed and said she would. So she wrote a story called, what else, "The Lizard" [see page 277], dedicated to me, and it was published first in the prestigious literary magazine, the *Southern Review,* and then it won an O'Henry Prize, and then it was collected in an anthology of the best stories from the *Southern Review.* Of course, the story wasn't entirely about a lizard that did yoga—that would have put it squarely in the realm of fantasy, a children's story, perhaps. What my mother did was to take this odd idea and put it into the head of an eleven-year-old boy, loosely based on me.

This was 1969 or so and I was spending several months with my grandmother and my great-uncle and aunt in their retirement community in Hollywood, Florida. My mother was teaching in Slippery Rock, Pennsylvania, and I hated the town and my school, so my grandmother said I could stay with her and go to school there. But before I moved in with my grandmother, my mother and I spent a few days visiting an old college friend of hers named Marge. They hadn't seen each other in years, and Marge turned out to be a real character. She lived in a house with a pool and a little sauna and survived on freebies given to her by clients of the small newspaper she worked for. She did restaurant reviews and so was always getting free meals. That's what I remember most. Marge impressed me because of all her freebies and her pool, but my mother, a writer and never much of a materialist, thought Marge was a bit unhinged. Marge once drove us the wrong way on a Miami freeway, nearly killing us—we had to dash across the median to avoid a head-on collision. And she was a terrible whiner, always complaining about her daughter, claiming the daughter was out to get her or, at the very least neglected her terribly. My mother took *these* details and meshed them with my dream of the lizard. She told the story from a point of view of a version of me at eleven, making Marge (transformed into Francie) the boy's grandmother. My sister Nola even had an oblique appearance in the story—she was transformed into the imaginative Aunt Sylvia (interestingly, my mother's middle name), the only relative the boy feels any connection to. In real life, my sister loved things of the imagination and the supernatural as did I, so the boy who saw the lizard was really battling between two conflicting visions of the world, the materialistic world versus the world of the unseen.

A lizard doing yoga is an improbable event, but my mother was able to make this idea believable by anchoring the idea in the consciousness of her protagonist. The lizard becomes an emblem of the boy's state of mind. Here's how she introduces the lizard:

> I thought, had the impression, wanted to believe, was all ready to believe that I saw the lizard doing an exercise. But it wasn't like the floor touching and jogging and belt-shaking of my grandmother. It seemed more like a pose or a dance to me. I looked back because I knew that if my grandmother saw me, if she called out in her bottom-of-the-bottle voice (did all women speak to their children like that?): What are you doing there? What are you watching? . . . always suspecting something that might please me and not herself . . . I might have to show it to her. And then she would say: Why, it's just a dirty old lizard dying!
>
> Nevertheless the lizard wasn't dying. Its legs were in the air, but that meant something else. Nor would it want to be turned right side up: it had the privilege of being on whatever side it pleased! The lizard's eyes shone golden.
>
> Half its body was in the air; it seemed to be bringing its tail down over its head as it lay on its back, the two forelegs implanted on the ground. I tried to think where I had seen something like it; my mother's only exercises were swimming, tennis, and golf. Then I remembered my aunt Sylvia, my father's sister who came to see me and take me out now and then. She was much younger than my

father, still at college, studying philosophy. I adored her laugh. She told fantastic stories.

I recollected having seen her stand on her head. And turn herself into a pretzel. She had started to teach me a few things. Oga? I thought. No . . . yoga. A lizard doing yoga.

Notice how she uses both salient detail and a close observation of the main character's consciousness to make a bizarre idea not only believable, but in its own way, revelatory. With a mother who paid attention to her son's dreams, it's no wonder I wanted to become a writer, too.

So-What Stories

Any of the types of stories mentioned in this chapter can be so-what stories. A so-what story is one based on a job or your childhood in which the only thing that's important about it is that it really happened or it's shocking or it has a punch line. Or it can be a dream story in which the protagonist wakes up at the end, automatically trivializing all the drama of the dream. A so-what story is the story about how much you've always loved Corvettes, and one time you found a great deal on one, but it needed a lot of work, so you spent the whole summer fixing the car—and you did it! It was a beauty when you finished.

Good for you, but so what?

Or you read a newspaper account of some horrific act of violence, a serial rapist/murderer on the loose. You decide to write a story in an attempt to "get into the head" of this character. The results are sadly predictable, an account of a serial rapist/murderer from the point of view of the rapist/murderer. Instead of transforming the story as Joyce Carol Oates did, you simply rely on what we already know, cheap sensationalism, graphic violence, and sociopathic reasoning. So what?

Or the time you had a premonition about someone dying, and you told her, but she didn't believe you, and then she really died! Or she didn't!

In either case, so what?

Or a story based solely on feelings of nostalgia. The fact that you feel teary-eyed about the corner malt shop you frequented in the 1950s in Riverdale is not necessarily the basis for a great short story or a novel.

Or the time your roommate stole your Corvette, kidnapped your grand-mother, and they both died in a fiery crash!

I think you get the point, but if you don't, go back to chapter two. You might want to bone up on the forms of fiction, and the difference between these and anecdotes and memoirs.

A Caveat

Of course, all of these categories of writing about yourself are more or less arbitrary forms. A job story can be a childhood story. A family story can be a tell-it-like-it-is story. Or your story might be none of these. The story might be completely fictionalized except for one or two details from your own experience, but that, too, is writing about yourself. In any case, don't take these categories too seriously. They're meant to give you a jump start, not to confine you in any way.

EXERCISES

1. Use indirection to write a scene based on something trau-matic that you witnessed, that happened to you or someone you know. In other words, create some distance by not letting us know everything about your protagonist right away—her motivations, feelings, suspicions. Or take the trauma and transform it to such a degree that it bears little resemblance to the actual event. Remember, the scene should not depend so much on simple outcomes as on character development and understanding.

2. Take the same trauma or a different one and write about it using the head-on approach. Still, you'll need to transform, to cut out unnecessary details and characters.

3. It's true, as Bret Lott says, that the best family stories are often the ones that have been around for ages. Write in your journal any family stories you remember, especially the ones that might get you in trouble. Those are probably the good ones.

4. Write a scene based on a dream. Even if the situation is strange, you'll need to make it believable through salient details and believable characters. Whatever you do, don't tell the reader it's a dream.

5. Pick up today's newspaper and find a story in it that you think could be transformed into a short story. Sketch it out. Who are the main characters? Who is the protagonist? What is the central conflict? Is the conflict something that's been left out of the actual newspaper account? Again, focus on the characters, and transform.

CHAPTER SIX

▼

Real Places

Sometimes a place we've visited fascinates us, and we can't seem to get it out of our system unless we write about it. That's fine as long as the story or novel is more than a thinly disguised travelogue. A story about a family trip in high school to Hawaii is probably not going to mesmerize an audience.

Every once in a while an Arctic-tundra story crosses my path. These are usually tales of high adventure in which two characters, usually men, fly around in a plane somewhere in Alaska, when the plane suddenly loses power and down they go. The rest of the story deals with their attempts at survival. We are informed that the Arctic tundra is freezing and that it's very white. Does that convince you that you're experiencing the Arctic tundra along with these men? It doesn't do it for me. It's your job as the writer to convince us that we're in the world you've created, not the reader's job to believe, and you convince the reader through the sensory details you choose to convey a place. Inevitably, such stories focus solely on unbelievable plot developments, and the characters tend to be about as believable as the descriptions of the frozen waste. But place or setting in a work of fiction can be a vital element. Often, the setting functions as almost a distinct character in the work, with its own personality. If you write convincingly about a place, this might be the secret ingredient to make your story or novel come alive. In this chapter, we'll discuss strategies for writing convincingly about real places.

Places in Memory

The places we remember are often the richest sources for our fictional settings. Just as childhood memories can serve as the springboard for our

< 133 >

stories, so too can our childhood homes and neighborhoods inform and inspire these stories. Before beginning to write such a story, ask yourself a few questions. What do you remember most from your childhood home? List the furnishings. Take a mental tour, first starting at the front door and going through all the rooms. Take your time. Lift your grandmother's teapot off the mantel—you know, the teapot that played "Tea for Two" when you lifted it. Notice the aromas. What's your grandmother cooking? Take a peek outside. If it's a fair day, take a walk. Go through the neighborhood. Wave to your friends and acquaintances. It's been a long time. "What's that you're carrying?" they might ask.

"Oh, it's my journal," you tell them, scribbling a few notes as you chat.

"Oh … well, say hi to your grandma for me," they say.

"Sure thing."

If you do this exercise, a flood of memories is bound to come back to you. You'll be surprised by how much you remember. Write down every detail of this place. When you write your story or novel, many of these details will come in handy and help transport your reader to this place in the same way you were transported.

Of course, you won't recall everything. Some things you'll remember incorrectly. Sometimes you'll remember too much. As with any kind of fiction, you must learn to choose. Use only those details of your setting that are necessary to convey the place to the reader.

The writer Xu Xi grew up in Hong Kong in a family of "Overseas Chinese" who had previously lived for generations in Indonesia before "returning" to China. Her father's family had intermarried some with Indonesians, but her mother's family, through the generations, had not. When they moved to Hong Kong, they didn't quite fit in—her parents spoke Mandarin and English, but not Cantonese, the lingua franca of Hong Kong. Xu Xi's name in Mandarin was considered beautiful by Mandarin speakers, but seemed strange to those who spoke Cantonese. Growing up, she felt different from other Chinese people in Hong Kong, part of a minority within the city, and it wasn't until she moved away that she started to write about the city, in novels, in stories, in essays. In the 1970s, she moved to America, but Xu Xi splits her home these days between New York, Hong Kong, and New Zealand—she is, in the parlance of Hong Kong, an "astronaut," a term first used to describe those Chinese from Hong Kong who, in advance of Britain's return of the city to China, obtained Canadian passports and now split their time between Hong Kong and Canada, particularly Vancouver (though in Xu Xi's case, she became an American citizen, not Canadian). With such a background, it's not hard to see why Xu Xi in her fiction is fairly obsessed with issues of identity and belonging.

"This is the city I couldn't wait to get out of," she says of Hong Kong. "I was born and raised here. I couldn't wait to get away from it, yet once I got away, I found how important it was to delve back into it until I physically came back. I found that when I was working on my MFA [which she earned at the University of Massachusetts, Amherst] and writing and living in America, all I wrote about was Hong Kong, or Asia I should say, but mostly Hong Kong. Through my writing, I discovered how much more of a connection to Hong Kong I had than I thought I had. I always felt a little bit outside the mainstream here. Then, of course, I go to the United States, where I'm obviously a minority, too. This was at a time when I was becoming an American and trying to understand America and learn about things like baseball." Even so, she found herself drawn to Hong Kong and its complexities. She began to study Mandarin because she knew that eventually Hong Kong would be returned to China. At that time, in the early 1980s, Hong Kong's official languages were Cantonese and English, but she knew that Mandarin would become dominant once China took control once again. Oddly, the language that Xu Xi's father had spoken when he emigrated to Hong Kong from Indonesia and had added to his family's sense of displacement, would soon become the language of choice, and the Cantonese speakers of Hong Kong would eventually find that they were the minority within the larger country that was poised to reclaim them.

Eventually, Xu Xi returned to Hong Kong and began her career as a professional writer, publishing her books, but it wasn't until she left Hong Kong again that she wrote what she calls her most definitive Hong Kong novel, *The Unwalled City*. "I didn't even know as I was writing it that it was about place," she says. "I thought I was writing this story about these lives of people in Hong Kong. I thought I was going to be focusing on these characters, and, of course, I did have four main characters, but when I finished the book and showed it to my agent, I realized that the city was my main character. And that was a very profound discovery for me. I didn't even know until I finished the book."

When she first started writing about Hong Kong, the central issues were those of personal identity as she mined her sense of what it meant to her to be from Hong Kong. She wanted to know who she was. But as she continued to write, her sense of what she was mining changed. If Xu Xi was something of a displaced person within this community, then so, too, was Hong Kong a displaced city in the world as a whole. Never independent, never a city-state, what exactly was and is Hong Kong? Xu Xi wondered. "Who are all these people around me in this place?" she asked by way of her writing. And lately, the issue has become more political as Hong Kong as a separate entity is threatened increasingly with erasure. In the 1970s, a Hong Kong local identity started to be fostered in the arts, and at that time, the British were seen as the ones who "took away our Chinese identity, and now we're going to reclaim it." Now, she says the opposite has happened. "Now that Hong Kong people have this Hong Kong Chinese identity, there's this sense that China is coming in and sweeping it out of the way. Now Mandarin is one of the three official languages. In school, they're supposed to learn all three, but the truth of the matter is that the elite are learning English and Mandarin. It's just so ironic. Cantonese is still the lifeblood language of this place, but it's getting stomped on in a sense. And now it feels like I've got to record this place. I've got to make sure it doesn't disappear entirely."

As we can see from this one writer, there are many ways and reasons for writing about place. We write about place in order to secure our personal identities through the medium of fiction. Or we write to make sense of it in some larger sense, to understand a place in relation to other places, or to preserve it, to chronicle it and to say, in a sense, at this time this is what it was like to live and love and struggle in this place that will never again be as it was once. Nostalgia, yes, but a serious writer of fiction does not simply write out of nostalgia. Simple nostalgia risks sentimentality, and this kind of treatment tends to reduce a place to those things you loved rather than those things that troubled you. Most often, our relationship to a place, whether the place in which we live now or a place in memory, is complex and difficult to define.

But notice that it was only when Xu Xi moved away from Hong Kong that she was able to write about it. When you are emotionally, temporally, or geographically distant from a place, you are often more able to see it with the clarity of a frieze. You will not remember everything, but you will remember what's important to you. What you remember about a place is the feeling it gave you, and the details are imbued with that feeling. Writers are essentially myth-makers, and the myths they keep returning to are primarily concerned with origins. Where we grew up is the site of our own personal myth of creation, and when we write about the place of our childhood, we are concerned with creation, the formation of our own perceptions against the backdrop of this mythical world.

Places Close to Home

You can also write about a place you live in now, though it might be so familiar that you're unaware how rich a source it can be for your fiction. What you need is distance, the kind you naturally achieve in your memories. Sometimes it's difficult to see this place in perspective. So you need to step back, either physically or mentally. You could take a vacation and write notes in your journal while you're away. But that's not realistic for most of us. It's not often we take vacations, and when we do, the last thing we want to do is write about the place we just left. The best way to achieve distance is to do it mentally, by transforming either your point of view or your immediate surroundings. If you live in an old house, imagine who the original occupants were, and write a story from their point of view. E. L. Doctorow did this and came up with his famous novel *Ragtime,* a book set at the turn of the century whose primary setting is the house he was living in. Or take a walk around your block. Who's that elderly man who peeks out at you whenever you leave your house? Maybe you could write a story from his point of view. Eudora Welty was looking out her window one day when she saw an elderly woman crossing her field. She wondered where the woman was headed, and from that random sighting came her story "A Worn Path" about an elderly woman's journey into town for the sake of love. You might take a different path. Take a walk to the doughnut shop on the corner of your street with its red neon sign flashing. Go in and take notes. Order a few doughnuts and some coffee so you won't look suspicious. Look at the people in the back making doughnuts. Write a story from one of their points of view. You might need to interview someone who works there for accuracy, or you can rely on your imagination. In any case, there are stories all around you. Keep your eyes open.

The Role of Place

Above all, remember that this is a story or novel you're writing. Character, again, is what needs to be stressed, and while the place might become a kind of character in your narrative, don't allow it to overwhelm your characters and story. You might write an accurate and beautiful description of the town of Charlotte Amalie on the island of St. Thomas, but if you go on for page after page, you most likely will bore the reader. In fact, any description of a place should probably be anchored within a character's consciousness, and say as much about the character as it does about the place.

Take a look at the opening paragraph from Robert Onopa's "The Man Who Swam Through Jellyfish, Through Men-of-War":

> Kimo Akeo owned a cream-colored Cessna from which he spotted fish for his sons. In the clear Hawaiian air, he flew in an elegant, extended zigzag pattern over waters he had set nets in when he was young: those of the Kaiwi Channel from the westerly shore of Molokai to the easterly shore of Oahu; from Makapuu Point in the north, south to the Penguin Banks. In the moving waters of the channel—seas blue-green and brilliant whose vast bulk was furrowed by the wind and heaved by swells—his fifty-year-old eyes could distinguish schools of nehu, anchovies, swimming in shimmering circles just beneath the surface, or aku bonita, whose fins breaking water turned it foamy white in circles a hundred yards wide.

Note that this description shows a lot about the character of Kimo Akeo. What is it that this character focuses on, to the exclusion of almost all else? Fish. There isn't a description in this paragraph that ends without a mention of fish. If Onopa had chosen to describe at length the clouds in the sky above the Cessna, he might have lost his focus and diluted our understanding of Akeo's character.

Here's a question that might seem out of left field, but it's pertinent to our discussion: Does cultural identity or ethnicity have any bearing on your ability to write authoritatively about a place? Could and should a non-Yanamamo Indian write about the Amazon from a Yanamamo point of view? How about a non-Haitian writing about Port-au-Prince or the Haitian enclave in Miami? If your answer is no, you're discounting the role of the imagination in literature, and what you really want to read and/or write is nonfiction. If you demand that the writer of a fictional work be, in the narrow sense, what he is writing of, you have very little understanding of what fiction is. Of course, we make assumptions, rightly or wrongly, about a writer based on his or her name. If the writer's first name is Elizabeth and she's writing from a man's point of view, we pay closer attention to how accurate the point of view seems. If the writer's last name is Dominguez and she's writing about the town of Merida on the Yucatán Peninsula, we think, "Ah, Dominguez. She must really know the Yucatán with a name like that!"

But that's a silly criterion to go by. Just because you were born in Charleston, South Carolina, or grew up there, or buried two sets of great-grandparents there, does not mean you can write worth a lick about the place. In fact, as shocking as this might seem, a native New Yorker might be able to write about Charleston better than you.

Take Robert Onopa, for instance. What assumptions did you make about him when you read his name and then read the passage from his story? Let's see. Onopa? Is that a Hawaiian name? Could be. Sounds kind of Japanese to me. Well, you know there's a large population of Japanese Americans in Hawaii. The fact is, Robert Onopa, who teaches in the English Department at the University of Hawaii, is a *haole* (if you don't know what *haole* is you'll just have to go to Hawaii to find out), and his last name is Polish. Does that change your opinion of the passage of his story I quoted?

It shouldn't.

As I've said, people often feel a sense of ownership of their experiences. They feel the same about the place they grew up, especially if it has some history like Charleston or a cultural uniqueness like Hawaii. When someone's ethnic identity is closely tied to a place, she might feel violated or exploited by your making fictional forays into her territory—no matter how convincing the portrait might be. Sometimes people feel that their territory is being co-opted when an outsider writes about them from their point of view. One well-known writer, serving as a judge on an arts panel, not only refused to award money to an artist who she learned was not of the same race as her fictional characters, but went so far as to call the surprised writer on the phone and castigate her for having such temerity. And a major magazine once rejected a story that they had previously accepted after learning that the race of the writer and his characters did not match.

As Margot Livesey insightfully remarks in her essay "How to Tell a True Story," "In the current climate, a novel set in Vietnam, written by someone who had not been there, would be unlikely to meet with the rapturous reception of *The Red Badge of Courage.* Certain experiences—war, other races, some illnesses, perhaps other sexual orientations—are no longer deemed appropriate territory for the imagination. We want the writer to be writing out of memory." But, of course, this expectation is ridiculous. Neither experience nor imagination should be privileged over the other. A fiction writer is not a nonfiction writer. If we ask our fiction writers to simply write about what they "know" in the narrowest, most corporeal sense of that word, we should also require actors to stop acting and painters to stop painting—unless they paint strict representations of their lives. Charles Johnson, author of *Middle Passage,* a novel about a slave ship that won the National Book Award in 1990, concurs. In an interview in the *AWP Chronicle,* he says, "Writers have always been able to transpose themselves into not just the racial other, but the sexual other and also into other historical periods. . . . Writers have always done that and always will do that regardless of people who, for one political reason or another, feel that their territory is being appropriated. . . . That other argument means knowledge is racially bound. That's scary. Ultimately, that is racist."

To which I might add: You cannot co-opt the territory of the imagination because it is a limitless territory without boundaries, without rulers. The story you write will always be different, without exception, from the story I write, regardless of whether our source material is the same.

Let's take this a step further. Can you write about a place you've never been? Nobel Prize winner Saul Bellow wrote his novel *Henderson the Rain King,* a book about an eccentric American millionaire's adventures in Africa, without ever having set foot on the continent. Robert Louis Stevenson wrote *Treasure Island* before visiting the South Pacific (where he later went to live). And what about novels that take place in a different time period? T. Coraghessan Boyle's novel, *Water Music,* about a Scottish explorer, is set several hundred years ago in Africa. Obviously, an act of the imagination is necessary to transport oneself and one's readers back into time. The late Robert Fox, a writer from Ohio, wrote a story, "Her Story-His Story," that won a prestigious Nelson Algren Award, from the point of view of a black inmate in prison. Fox had seen prison, but only as an outsider, as a teacher and workshop leader. A group of inmates upon reading his story were shocked when they met him and saw he was white. Their reaction, however, was overwhelmingly positive. What shocked these inmates more than Fox's race was how well he described the prison. In his story, Fox describes the prison as it was twenty years ago and how it's changed since then. For that portion of the story, he relied completely on his imagination. He hadn't seen the prison twenty years ago. One prisoner could hardly believe that. He was something of a prison historian and claimed that Fox had the details exactly right.

In his essay "Autobiographophobia: Writing and the Secret Life," fiction writer and poet David Jauss relates two calls he had from people who believed the places and characters in his stories were real.

"One [call] was from a man who told me he had just read a story of mine called "Rainier," which is about a divorced alcoholic whose son dies in a car accident. 'The same thing happened to me,' the caller said, then proceeded to tell me about the anguish he suffered after the death of his son and how AA had helped him overcome not only his alcoholism but his grief. He did not cry, but I could tell he was fighting tears. When he finished telling me his story, he paused, then said, 'I just wanted you to know that you're not alone.'

"I couldn't tell him that *he,* at least at that moment, was alone. My story is not autobiographical. I have never lived in Montana or Wyoming, where the story takes place; I am not now, nor have I ever been, divorced; I am not an alcoholic, recovering or otherwise; and my son, I'm happy to say, is very much alive. Nothing in that story happened to me, or anyone I know. I made it up. I didn't have the heart to tell the caller this, however; for the duration of the phone call, I pretended that the story was true and that I shared his grief, not only imaginatively, but literally.

"The other phone call was from a Vietnam vet who had read my short story 'Freeze,' which is about a soldier in Vietnam who steps on a mine that doesn't explode yet nonetheless has devastating effects on his life. The caller wanted to know if we'd ever met. 'I remember the guy you wrote about,' he said. 'The lieutenant. And I think we must have been at *Lai Khe* at about the same time. Did you know Larry Kelvin? Or Rick Hammond?' When I told him I'd never been in Vietnam, or even in the military, he was more than disappointed, he was outraged. 'What gives you the right to write about a war when you weren't even fucking *there?*' he demanded. Clearly, he felt as if he'd been taken in by a con man. And in a way, he had, for what is a fiction writer if not a confidence artist, someone who trades words for your trust, and for your money?"

Exactly. It's the writer's job to make the reader believe. This is how "Freeze" opens:

> At first Freeze Harris thought Nam was a crazy nightmare, an upside-down place where you were supposed to do everything that was forbidden back in the world, but after a while it was the world that seemed unreal. Cutting ears off dead NVA had become routine; stocking shelves at Kroger's seemed something he'd only dreamed. Then, on a mission in the Iron Triangle, Freeze stepped on a Bouncing Betty that didn't go off and nothing seemed real anymore. It was like he'd stepped out of Nam when he stepped on the mine. And now he wasn't anywhere.

Here is David Jauss's story as his irate caller would have preferred:

Jauss's critic would have preferred silence, for the story to have remained unwritten. And yet, had the caller examined his own reactions, he might have been more generous toward Jauss. In Jauss's story, the veteran had made a connection, had recalled a similar event and felt sympathy with someone else's vision of the world. To me, that's the opposite of being alone and in fact, is the best justification possible for the writing of fiction, if any is needed. Through fiction, the writer imagines a world in which we can simultaneously and successively inhabit multiple consciousnesses and visit places we might only dream of.

This approach is not universally successful by any means. There's nothing worse than a clumsy story that relies on stereotypes about a place one has never been and a point of view one has never known. But the imagination is a powerful thing. "I've written about places without having been there," says Barry Hannah. "And when I got there, I had guessed pretty well. I think that the foreigner or the alien often has a point of view that is more precise than the native. I used to not believe that but I do now. It's good that a New Yorker would cover the South and that a Southerner would cover New York."

I'm not saying it's good to be ignorant of the place you write about. That's absurd. The contrary is true. It's important to find out as much as possible about a place before you write about it, and it's important to strive for authenticity, something we'll discuss in the next chapter. All I'm saying here is that it's possible.

It's all in the details. If you rely on the obvious and the stereotypical when writing from a point of view that's not your own, about a place that's not your own, you will not be successful. Even those who know a place intimately sometimes rely on the stereotypical in writing about that place. Think of it as a test of your imagination. If you set a story in New York, don't have your character stand in front of Trump Towers, arms over his head, yelling, "You crazy, wacky city! I love you!" If you write about New York, better to include lesser-known landmarks, a particular Korean grocery on Broadway or a dry cleaner. The more particular and individual the details, the more believable they seem.

Adopting a Place

As I've stated, many writers adopt a locale to write about in their fiction. It might be a place they live in now but weren't born in, a place they've passed through, or one they've never been to. Success depends on the imagination and skill of the writer, not on his physical ties to the place.

Sometimes a place you've never lived in captures your imagination, as it did with Philip Gerard when he wrote *Hatteras Light,* a novel set in the early part of the twentieth century about a lifesaving crew on the Outer Banks of North Carolina. Now Gerard lives in North Carolina, in Wilmington, another coastal town, but when he wrote about Hatteras he was living in Arizona. He'd spent a lot of time in Hatteras and says, "The land had kind of whipped into my bones. I kept on dreaming of it and thinking about it." Gerard's book *Cape Fear Rising* is set in Wilmington in 1898. He says the same thing happened to him with Wilmington as Hatteras: "As I began walking around the streets the ghosts started coming out of the cracks in the sidewalk and the river. There's this tremendous feeling of place. There's this weight of history. And the closer you get to the heart of downtown Wilmington the thicker the air gets with those spirits. And in certain buildings it's practically overpowering." To write successfully about a place, you must be overpowered by it. If it doesn't "whip into your bones," your treatment will most likely be superficial or naïve or overly romanticized.

The writer Philip Graham was born in Brooklyn, and yet the places that have exerted the strongest influences on his imaginative life and hence, his fiction, are West Africa and the Midwestern United States. Graham has lived in Champagne/Urbana, Illinois, for the past two decades, but he's also spent quite a lot of time in the Ivory Coast, supporting the research of his wife, anthropologist Alma Gottlieb. Both have lived with a minority group called the Beng for extended periods of time and co-authored an award-winning travel memoir about their experiences with the Beng: *Parallel Worlds: An Anthropologist and a Writer Encounter Africa.* After living in Africa for over a year, Graham found that not only had Africa become familiar to him, but in the process, America had become unfamiliar. "Home wasn't anymore what I imagined it to be," he says. "It was not the world I had left. I was now returning to *a* world called America. The fact that it was a *particular* kind of culture and place was nothing I had really considered before. I was part of it. It was everything that I breathed and lived. You know, you have a very complicated relationship to where you grow up and the culture you're brought up in. It just seems like that's the way the world works. I never really returned to the America I had understood before I left for Africa. That gave me this double-vision that I didn't realize was a real blessing for me as a writer. Things just jump out at you because you know what it's like in a very different culture."

In other words, Graham had learned how to observe his own culture with a new sense of curiosity and remove. The best writers are often the best observers. What others take for granted, the writer sees as though seeing it for the first time. The Beng live in compounds in which all the daily living is done in the courtyard—consequently, life is much more communal than in America, and when you walk through a village, you essentially must pass through the living rooms of your neighbors in order to reach a particular destination. The Beng have no word for privacy. If you and your spouse have an argument, the rest of the village comes to watch. In comparison, everything in America is private. You don't walk through a neighbor's house, you don't show up uninvited. You must, in fact, make appointments to visit. The private worlds of Americans seemed somehow unnatural, even chilling to Graham when he returned. Coming back to this country, he started to realize how isolated Americans are in their private lives from one another. The same kind of wildness of the courtyard that Graham observed in the African village in which he lived was also going on in American homes, with the difference being that in America, one rarely glimpsed it from the outside. Americans, he observed, had built their own little private caves to decorate and design and, in a sense, hide from one another.

Africa informs every story he writes, Graham says, though virtually all his stories are set elsewhere. While he was living with the Beng, Graham's father died and there was no way he could possibly make it back to the States in time for the funeral, so he held a Beng funeral for his father. In the Beng concept of the afterlife, the dead inhabit a parallel world in which they continue their everyday existence, though invisible to the living. From this idea sprung a group of stories about the afterlives of ten American ghosts all existing in an American version of the Beng afterlife. Filled with stories of spirits speaking to Beng diviners, he essentially transposed this idea to his story "Angel."

In a sense, Graham adopted Africa or it was the other way around, and yet, the Midwest, another adopted home, figures prominently in his fiction as well. His story, "Interior Design" [see page 287], while set in the Midwest, is basically an extended meditation on his notions of the caves in which we Americans live. Told from the point of view of a woman who is an interior designer, the story has its origins in two different triggers. While visiting some friends in D.C. who were buying a new house, they showed him the brochure supplied by the builders, depicting the display home. At the bottom of the brochure was the disclaimer, "All furniture in display rooms are ¾ size." Why? To make the rooms seem larger so that prospective buyers would think they were buying more space than they really were. The second trigger was a visit to a farmhouse in rural Illinois where a baby shower was being held. The industrious owners of the house had built a Polynesian-themed room with a pool and an elaborate maze of underground tunnels for the farm cats who lived in the barn so they could enter the house at will. While in the bathroom, Graham was surprised when a little trap door opened in the floor, a cat poked its head out, and then popped back into its tunnel. What passerby could guess what a bizarre interior life this non-descript Illinois farmhouse held?

Graham tells his story, "Interior Design," from the point of view of the daughter of a builder who used ¾-size furniture to fool his home buyers. Her own passion for design is fueled in large measure by her desire to make expiation for her father's sins. One of her assignments, though it gets brief mention in the story, is just such a "Polynesian Splendor room" as Graham saw at the baby shower he attended. And the way in which the main character thinks about furniture, about living space, is completely influenced by Africa, once you understand the influences of her author. Take, for example, the following exchange between the protagonist and her husband, Frederick:

> It was October and I had just sketched a giant stadium on the porch, with baseballs flying out—all of them homers for our team. While we watched the Series, a huge bowl of popcorn between us, I said casually, "Hon, did you know there's a country where hosts polish their chairs incredibly carefully, so when a visitor sits on one its smoothness rubs off and makes him a good guest?"
>
> "Shhh," he said, "A three and two pitch."
>
> I waited until the strikeout before trying again. "Y'know," I said, stretching back a little, hoping he'd glance at me, "I read somewhere there are people in Africa who believe your soul lives in your chair. No one else can sit there. And when you're not sitting on the chair you tip it over. So your soul can't be stolen."
>
> "Imagine that," I said, " a chair isn't just a chair, it's what people *think* a chair is."
>
> He grabbed the control away from me and mumbled through his popcorn, "Well, that's certainly *one* way to look at it."
>
> That stopped me. I always told him there were many ways to see something, but it was true I wanted him to see it *my* way. . . . "

When she eventually leaves him, she first knocks over all the furniture in the house so *her* soul can't be stolen.

One normally wouldn't pair the Midwest and Africa, but that's why

Graham sounds unlike any other writer you'll encounter, why his stories are familiar and simultaneously extraordinary.

Disguising a Place

Just as one can write a composite character, one can write a composite place. Often, the disguise is a thin one, meant to fool no one. All the same calling your great Eastern city "Metropolis" instead of "New York" gives you all sorts of freedom. First, you're signaling the reader, the persnickety one I mentioned earlier, the one who won't go beyond the accuracy of the details when reading your book. You're telling everyone, including yourself, that this is a book of fiction, and the place you're writing about is as mythical as the home of the gods, Mt. Olympus—which, of course, is also the name of a real mountain in Greece. And by a strange twist, you're actually appeasing this reader by using this strategy. You're turning the tables on her. Instead of saying, "Ferret out all the inaccuracies in my book," you're appealing to this reader as a fellow insider who's not fooled one bit by your thin disguise. You're telling her, "Guess what's really true in my story." And before you know it, that reader will think she has it all figured out. "Why, that's Mr. Simpkin's house," she'll exclaim, even if you have no idea who Mr. Simpkin is, much less where he lives.

But there are other reasons to disguise a place in your fiction. Perhaps you don't want to hurt the feelings of your friends and family who live in your hometown, who you believe will be devastated by an unflattering portrait of the place. Or maybe you once witnessed a knife fight in a bar in Chicago, and you've decided to include a scene based on that memory in your novel. Chances are slim, of course, that the owners of that bar will read your book, but you never know. If you've written an unflattering portrait of the place, the owner might become angry enough to sue you. I'll talk more about that in chapter eight, but the point is, don't leave yourself vulnerable to legal action. If you're in doubt, change the locale. Base it on the real bar, but place it in another city. Change the name. Invent another city. Maybe the knife fight doesn't need to take place in a bar at all. Transfer the knife fight to an upscale restaurant and see how that changes the story. Turn the knives into water pistols, pads of butter, croquet mallets. As with anything in fiction, be willing to be flexible with real events and open to the transformation process.

EXERCISES

1. Write a scene with a character based on someone you know well in an unfamiliar setting (unfamiliar to this character but familiar to you)—Aunt Betty from Tulsa riding the Chicago El or Uncle Lou from New York showing up unannounced at your apartment. Write this scene from this character's point of view. Now switch. Tell the story from your point of view. How does your description of the setting change from one point of view to the other? Are some details missing in the version based on your point of view? Why?

2. Take a mental tour of the neighborhood in which you grew up. Pay attention to all the details. Get reacquainted with the place. Are there any stories lurking in the streets, the houses, the fields of your past?

3. Take a mental tour of your present neighborhood. Where are the stories here? Pay attention to every sight and sound, and sniff out the stories.

4. Write a scene from the point of view of the person who lived in your house or apartment originally (as E. L. Doctorow did in *Ragtime*), or the person who lived there right before you, or even the person you imagine will move in after you. Have you left anything behind, forgotten anything—clothes, furniture, money—that the next resident will wonder about?

5. Disguise a place you know well. Write a scene about this place, changing whatever aspects of the locale will make you feel free to explore the terrain with your imagination. Think of the place symbolically. What symbols will best convey the feeling or tone of this disguised locale?

▼

CHAPTER SEVEN

Writing (and Rewriting) with Authority

Throughout the creative process, you must try to mold your story to the specifications of fiction. As in the other stages of writing, your revisions involve a constant search for structure, flexibility, distance, and the right point of view. Everything you write won't be immediately brilliant. In fact, very little will be. The real art of writing is in the fashioning, the revision of the story. If you don't give up, if you're persistent, you can turn almost anything into a good story. In this chapter we'll discuss the strategies for making your story as good as possible, from research to revision.

Research

Obviously, you don't have to write from your own experience. The standard advice used to be to "write what you know," but what does that mean? What you know is not a static thing. We're all capable of learning more. And that's where research comes in. If you don't know something, find out about it. A lot of fiction writers use research in their work—everyone from the late James Michener, who had a researcher working for him on his mammoth epics, to lesser-known writers working on tiny short stories.

Research for a fiction writer can involve just about anything. When we think of research, we think of someone cloistered among the stacks of a library, poring through dusty texts. But that's only one kind of research. There are two categories of research: *primary* and *secondary.* Primary research involves traveling to a place you're writing about, actually running with the bulls in Pamplona or interviewing one of the Watergate conspirators. Secondary research involves reading a book about the place you're writing about, watching a film of the running of the bulls or listening to an

< 149 >

interview with Gordon Liddy. Both types are equally valid for the fiction writer, as long as the final product seems authentic to the reader.

Remember what we talked about in the last chapter? Even if you've lived somewhere does not mean you have the ability to write convincingly about the place. The opposite is true as well. Even if you haven't been somewhere doesn't mean you're unable to write convincingly about the place. As I mentioned, if that were the case, historical novels would be impossible, to say nothing of science fiction. Travel isn't necessary to write convincingly about a place, provided you do your research and are able to use it authoritatively in a fictional context. But those are major provisos.

If you want to write a novel set in Borneo, find out as much about Borneo as possible. Read about the culture, the flora and fauna, the climate. You can learn a lot about a place from a book or photographs. Watch a documentary on Borneo. Learn from the experience of others; interview people who've spent time there. Look at the microfilm of the *Borneo Times* or another paper in the library. If your story takes place in 1955, find out about the time. But don't just look at the articles. Look at the ads, what people were wearing in Borneo, what was playing at the movie theater.

Knowing When to Stop

The problem with research is that you never know when to stop. Naturally, you want things to be accurate, and most good writers are perfectionists, so you keep on reading about Borneo until you've read twenty-five books on the subject, have amassed a video library, and can speak every dialect on the island. But you still haven't started your novel. If you're not careful, you never will—and your research will become a kind of crutch.

It doesn't matter how you organize your research. Index cards, your journal, a tape recorder, a photo album. What's important is for you not to let the research get out of hand. This might sound a little strange, but in your first draft rely on nothing but your imagination, especially if you find yourself bogged down in interminable research. Your imagination, if it's working properly, is a pretty amazing tool, and sometimes fact and imagination coincide. Then, after you have a workable draft on paper, go back and fill the gaps with research. This method works perfectly well. You just have to slog through and be unabashed in your ignorance during the writing of the first draft. You can change it later.

In rare instances, if your imagination is powerful enough and the world you've created is believable, it doesn't necessarily have to be authentic. A number of years ago, I read a review in the *New York Times Book Review* of a novel written by a French woman. The novel was set in Greenwich Village, where the novelist had never set foot and didn't know much about. Nevertheless, the reviewer, though somewhat bemused, gave the book a favorable review, saying that this was a strange hybrid of Greenwich Village and a neighborhood in Paris, but it didn't matter because the book was engaging and believable within the context it had created.

And the French artist Henri Rousseau was a postal clerk in Paris whose paintings all depicted scenes from Africa, where he had never set foot. The giant plants in his jungle scenes were merely large-scale versions of plants that could be found in France. Rousseau's paintings have a fairy-tale quality, but the scenes they depict seem authentic in their own way, just as a good fairy tale will draw the reader in and say something authentic about the human condition.

Incorporating Research

When I wrote *The Last Studebaker,* I found all kinds of books about Studebakers and lined my shelves with them. I also had a videotape of a documentary done on Studebakers and pamphlets on various homes the Studebaker family had owned in South Bend, Indiana, where the Studebaker plant was located and the novel is set. I put a map of South Bend on my wall, bought a weather calendar, drank coffee out of a Studebaker mug, had a Studebaker refrigerator magnet and a Studebaker T-shirt.

I read these books, pondered my map, rewound the videotape, and diligently drank coffee from my Studebaker mug. After a while, I knew a good deal about Studebakers. The problem was that I wasn't writing a history of the Studebaker car or family; I was writing a novel. And while Studebakers are an integral part of the novel, they function primarily on the level of metaphor. The heart of the novel is about a family who lives in present-day South Bend, twenty-five years after the shutdown of the Studebaker plant. The main character's father used to work at the plant and suffered a breakdown when it closed, but there are other concerns in her life besides the ancient legacy of Studebaker.

Still, there was plenty of lore I wanted to include in the book. For instance, in the annual Christmas parade through downtown South Bend the year before the plant closed, the organizers flocked a Studebaker. I loved this image of a flocked car, but unfortunately, I just couldn't fit it in. There were also wonderful facts about the company, some of which I was able to incorporate, some of which I couldn't. One early draft had a restaurant scene between my main character, Lois, and her ex-husband, Willy, in which Willy rather baldly spouts facts about Studebaker to his bored ex-wife and bored reader. I knew it was bad the moment I wrote it, but I guess I just needed to get it out.

This is what's commonly referred to as *exposition disguised as dialogue.* It's not necessarily bad to incorporate your research into your dialogue, but your dialogue should never seem as though it was written for the sole purpose of conveying information. Likewise, you don't need to incorporate all your research in one large, undigestible chunk. Weave it through your story. Exposition slows down a story, so use it sparingly so that you don't bog down the reader. Also ask yourself why you want to incorporate this or that fact in your novel or story. Is it simply because it's an interesting tidbit? Or does it enrich the story? In a novel, you have more leeway than in a short story. You can be a little more self-indulgent, throwing in a few tidbits—whether about Studebakers or Borneo—simply because you like them. I placed many of my tidbits in the mouth of an auctioneer as he auctions a classic Studebaker toward the end of the novel.

A related problem is that you must find the right way to convey the information gathered in your research. Sometimes a story becomes more like an essay when you try to incorporate the facts you've found. Are all of the facts you've found absolutely necessary to your story? Is it essential that we know the per capita income of Borneo residents? Many details in a story or a novel are not absolutely crucial for the reader to know. And even if they are crucial, you must find a way to trick the reader into not noticing he is learning about a different time or place.

Writing with Authority

What the French novelist writing about Greenwich Village succeeded in doing is commonly known as *writing with authority.* Terms like this and *writing honestly* are often bandied about in workshops without anyone really knowing how to achieve either state, except instinctively. As for writing honestly, that's a potentially dangerous term (though I've used it myself) that could lead writers to gush all over the page or write something autobiographical without transforming it at all. Writing with authority is an equally mysterious term. You can get all the research right. You can know your subject. But when you start writing, it doesn't seem convincing, for any number of reasons, perhaps as numerous and individual as the number of writers who have written stories that didn't ring true. But one overwhelming reason has to do with what David Huddle in *The Writing Habit: Essays* calls writing with the "false self." He explains that most often "the false self is an overly literary fellow, a user of fancy diction and elaborate syntax, a manipulator of characters who are too good and beautiful for this world or else . . . thoroughly terrible and evil." The writer of such a story is perhaps more concerned with being literary or appearing smart to be bothered with an understanding of her characters. Often, such a writer is trying to imitate another writer she admires. This is fine; learning through imitation is a perfectly respectable avenue—as long as you eventually cast off the imitative voice and find the voice that's most natural for you.

Ian MacMillan is one writer who writes authoritatively about a time and place he did not experience. He grew up in upstate New York and has taught for many years at the University of Hawaii. Sometimes he writes what he calls "cows and chainsaw stories" about New York, but most often his subject is Eastern Europe during World War II. His novel *Orbit of Darkness* is an amazing exploration of the human spirit pushed to extremes, and it unblinkingly explores the war from disparate points of view. One constant character in the book is the historical figure Maximillian Kolbe, a Franciscan priest who volunteered to take another man's place in a starvation cell at Auschwitz. Another story in the novel is from the point of view of a Ukranian separatist fighting the Germans, and one of the most powerful chapters of the book is from the point of view of a young Russian boy traipsing across a frozen wasteland littered with corpses, in the company of his half-dead sisters, and his grandfather who miraculously manages to feed them. MacMillan is not for everyone. His vision is often harrowing. But it is so precise and, at its core, humane, that his work never treads on the sensational. The chapter from the point of view of the Russian boy is titled, "The Provider." Here's how it begins:

A long way from our village we found a building, and next to the
building there was a bench with four, naked men sitting on it, and
their feet were in a horse's drinking trough. Frost covered their hair
and faces and hunched shoulders. We walked past. Grandfather
Saburov went close. "They're tied to it," he said. "Their feet are tied
in the water. I mean ice."

This short passage is written with authority. You can find the entire story
on page 301. Remember that the best way to incorporate your research is to
anchor your "facts" in the consciousness of your main character. The details
MacMillan uses are specific, the voice simple but commanding, the action
immediate. Admittedly, this story, as many of his others, contains some
gruesome and disturbing images, but nothing beyond the pale of human
experience during World War II, and much of it strangely beautiful.

The Revision Process

One aspect of writing with authority is the revision process. In fact, the
revision process, for most writers, is perhaps the single most important
ingredient in writing believable fiction. It's here that the real art happens,
that the necessary adjustments and overhauls are made to your story. A bad
ending, for example, can ruin an otherwise good story. Often, in revising,
you find the right ending for your story, and afterward you can't imagine it
ever having ended differently. Or perhaps you need more details. Or maybe
you've included an unnecessary character in your story, one who played
an important role in the real event but who now seems to serve no real
purpose. And of course, nearly every time you add something to a piece of
fiction, something else has to be taken away to maintain the story's balance.
And nearly every time you take something away, something new needs to
be added.

When I was twelve, I bought props for practical jokes out of catalogues.
Fake vomit, fake dog doo, snapping packs of gum, cigarette loads, itching
powder. You name it. But the best thing I got that year was something called
the Big Ear. This was a listening device, a giant orange cone with a tripod
and a little ear plug to listen with. With the Big Ear, I could listen to conversations almost five hundred yards away. My mom and I lived in Columbia,
Missouri, at the time, where she taught at Stephens College, and I used to

take the Big Ear out to Stephens Lake and point it at couples making out. Sometimes they'd look up at me and wonder, *What's that kid doing?* Then I'd tip the cone up toward the sun and pretend I was conducting some serious scientific experiment.

Stephens was an all-girls school, and I had crushes on my mom's students. My favorite was a woman named Nan. Nan smoked a lot and I was against smoking, so one time when Nan came over, I placed a cigarette load in one of her smokes, thinking she might get the message that smoking was bad if the cigarette blew up in her face. I also thought it would be funny. It was hilarious. I caught her dress on fire, but luckily Nan wasn't hurt, and she still miraculously liked me.

One time, my mom left me for a few days with one of her students, a woman named Robin. My mom was going to Denver for an ear operation. An old boyfriend of Robin's found out where she was staying and kidnapped both her and me. He drove us around for a while, babbling and getting angrier and angrier. I didn't know what was going on. He stopped on a dirt road and told me to walk up the road out of sight. I didn't hear anything for about fifteen minutes. Finally, Robin came and got me. "It's all right," she said. "He's going to take us home." And that was the end of it. After the man dropped us off, Robin didn't call the police and she made me promise I wouldn't tell my mother what had happened. I promised because I really didn't know what *had* happened. I forgot the entire experience until I started writing a story about the Big Ear some twenty years later.

I thought this incident and the one involving Nan somehow fit together— the way men sometimes treat women, the aggression that we grow up with, the way some men have the anger wire crossed with the love wire. So I combined Nan with Robin and made the situation similar to the way it happened, but in the story the mother leaves to visit a boyfriend, not to have an ear operation.

The opening of my first attempt began this way:

The Big Ear, nearly as large as Peter, and brightly colored, stands out wherever he takes it, but no one really knows what it is, unless they ask. Peter practices withering looks on the people who ask, especially if they're kids. With the seriousness of purpose and steadiness of a Civil War photographer, he stands beside his Big Ear on its black tripod. He pretends to make fine calibrations on the plastic orange cone, bending into it and tapping it with a finger. Most people never get close enough to bother him with questions. That is one of the wonderful things about the Big Ear; it is a powerful device. You can set it up almost as far away from people as you like, two hundred yards, and it still picks up what they're doing. It can listen through windows. It can penetrate plaster walls.

Not a bad beginning, but the story went seriously astray with the kidnapping. I knew what I wanted to do, but I just couldn't do it.

Structure

As stated earlier, stories that come from memory can be too episodic. Instead of a chain of events with a clear cause/effect relationship, you might be tempted to string together a bunch of loosely connected episodes from your life and call it a story. The cause/effect relationship doesn't need to be obvious, but it needs to be there to some extent. Otherwise, it's not a story in the traditional sense.

A story needs direction. So if you go from your watermelon party when you were ten to a time when you caught sixty blue gills in the lake to the time you kissed your cousin in your grandma's tool shed, you might have "Scenes from a Happy Childhood," but you don't have a story. In stories based on real life, difficult distinctions must be made between what is necessary and what is merely an interesting but extraneous side note.

If your story seems too episodic, consider its structure. See how it all fits. List the scenes and what happens in them and see whether they're connected. Try structuring the story in a different way. Be flexible. Write five different titles. Write five different beginnings. Write five different outlines. Write five different outcomes. Loosen up, and don't berate yourself if it doesn't work the first time.

The kidnapping in my Big Ear story, even though it had happened, didn't seem to belong. It almost seemed like another story. I was introducing another character late in the story, while before it had just been about Peter and the woman based on Nan.

This draft of the story ended in a silly fashion that I should be too embarrassed and intelligent to relate. But I'll relate it anyway. Remember the cigarette loads I mentioned earlier? They play a contrived role in this version.

They tell him to go up the path, to stay in view. They've pulled off the road by a demolished building. It's only a pile of bricks and rusting furniture. Large spools of thread—red, white, and yellow—stick out among the bricks. Peter walks to the other side of the heap. He can make out Sandy and Charlie's heads, but not their bodies. There's a long shack made of faded boards, one wall torn out, and inside are more spools of thread, the signs of a campfire, and broken school desks. He could run, he thinks. If their voices rise or if they're silent, he'll run. If they disappear from view, he'll run. He can run along the road or through the woods, though he knows this gangly man, who looks like a long distance runner, might easily overtake him, despite his smoking.

He hears their voices, but can make no sense of them. He wishes he had his Big Ear. But the pain comes through clearly, even if the words make no sense. Was that all he needed to understand, the pain they caused? That it was private, theirs alone, and he could never enter it? The clearest sound is the rustling of dry leaves, as sharp as breaking glass. The in-suck of breath from the lit cigarette.

He hears a pop and then Sandy says, "Oh God," and both their heads disappear behind the rubble of the broken building.

Peter runs toward the sound rather than away. He races around the bricks and spools of yarn and stops.

Charlie seems stunned. He stands there with the exploded cigarette in his mouth, and then he gets a reflective look and begins to cry. Sandy stands there with that same reflective look, and her shoulders begin to buckle, and she buries her face in her hands.

Peter wonders what he should do. He had hoped the exploding cigarette would divert Charlie's attention and give Sandy the advantage. But neither she nor Charlie seem to want the advantage now.

"I could never hurt you," he says.

"I know," she says, trying to quiet him.

Peter takes a step back. I've just been kidnapped, he wants to scream, but he's silent, trying his best to understand, though he knows now it's impossible to understand completely.

Then Sandy notices Peter. "You little fool," she yells at him.

He doesn't understand the rest of what she yells.

But I thought you were afraid, he's thinking, unsure of what could have gone wrong.

When his mother returns from Atlanta, he won't ask her about Guido. He doesn't want to know. And if she asks him about his week, he'll just say it was fine, and change the subject, and talk about what he wants for Christmas, a new fishing pole.

Peter stands there, blinking his eyes at Sandy, like it's some lost code between them.

She takes a step toward him, and Peter turns and runs.

I knew this wasn't very good about two seconds after I wrote it. There are some good details, but the action seems contrived and the dialogue seems melodramatic. Still, it's better to finish a draft of something terrible than to give up. At least then you have something to work with. If you don't complete a draft, you might easily get into the habit of abandoning your work before giving it a chance to gel.

Changing Point of View

I decided to try a new approach. I thought maybe I was sticking too close to actual events, so I thought, *What if I tell it from a different point of view, say, a young girl's instead of a boy's? And what if I change the mother into a father? Maybe he's teaching at this all-girls' school and is having an affair with one of the students! Yeah, sure.* I also remembered something else from childhood, a neighbor kid from when we lived in Athens, Ohio. His name was David Roger Biddle. I'm telling you his full name because that's how he always referred to himself. He had a strong country accent, and no matter how many times he spoke to you, he'd always introduce himself: "Hah, my name is David Roger Biddle." David was a very gullible kid. No matter what you told him, he believed it. Of course, being the fledgling writer that I was, I tended to tell him a lot.

Then I remembered something else, this time from Columbia: these two girls I used to play with and their missionary father and mother. What if I combined David Roger Biddle with them and made his mother the student the narrator's father fools around with? My main problem here was that I didn't know my characters well enough. I had a situation in mind (boy with listening device, not understanding adult goings-on), but I didn't know who any of the characters were besides this boy. He was me when I was twelve—though not completely. He was me exaggerated. But with the other characters I was floundering. Here's what I came up with this time:

> "Hi, Justine, my name is Bobby Bradley Biddle, Bobby said to me when I opened the door. He had a strong accent, so what he said to me actually sounded like, "Hah, Justine, mah nayem's Bobay Bradlay Beetle."
>
> He'd only been to my house a million times, but this was a strong habit with Bobby Bradley Biddle, announcing his full name wherever he went, like he was sure people would forget him the moment he left their sight.
>
> Bobby smiled shyly at me and said, "Remember me?"
>
> "Elvis Presley?" I asked.
>
> "Nope," he said.
>
> "Duke Ellington?"
>
> "Nope," he said and laughed. "I don't even know any Duke Ellingtone."
>
> "Then you're going to have to leave. I don't know you."
>
> "Sure you do," he said, but he didn't laugh this time. He looked ultra-serious. "Sure you know me," he said. "I'm Bobby Bradley Biddle."
>
> "What was that middle name?"
>
> "Bradley."
>
> "Oh, now I remember you," I said, and let him in.

Fine, but what happened to the Big Ear? I decided to scrap this version as well. Okay, back to the kidnapping. Maybe if I started the story with the kidnapping and changed the point of view again it would work. Worth a try, anyway.

> In the car, Joe asks Anthony if he's kidnapping them. Nora, still dressed in her heavy tae kwon do *gi,* tied with a yellow belt, stares

out the window, which is wide open. Anthony didn't even give her a chance to change at the house. "No one's kidnapped anyone," Anthony says softly. "I just don't want to let you go." Anthony seems, to Joe, like a nice guy, not like someone who wants to or could harm anyone. He told Joe before he worked with mentally challenged children. He said it was sometimes rewarding, sometimes heartbreaking.

I guess I can't write good kidnappings. My heart just wasn't in it. To me, it didn't ring true at all, which brings up an interesting point: I *was* actually kidnapped at that age (albeit briefly), but it seemed less "true" than many of the events I imagined for the story. When I say it doesn't ring true, I mean that it doesn't ring true to me. Perhaps if I showed it to someone else, he might say it looks perfectly fine. In some ways, we're not talking about the authenticity of the event; it might seem like a perfectly authentic kidnapping. But the scene didn't ring true to the story I wanted to write, even if I wasn't completely sure what that story was. It didn't fit. It seemed to take the story away from the central character too much. It worked against the focus of the story, which was Peter. So I had to take it out.

Getting Distance

The distance I'm talking about means setting aside your draft for a while, for however long it takes so you can see it with a clear perspective and a cool eye. Don't rush your revisions. If your story takes two or three years to gel, allow yourself that time.

I gave up on the story for a year or two. That might have been the best thing I could have done. It gave me time to get distance. I was too close to the material, even though it was by this time far removed from my real-life experiences.

Finally, when I was ready I went back to Justine and Bobby Bradley Biddle. This time, I decided to get back to the Big Ear and make sure it was an integral part of the story.

Now I'm in my activist phase, but I used to be big on party gags.
"By the time you grow up, Justine," Mom says, "you're going to

break the Guinness world record for most phases." She's wrong. Petition drives, environmental issues, the nuclear thing—that kind of stuff is what I'm making my life's work. But back when I lived with my dad half the year, I clowned around all the time. It started with this catalogue I found an ad for in the back of a comic book. The ad showed a little cartoon guy with a big head and electrocuted hair poking his finger into a light socket. A bunch of other cartoon guys who looked just like him surrounded the little guy, and they were bent over double, pointing their fingers at him. "HA HA HA!" was written in bold black letters all around the ad, and in smaller letters were the words, "Thousands of gags for incredibly low prices!"

What I really wanted from the catalogue was the Big Ear, an electronic listening device, so that I could go out to Stephens Lake and listen to all the couples making out on their blankets.

My dad didn't like teaching at Stephens and used to complain about its reputation as a finishing school for Southern belles, where women majored in subjects like equestrian science. Once, when he was getting ready to leave for school, he gathered up his scattered things around the house by galloping like a horse.

"Where are my keys?" he shouted. "Come on noble steed or we'll be late for class." He clucked his tongue and shook the reins.

I pointed to the Big Ear and said, "Do you think you could afford this for my birthday?"

My dad bent down and said, "We'll see, Justine."

He turned his attention away from me and started scanning the kitchen counter, then sifted through the tons of paper, rubbing his hands across the surface like a miner sifting for gold in a stream. "I can't leave without my keys," he said finally. "Did you see them?"

"You're always losing your keys," I said. "I should get you an electronic keyfinder. They have one in the catalogue. When you lose your keys you have a little beeper that finds it for you."

Not a bad voice, but this one wasn't right either, so I went back to the kidnapping. Finally, I got so sick of going back and forth that I looked at my story with a cold eye and thought, *How many stories am I telling?* By my count, about half a dozen.

Telling One Story Well

What I needed to do, I finally figured out, was to drop all the extra memories and tell one story well, not six stories poorly. So, I dropped the kidnapping altogether. I went back to the male narrator. I dropped Bobby Bradley Biddle. I focused on the Big Ear and the main character's relationships to his mother and the character based on Nan. I began the story with the same beginning I'd started with, but this time I stayed focused. And, in the end, the story did everything I'd wanted it to do. My main character, Peter, basically listens to other people's pain. His mother is trapped in this going-nowhere, long-distance affair. The woman he was staying with, however, is somewhat stronger than Peter's mother. And, in the end, Peter comes to some understanding of what he's been listening to all along. The story is smaller, in some ways, in its conception than it was originally, but now it's more successful, I think. It doesn't end with a bang, but it ends more realistically. And I replaced the kidnapping with a remembered incident of being abandoned in Europe that a woman once told me when I was in college.

Now would be an excellent time to turn to page 315 and read my story, "The Big Ear," in its entirety. When you're done, just return to this spot.

That wasn't too painful, I hope.

By the way, a line or two that Sandy says is something that a friend told me one day during the time I was working on that story. "All my life I've been involved with murderers. Part of the attraction of the relationship was the pain." When my friend told me this, I nodded my head sympathetically, then I asked him if I could use it. Perhaps, now that I've alerted you to the theme running throughout the story—pain in relationships—this passage, too, might seem like so much scaffolding. But if you come across it naturally in the course of Sandy's dialogue (and haven't read my previous drafts), I don't think it will stick out too much.

Sharpening the Knife

There's no set way to go about revising. It's a matter of trial and error. With material from real life, people have the natural tendency to include the kitchen sink and see everything they've written as crucial to the story simply because "it really happened." To you, the writer, the connection between remembered events is implicit: They're connected because they happened to you. But that's not the way it will work for everyone else reading the story. It's not important to anyone else simply because it happened to you. If you write fiction, you must learn to be brutal with your work—and your life. Many times, other people to whom you show your work either aren't invested enough in what you write to offer you truly helpful suggestions, or else they're simply at a loss as to what you can do to improve the story. So you must rely on your own instincts eventually and become your own strongest critic.

EXERCISES

1. Count the number of words in a story you've written from real life, perhaps one you're having trouble focusing. Now cut the story in half. Cut it in half again. What you're left with will be the essentials of the story, and you'll be able to see it more clearly.

2. If your story lacks focus, if it seems to ramble from one episode to another based on your life, change the point of view. Make it not your life.

3. Try writing a scene based on your life in a different genre. Turn it into a science fiction piece. Turn it into a thriller, a horror story, a comedy.

4. Write a two-page description of the area you now live in—your city, town, or neighborhood—as if you plan to use this area as the setting for a piece of fiction. Try to evoke a vivid sense of what this place is like today. Next, research the area at the local library, at the area historical society, or by interviewing longtime residents of the place. Then rewrite your description, enriching it with the facts, details, and anecdotes acquired through your research.

5. Go to the microfilm section of your library and find a newspaper from fifty years ago. Examine it from front to back and use this

paper as a guide for setting a scene on this exact day fifty years ago. Ignore most of the headlines. Look at the small stories and the ads. Use the advertisements to dress your characters. Use the classifieds or the movie section or the funnies to give them something to talk about.

▼

CHAPTER EIGHT

Legal and Ethical Concerns

Recently, I was approached by a woman who had a story that "needs to be told." Actually, it wasn't her story, but the story of a friend of hers. The woman whose story it was didn't know that the other woman was planning to tell her story and perhaps would be angry if she knew about it. In other words, the woman's story *didn't* need to be told. Frankly, no story *needs* to be told. A story is not a concrete thing—not something you can bring home like a baby from the hospital, feed it, nurture it, and then send it out into the world where it can be told. A story depends on the teller. The woman "whose story needs to be told" doesn't know that her story needs to be told, perhaps doesn't care except that it might embarrass her if people she knew connected her with the story. For her, it's not a story. It's a life.

I asked the woman why the other woman's story needs to be told, and she answered, "Because she's going to die soon." That's not really a reason for telling a story, since we're all going to die soon, relatively speaking. "It's about teen violence," she went on, "and it's important because there's so much of it going on today." I asked her if it needed to be written as fiction, or if it was better suited for nonfiction. She knew nothing at all about fiction, she said, but she wanted to write it as fiction because she wanted to disguise it so the woman whose story "needs to be told" wouldn't be able to "prove anything."

All of this is tricky territory, but a lot of it depends on one's personal sense of ethics. On the one hand, you can't copyright an anecdote told at a party, a secret told in confidence, or any other life experience. But you should be aware of other people's feelings and realize that what you write might inadvertently hurt someone in your family or ruin a friendship.

The word "inadvertently" is important here because some people are

< 165 >

thin-skinned and don't understand what fiction is. Your mother, perhaps, sees herself in every story you write. You have a story in which the mother slaps her child. "I never slapped you!" your mother screams when she reads the story. "It's not about you," you say. "It's fiction." A little later, she shouts, "I didn't know you smoked pot in high school!" " I didn't, Mom. It's a story." Sometimes, when you *have* written pretty directly about your friends or relatives, they don't recognize themselves at all. That's really not so amazing. You might see your aunt Imelda as avaricious and petty, but she sees herself as the most generous-spirited soul alive. And who's to say who's right? Maybe you're the avaricious and petty one, and you're just projecting your shortcomings onto Aunt Imelda. In any case, Aunt Imelda reads your story and thinks it's precious. She's just proud that you've written a story, and she tells you she's going to brag to her friends about you. Now, don't you feel guilty?

Disclaimers

Here's a secret: Those disclaimers in the front of novels that read, "Any resemblance to persons, living or dead, is purely coincidental," don't mean a thing. In a legal sense, disclaimers do not provide protection from or defense against lawsuits. If someone feels your characterization is not in the least coincidental and decides to sue you for libel or invasion of privacy, pointing to your disclaimer won't help. In a creative sense, and let's be honest, the resemblance is not coincidental at all. Every writer uses real people as the basis for fictional characters. There's even an encyclopedia of real people who were models for fictional creations. The book is called *The Originals: An A-Z of Fiction's Real-Life Characters,* by William Amos. For instance, look under "M" and you'll discover that Miss Marple, at least in part, was based on Agatha Christie's grandmother. Look under "T" and you'll discover that Elliott Templeton in W. Somerset Maugham's *The Razor's Edge* is based on Sir Henry ("Chips") Channon, the son of a Chicago businessman, who wanted to "become more English than the English."

Characters rarely come from nowhere, though they aren't always based on one person. As I've mentioned previously, characters most often are composites of several people we've met in our lives. Maybe you met these people by chance, but that's about as coincidental as it gets. Even Maugham's friend Chips was a composite. Apparently, Chips *wanted* to be portrayed by Maugham as Templeton, but Maugham delivered more than Chips bargained for. Chips explained, "[H]e had split me into three characters, and then written a book about all three." I suppose that makes Chips not a composite but the opposite, a real person split into three characters. Perhaps a prismite?

Still, the disclaimers are part of the business and on occasion have risen to an art form. Frederick Exley has one of the best in his book, *Fan's Notes:*

> Though the events in this book bear similarity to those of that long malaise, my life, many of the characters and happenings are creations solely of the imagination. In such cases, I, of course, disclaim any responsibility for their resemblance to real people or events, which would be coincidental. The character "Patience," for example, who is herein depicted as "my wife," is a fictionalized character bearing no similarity to anyone living or dead. In creating such characters, I have drawn freely from the imagination and adhered only loosely to the pattern of my past life. To this extent, and for this reason, I ask to be judged as a writer of fantasy.

Hemingway, in *To Have and Have Not,* also used the disclaimer to good effect:

> In view of a recent tendency to identify characters in fiction with real people, it seems proper to state that there are no real people in this volume: both the characters and their names are fictitious.

Hemingway was being coy. A number of his characters were based on real people, including very unflattering portraits of John Dos Passos and his wife, Katy Smith Dos Passos—so unflattering, in fact, that Arnold Gingrich, publisher of *Esquire,* urged Hemingway to take out the potentially libelous passages from the book. Gingrich claimed that the characterizations were so transparent and vicious as to invite legal action.

In the passages, Hemingway characterizes Dos Passos as a hypocrite who pretends to be "incorruptible" and borrows from his friends on the basis of his sterling reputation, with no intention of paying them back. It's "like a trust fund," one Hemingway character says to another. Katy Dos Passos comes off even worse. She's characterized as a kleptomaniac who "likes to steal as much as a monkey does."

According to Robert E. Fleming in *The Journal of Modern Literature,* Hemingway took Gingrich's advice and expunged the offending paragraphs from the manuscript. He even changed the description of the character based on Dos Passos, making him a handsome man when, in fact, Dos Passos was balding, skinny, and wore thick glasses that hardly made him the Hemingway model of male perfection. (Fleming notes that it's possible Hemingway simply removed the paragraphs for artistic reasons rather than worries of a libel suit. Hemingway tended to write vicious attacks on former friends, attacks he never intended to publish, such as *The Autobiography of Alice B. Hemingway,* in which he attacks Gertrude Stein.) In any case, what prompted this attack of vitriol on Hemingway's part? Poor fishing off Cuba? Bad hair day? No, apparently Hemingway was one of those unfortunates who had loaned Dos Passos money, $1,000 in 1933 when Dos Passos was convalescing from rheumatic fever. Dos Passos did have a reputation of incorruptibility, someone who wouldn't follow the latest trends, who attacked the moneyed interests of J. P. Morgan and William Randolph Hearst and who, according to Hemingway, "wouldn't change a comma if you put him on the rack. You could break him on the wheel but the word *merde* stays in, you know." Fleming claims that by attacking Dos Passos's integrity, Hemingway supposed he was slamming his former friend where "it would hurt most."

Writing Well Is the Best Revenge

Hemingway isn't the only writer who gets revenge on the real world in a fictional one. This is perhaps not the noblest of reasons for writing about someone else, but almost every writer tries it at one time or another. Nora Ephron got ex-husband Carl Bernstein good in *Heartburn.* Perhaps revenge wasn't her motive, but the portrait of him is certainly scathing, and it definitely steamed him up. This is perhaps the most common type of revenge, casting a former spouse in a villainous role, and publishers cringe at the thought of such portraits and the attendant lawsuits that sometimes follow. Even if your motive isn't revenge, it still might not be the wisest idea to write about a former lover or spouse in a disparaging way, especially someone who might not hold you in the highest regard, either.

Terry McMillan found this out when she based a character on her former boyfriend in her novel *Disappearing Acts*. In the novel, she gave him the same occupation, the same education, and he even ate the same breakfast cereal. But the man in the novel also abuses alcohol and drugs and beats his girlfriend. That characterization upset Leonard Welch, her ex-boyfriend, and he sued for nearly $5 million. The judge dismissed the case. According to the *Wall Street Journal,* the judge, in his decision, wrote, "[A] reasonable reader couldn't possibly attribute the defamatory aspects of the character [Franklin Swift] to Mr. Welch, even though the character seems to be modeled on Mr. Welch. . . . But the man in the novel is a lazy, emotionally disturbed alcoholic who uses drugs and sometimes beats his girlfriend," said Judge Spodek, while "Leonard Welch is none of these things."

Another apparent revenge case was that of *Springer v. Viking Press* in 1993. Lisa Springer, a college girlfriend of Robert Tine, claimed the novelist added a character, Lisa Blake, to his novel in revenge for the breakup of their relationship. Lisa Blake was exactly like Springer in her physical description, where she lived, her hobbies, her vacations, even her jewelry. The only difference was that Lisa Blake was characterized as a high-priced prostitute.

Perhaps a little tacky and juvenile on Tine's part, but the courts found, as in the McMillan case, that no reasonable person who knew Springer would believe that she was indeed a prostitute.

Despite the fact that the novelists won in these cases, it's better to avoid the mess by doing something more aggravating to your exes than dumping them in your fiction. How about signing them up for all those aircraft-technician schools you find on matchbook covers? Now *there's* a more mature revenge.

Of course, I'm not above a little revenge. I put the last names of some people I didn't like on tombstones in *The Last Studebaker.* There's nothing defamatory in that, except they're dead. I also got mild revenge in the same novel on a restaurant that wanted to serve my wife fish and chips without French fries. The absurd conversation that followed was lifted nearly verbatim from the actual occurrence, including the manager's contention that, "We don't mean fish *and* chips. We mean fish cut *into* chips." Yes, someone literally said that. So, while I'm not in favor of getting revenge on exes in print, I'm all for going after bad restaurants and banks and anything else that contributes to the myriad frustrations of contemporary life. Even so, it would be wise to change the name or locale of the offending institution.

So Sue Me!

It might seem as if you can't write about anyone without the fear of being sued for libel, but that's not true. McMillan said, quite rightly, after the judge's decision in her case, "Every writer takes things from his or her own life, but you alter them. I hope this decision will reassure other authors, too, to just exhale and get on with what we do." This was considered a major victory for authors and publishers, primarily because it dealt with one of the main characters in the book, not a minor one as in past cases.

There's a great catch-22 at work here for the fiction writer. Obviously, the suit is without merit, goes the logic of the decision in the McMillan case, because the characterization is so blatantly false. On the other hand, if Welch *were* a drug addict and a girlfriend beater, the accusations would be true, and therefore the suit would likewise be without merit, since true accusations are not defamatory.

You can be sued for almost anything, though that doesn't mean the lawsuit will stand up in court. If your mother sues you because your character who slaps her children is loosely based on her, your lawyer counters by saying, "That's why it's called fiction. Everyone who knows you knows you'd never slap your children." And then your mother drops her lawsuit because she is, after all, your mom.

According to an article in the *New York Times Magazine* by Judge Irving R. Kaufman, things can and have gone the other way, using just the *opposite* logic of the above catch-22. The plaintiff shows the similarities between himself and the character in a novel or short story, and then shows any deviation as evidence that the portrayal is false.

In 1979, Gwen Davis wrote a novel based on a nude encounter group in California. She had signed an agreement with the leader of those sessions, psychologist Paul Bindrim, that she would not write about the group, and she didn't. She fictionalized it. In her book, the head of the encounter group was described as a "fat Santa Claus type with long white hair, white sideburns, a cherubic rosy face and rosy forearms." Bindrim, however, was short-haired and clean-shaven.

Bindrim sued, claiming that she distorted the events of his group. Bindrim won, and his suit was upheld on appeal, the majority of the judges finding "overwhelming evidence that plaintiff and Herford [the name of the fictional character] were one." However, the lone dissenting judge noted in his opinion, "the fictitious Dr. Herford has none of the characteristics of plaintiff except that Dr. Herford practices nude encounter therapy." This decision set an absurd precedent. As Judge Kaufman points out in his *New York Times Magazine* article, it boils down to, "When you criticize my occupation, you libel me."

Bindrim collected $75,000 in damages from Davis and her publisher, Doubleday. Though that's not a vast sum by today's standards, it completely shocked the publishing industry. Partly as a result of that decision, publishers responded nobly and rallied round their authors with equal parts of self-protection and cowardice and made them sign contracts that basically said, "If you're sued, you're on your own." These "waivers of idemnification," as they are called, do not protect the publishers from lawsuits; they protect publishers from responsibility for lawsuits against the writer. Litigants, knowing where the big bucks can be made, almost always go after the publishers as well as the writers.

Today, most publishers have libel insurance and will go to bat for you, provided you disclose to them before publication anything that is potentially libelous. This is a key point. If you have a book accepted for publication, it's imperative to inform your publisher of any portrayals of real people in the work so the publisher's attorneys can review it against any potential libel claims. Disclose everything. If you have any doubts, err on the side of full disclosure. Ultimately, this will protect you.

In a similar case, Dr. Jane V. Anderson sued over the film version of Sylvia Plath's *The Bell Jar*. She and Plath had been patients at the same mental hospital, and she contended that she was the model for the character Joan Gilling, a suicidal lesbian. In court, her side argued that Anderson had never, in fact, made sexual advances toward Plath. "I also never made any suicide attempts or had scars on my breast. And certainly I never hung myself." That last statement seems a given. But if she *had* hanged herself, just imagine how much more potent her testimony would have been. The defense argued exactly the same thing. You're alive. You're here in court. Therefore, the character is fictitious.

This case was resolved in an out-of-court settlement. Who knows who would have won or what precedent it might have set, but it's understandable that both sides settled. The costs of such actions are so exorbitant that no one wins in the end.

Perhaps the most ludicrous literary libel case was the 1982 case of the former Miss Wyoming who sued a short-story writer for a story that appeared in *Penthouse.* In this case, a fictional Miss Wyoming was characterized as performing all kinds of farcical sexual activities. The description of this Miss Wyoming was very stereotypical, something like blond hair and blue eyes and she was a baton twirler. By coincidence, the real Miss Wyoming fit the story writer's portrait, and she sued. She won, too—$28 million! But the case was overturned by a federal appeals court, ruling that the sexual escapades were so bizarre that no one would believe a real person (not even from Wyoming) could perform them.

Again, that catch-22.

More recently, in 1996, a Harlem librarian, Daria Carter-Clark, sued Joe Klein, the author of *Primary Colors,* for libel. In the novel, the presidential candidate based on Clinton visits an adult-literacy program in Harlem and sleeps with the librarian. Carter-Clark cried defamation. Like the character in the book, she ran an adult-literacy program in Harlem that had been visited by then-presidential candidate, Bill Clinton. Unlike the character, she had *not* slept with the candidate. The case was eventually dismissed for the usual reasons. The court decided that one couldn't hold a work of fiction to the standards of nonfiction and that anyone who knew Carter-Clark wouldn't attribute the behavior of the fictional librarian to her. Yet, of course, nearly everyone attributed the behavior of the fictional Jack Stanton in the book to the real-life Clinton. That was much of the appeal of the book. So why not likewise assume that Carter-Clark indeed slept with Clinton? Klein dodged a bullet.

Not so the editors of *Seventeen.* As part of their New Voices in Fiction contest, they published in 1991 a story by Lucy Logsdon of Southern Illinois whose high school protagonist characterizes another student identified only as Bryson as a "slut." As bad luck would have it, Kimberly Bryson, also of Southern Illinois, decided that the slutty Bryson of the story was, in fact, her and that she'd been defamed. She sued and two lower courts agreed that this was simply a case of one fictional character uttering an opinion about another fictional character. Sounds reasonable, but the State Supreme Court disagreed and overturned the lower courts' decisions. The Supreme Court decided, with one dissenting opinion, that because of the location and the "unusual" name, reasonable people might indeed meet Kimberly Bryson and exclaim, "Oh, you're that slut I read about in *Seventeen!*" This is a rather chilling verdict, especially considering that Bryson isn't THAT unusual a name—had Logsdon chosen a truly unusual name, say, Mxyzptlk, none of this unpleasantness would have happened. But then she might have been sued by Mister Mxyzptlk, a fifth-dimensional imp who has plagued Superman nearly his entire career. I mean, if one can be sued over fictional portrayals, it only follows that fictional characters are going to get into the act soon and start suing over their portrayals as well. So watch out.

Now that I've thoroughly scared you, let me give you cause for cheer. It's rare for fiction writers to be sued, and when they are, the courts rarely award damages. Furthermore, most courts have not followed the precedent of the Gwen Davis case, but have followed the model of Joe Klein's. But Bryson's case is a much more recent precedent than Klein's. Although the *Seventeen* story appeared before *Primary Colors* was published, it dragged on for years and was only recently settled. Regardless, the costs of defending oneself against a libel action can be expensive, as well as emotionally disruptive, so it's not a good idea to take too cavalier an attitude toward such concerns.

The Associated Press Stylebook and Libel Manual defines libel as "injury to reputation." So, what then is libel in fiction? According to Judge Kaufman, certain conditions must be present: "The reference must clearly be 'of and concerning' the plaintiff. It must not be mere opinion." In other words, just because you have a character refer to Ann Coulter as a neo-Fascist pedant who's got her head up her duffel bag does not give her the right to sue. Last, the offending work "must be made with actual malice." Malice, in its legal sense, means that you know something is false but publish it anyway with "reckless disregard," according to the A.P. manual.

However, private citizens, as opposed to public figures, need not prove malice in court. They must simply prove negligence, meaning that the writer did not take the necessary care in proving the veracity of information before stating it as fact. As a general rule, the more public the figure, the greater the burden of proof necessary to win a libel case. This rule is based, of course, on freedom of speech. The more public the information, the greater its protection by the First Amendment. So Ann Coulter needs to amass stronger evidence of your intentions than does your ex-boss, who claims you libeled him in your latest novel.

So while we all use real people as models, we must be somewhat careful. That a characterization of someone real appears in a work of fiction does not automatically protect it from libel concerns. Moreover, the legal precedents are somewhat hazy and contradictory. Although, as mentioned earlier, most lawsuits against fiction writers are eventually dismissed, the legal costs of mounting a defense are prohibitive, so it's much better to do everything you can to avoid being sued in the first place.

Your best defense is written consent from the person you have fictionalized. Here's a list of other points to consider:

- Is your character an easily recognizable real individual?

- Have you written an unflattering portrait?

- Do you seek revenge on this person?

- Are the transformations of the character simply superficial ones?

- Have you neglected to tell your publisher or editor about any potentially libelous material?

If your answer is yes to any of these questions, you must go back and transform your material. To be safe, transform your characters as much as possible. Change the gender or locale. Use composites. Better to err on the side of conservatism than to be sued later.

For journalists, the only absolute defense against a libel suit is that the facts stated must be *provably* true. For fiction writers, there are no unconditional defenses. But for a characterization to be libelous, it must be *clearly* of and concerning the plaintiff. That's the opposite of the journalist's defense. Your defense is that it's clearly *not* true, that it's fiction.

Real Names

A lot of writers have made the mistake of using someone's real name in a story or a novel. Some even do it on purpose. In the 1970s, John Irving was a visiting writer at the Iowa Writers' Workshop and had a student named Jenny Fields. The story goes that Irving wanted to use her name in his new book, *The World According to Garp*. Apparently, Fields was not pleased with this, and she went to one of the permanent faculty members to complain. "There's nothing you can do about it," he told her. Names are fair game, as long as you do not use the person, too.

If Jenny Fields could prove that Irving's character was based on her and the novel publicly disclosed facts about her private life, she could try to stop publication. If she could prove that her reputation was damaged by the characterization or, again, that private facts had been made public, she could sue. But since Irving used only her name, for a character with no other ties to her, she was left without legal recourse. Most suits involving the use of someone's name pertain to famous names that are used without permission to sell a product. If, for instance, you begin selling Michael Jordan candy bars without first asking Mr. Jordan, he can sue. Writers need to worry about name-appropriation suits only when they use the person to whom the name belongs.

Madison Smartt Bell learned this lesson when he inadvertently used a real name as well as the real person in his fiction. Libel insurance was new when Bell's first novel, *The Washington Square Ensemble,* came out, so he and a lawyer went over the book as closely as possible. "I confessed tiny, tiny details," he says. "We were changing things like the names of bars. That night I went to Studio 54—the only time in my life, because a friend took me. I go into the men's room and out walks this guy whom I'd known on a job, wearing a white tuxedo. He's giving me this big smile. I hadn't seen him in about eighteen months, and he was in the book with a very hostile characterization under his own name. I'd forgotten that this guy was ever real. He was not a friend. And he turned into this jerky character in the novel. Immediately after this strange and discomfiting encounter, I had to go back to my publisher and say there'd been this little oversight. As it happened, the characterization was just a minor role in the first chapter. I ended up deleting it. It didn't appear in the finished book. Regardless, writers have a great ability to delude themselves."

That's true. Sometimes, as strange as this might sound, you almost forget the boundary between your imagination and real people. You forget that people who really exist weren't made up by you. I know that sounds awful and solipsistic, but it's the natural result of living in your own little world half the day. So, something like that can easily happen if you're not careful. It happened to Oscar Hijuelos in his Pulitzer Prize–winning novel, *The Mambo Kings Play Songs of Love*. He used the name "Glorious Gloria Parker and Her All-Girl Rumba Orchestra." I know exactly why he did it, though I've never spoken to Mr. Hijuelos. He used the name because it's great. Who could make up a band name like that? This is pure conjecture, but he probably didn't know her whereabouts, didn't even know if she was still among the living, or maybe, like Bell, forgot this was a real person.

Glorious Gloria Parker was all too real and all too unhappy when she saw her name and former band portrayed in Hijuelos's book, and she sued him for $15 million for defamation of character. I love the supposedly defamatory passages in the book. One reads that the Mambo King "made it with three of the musicians who played with Glorious Gloria Parker and Her All-Girl Rumba Orchestra, among them a Lithuanian trombone player named Gertie." In the other passage, Hijuelos shows "Gloria huddled at a table drinking daiquiris," and then saying to the Mambo King, "Come on ya big lug, why don't you kiss me?"

Glorious Gloria was not amused, claiming she was now unable to find bookings as a result of being cast as a "character in that dirty book." She also claimed that she'd led an exemplary life and neither drank nor smoked. Obviously, this was not someone who would ask some big lug to kiss her.

The judge dismissed this case too, writing that, "It is difficult to believe that an average reader would consider either of the passages defamatory."

A lot of writers, including myself and most of my friends, occasionally use the names of their friends in their novels or stories. These cameo appearances are designed for the mutual amusement of the writer and her friend. These are always expendable, sometimes off-stage, characters. In *The Last Studebaker,* I made my friend Jurek Polanski the executor of an estate. David Shields often includes me in his books as some off-stage editor or other pesky character.

Sometimes writers find names in the phone book. There's nothing wrong with that, and it's unlikely that you'll be sued. Let's say you see the name Travis Boovy. You don't know Travis Boovy. You've never met the gentleman. You just like the name. So you don't know what he's really like, and you certainly can't maliciously and consciously defame the man. If you name a character John Smith and you make him someone who stuffs hash browns in his ears, are all the John Smiths in the world going to sue you?

Public Figures

Some writers use public figures in their books. Public figures are those people who are in the limelight: famous actors, politicians, musicians. This also includes ordinary people who have been thrust into the public spotlight through some newsworthy event. Here, we also encounter our privacy laws. According to the A. P. Manual, "When a person becomes involved in a news event, voluntarily or involuntarily, he forfeits the right to privacy. Similarly, a person somehow involved in a matter of legitimate public interest, even if not a bona fide . . . news event, normally can be written about with safety. However, this is different from publication of a story . . . that dredges up the sordid details of a person's past and has no current newsworthiness." As an example, the guide mentions the case of a prostitute who was tried for murder, acquitted, later married, and lived a happy life until a motion picture appeared that used her real name and was billed as based on a true story. This was found to violate her right to privacy.

Satire, of course, would be nearly nonexistent if we didn't have our First Amendment right to verbally draw and quarter our politicians and entertainers. This falls under the heading of fair comment, satire being a form of opinion. That doesn't mean it's impossible to be sued by a public figure, but as it is, they rarely sue the *National Enquirer*. Still, let's say you're sued by Liz Taylor or Michael Jackson because of the novel in which you portray Macaulay Culkin as their secret love child. Oh lucky day. Think of the publicity. Your book will probably be a best seller. Plus you'll win the court case anyway. No sweat. Still, if you're squeamish, go ahead and change the name like Joyce Carol Oates did in her novel *Black Water*. This book is unquestionably about Senator Ted Kennedy and the Chappaquiddick tragedy. But Oates changed the names and the time frame (probably for artistic reasons as much, if not more, as for reasons of legality). So Kennedy becomes The Senator and Mary Jo Kopechne becomes Kelly. There's no way one can read the book without thinking of Chappaquiddick, but it's not meant to be a literal account, simply a literary exploration.

On the other hand, consider *The Public Burning,* by Robert Coover. This absurd, farcical book is partly narrated by Richard Nixon and deals with the conviction and executions of Julius and Ethel Rosenberg. But in Coover's retelling of this chapter of American history, Nixon goes to prison to see Ethel Rosenberg, where he unexpectedly falls in love with her. They start making out in her cell, but they're interrupted and are unable to consummate their passion for each other. However, unbeknownst to Nixon, while his pants were off, Ethel scrawled the words, "I am a scam" in lipstick on his buttocks. Also, in Coover's telling, the Rosenbergs are executed in Times Square. In the middle of this public event, Nixon gets up onstage and his pants fall down, revealing to the assembled multitude the words Ethel wrote on his rear end. In the midst of the uproar that follows, Nixon is sodomized by the spirit of Uncle Sam!

Whew, loses something in the retelling, doesn't it? Nixon was none too happy about this novel, and his lawyers were nearly able to scuttle the book before it was published. In any case, they delayed the book's publication and undoubtedly made Coover's life uncomfortable.

There are no absolute protections for fiction writers writing about public figures. Knowing that you'll probably win a lawsuit brought on by such a person will not necessarily make you sleep better at night, again because of the legal fees you'll incur defending your book, as well as the disruption to your peace of mind. If you can thinly disguise such a person without destroying the integrity of your work, so much the better. If you feel you must use the real person in your work, steel yourself for any possibility. As I've said, fiction writers are rarely sued, and when they are, the lawsuits are usually without firm legal grounding, as in the case against Oscar Hijuelos. So there's no sure indicator whether you will be sued for your published work. Much depends on who wants to take issue with it. Of course, controversy has rarely hurt a book, but it might hurt you personally. Again, the rule of thumb is to transform when possible and discuss any doubts with your publisher.

Historical Accounts

Plenty of historically based novels have been written—Don DeLillo's novel *Libra,* for one, a fictional account of the Kennedy assassination in which he mixes fact and fiction freely, from the character of Lee Harvey Oswald to a fictional C.I.A. operative. *Schindler's List* by Thomas Keneally is another example, a novel and later a movie based on the life of a German industrialist who managed to save a number of Jews from the gas chambers. Of course, the main characteristic these books have in common is that most of the principals in the book are either dead or fictional.

That someone you write about is no longer living might not necessarily shield you from legal concerns, especially if the person is recently deceased. Consider his heirs who might be happy to sue you for defamation of character. A woman I know decided not long ago to write a nonfictional account of a highly publicized murder trial in North Carolina. She contacted the principals who were still alive as well as their relatives and was promptly threatened with a lawsuit. Perhaps the lawsuit would have been without merit, especially since this was an account of historical record, but it was enough to frighten her. The lawsuit's grounds would most likely have been the right to privacy, since the murder was no longer newsworthy.

So she decided to transform the account into a fictional murder mystery. This does not necessarily make her any safer, unless she transforms the characters as much as possible—changing the locale, using composites, etc. Sometimes the threat of a lawsuit is enough to make a writer give up a project.

If you are concerned that your story may be legally actionable in some way, contact an attorney. If you can't afford one, try Volunteer Lawyers for the Arts (VLA). This is a nationwide organization of lawyers who offer free or reduced-fee legal services to people in the creative arts on matters related to practicing art. To locate the branch nearest you, visit their web site at http://www.vlany.org/res_dir.html.

Even if you've based your story on a historical account that happened a hundred years ago, some people might still attempt to intimidate you, as happened to Philip Gerard with his novel, *Cape Fear Rising*. This novel deals with an infamous incident in the town of Wilmington, North Carolina, where Gerard lives. In 1898, a group of powerful white businessmen staged a coup, driving out the Reconstruction town government and massacring some of the town's black residents. Gerard opted to use real names in his book, prompting a great deal of controversy in Wilmington. When the book appeared, there were grumblings of suing him, though no one ever figured out any grounds for such a lawsuit. Gerard did what many writers do: He made a number of people very uncomfortable. That, however, is not something a good writer necessarily shies away from. Sometimes it's the writer's job to make people uncomfortable, especially if they'd rather sweep under the rug a shameful period of their history. "When I started writing the book," Gerard says, "I told virtually no one, because I knew that if I received pressure when I was writing it, the novel would have gone unwritten."

This also harks back to the idea of the outsider writing about a place. Often, the outsider sees the place with much more clarity and insight than the insider.

Mistaken Identities

Sometimes there are freak coincidences. A former teacher of mine once wrote a novel about a woman whose brother-in-law and sister worked behind the scenes, unbeknownst to her, to cheat her out of an inheritance. She made this all up, but it turns out that's exactly what her brother-in-law and sister were trying to do in real life, and the two sisters haven't spoken to each other since. Sometimes, as mentioned earlier, when you get to the emotional core of things, you brush uncomfortably close to what really happened.

More often than not, people don't recognize themselves in your work. On this subject, Madison Smartt Bell says, "My experience has been in cases where I did base a character on a real person, I showed it to the person to make sure it wasn't a problem, and the person would say, 'I don't mind, but this is not me.' But frequently people recognize themselves where you had no intention, in characters that don't resemble them at all. One woman's been angry with me for years, thinking this novel I'd written was all about her, and there were not even any women characters in the novel!"

The same thing happened to Steve Yarbrough, although his case is perhaps a little atypical of most writers. His literary landscape is well-defined in that he almost exclusively writes stories set in and around Indianola, Mississippi, the town in which he grew up. "I did a few book signings in Mississippi right after my first book came out," says Yarbrough, "and I was uncomfortable around my hometown. People had bought the book and read it, people who'd never read a work of fiction in their lives, and they were just reading it to see if they could find somebody they knew. One of my high school teachers called me up about two weeks ago. I hadn't talked to her in years and she told me she had read my first book, and she wanted me to confirm that this person was based on so-and-so and that person was based on somebody else. Very often her evidence would be something really preposterous like, "Well, I know that's so-and-so because you said he's more than six feet tall and his name starts with W." When you're writing about a town of nine thousand like I am, it makes people want to make really huge assumptions."

It is doubtful that, in most cases, such mistakes or assumed identities are legally actionable. An outraged neighbor in your hometown would need to prove that a character is a thinly disguised version of her and that she has suffered damages as a result of your characterization. She must also prove that you have publicly disclosed private facts. "Private" is a key word here. You may write of a town figure who regularly gets drunk at the corner bar and starts fights—because he does this in a public place and his behavior is known to the public. But if this thinly disguised character goes home and beats his wife—or, like Miss Wyoming, engages in bizarre sexual behavior— he could have a case. Miss Wyoming, after all, won hers.

Begging, Borrowing, and Stealing

Two writers whom I interviewed for this book told me cases of writing about friends or acquaintances, but they wouldn't let me tell you their names or give you the exact circumstances of the genesis of their stories. And for good reason. In one case, the writer had written a story based on a rather insane acquaintance of his, someone he suspected of being slightly dangerous, and however remote the chances were that this man would ever read this book, the writer did not want this guy to know he'd written a story about him. Another writer I spoke with recounted an anecdote in which her child had been bullied by another child in the presence of the other child's mother. She had wanted to scold the friend's child but hadn't, and the friend had simply ignored the incident. This sparked a story, and in this case the writer didn't want her name used because she was afraid her friend would somehow connect herself to the incident and be angry.

We're all a bit sheepish when it comes to talking about where we get our material. And a bit paranoid. The fact is, real life is the stuff of fiction, and real people are the stuff of life. You can't avoid writing about real people, nor should you be expected to. The problem is that fiction deals with moments of crisis and with secrets. It deals with exactly the types of things real people would rather not have known about them. So how do you get around ruining a friendship? First, I must stress that not everything you write about another person could conceivably upset the person you're writing about. Most often, people are flattered that you think there's something in their lives worth writing about, and that's as it should be. But in answer to the question about preserving a friendship: I don't know.

Some writers, like Madison Smartt Bell, check with their friends before writing about them, but I'd bet he's the exception. Most writers just write and hope their friends or family won't mind. Some writers don't even care. Faulkner said a writer is "completely amoral in that he will rob, borrow, beg, or steal from anybody and everybody to get the work done."

While not all of us are as callous as Faulkner, fiction writers are not necessarily great humanitarians. Writers sometimes unfortunately feel that their ambition justifies nearly anything. There's nothing wrong with ambition. It's necessary to some extent. But writers do not necessarily give a hoot how you feel about their writing your life story or stealing your ideas. If you don't want something from your life written about, don't tell a writer. Otherwise, you're asking for it. And, as I said before, you can't copyright experience. If you tell a writer about the time you almost drowned and he thinks it's a great story, don't blame him. Blame yourself for blabbing it to him.

So I'm giving you fair warning. My sense of ethics and fair play shift from story to story, depending on how much I like the idea. Sometimes (most times), I'm ready to relinquish or radically change a story idea so as not to embarrass someone, even if I know no one will ever know it's based on her except for the person in question. Other times, I'm willing to give up a friendship over a story. In fact, I have. I'm not happy about it. I'm not sure the story was worth the friendship. Probably not. But at the time, I was just as selfish as that woman who claimed she had a story "that needs to be told."

It's hard to be a writer and not alienate someone along the way. On this subject Steve Yarbrough says, "I suspect that one friendship was ruined by a story in my first book. The friend was someone who used to call me a lot, but he stopped calling about a year after the book came out. He lived on the East Coast, but the story is set in Mississippi. Still, I have the feeling that he saw himself in the story, and that may have ruined the friendship, and to tell you the truth, I feel terrible about it. I thought that I'd altered enough of the facts of that character's life that he would never see himself in the story. I don't think anyone but this particular individual would ever have matched up the character with him."

David Huddle puts it very well in his book *The Writing Habit,* when he writes:

> I believe the writer must do whatever he can to avoid . . . trouble, to keep from hurting feelings, but I believe finally he cannot allow the opinions and feelings of others to stop or to interfere with his writing. Maybe this is the ultimate selfishness, to say that one's own work is more important than the feelings of family and friends. Autobiographical writing will bring you to the point of having to make not just one but a number of hard choices between the life and the work.

I wish I could tell you that if you're careful and a nice person, you'll never run the risk of hurting someone's feelings in your writing. But, of course, I can't. If people see themselves in characters you never intended to base on them, how can you predict how they'll react to the characters you *have* intentionally based on them? If you're meant to write, your desire to write will eventually overcome all other considerations, and you'll write, regardless of what anyone else might think. Says Yarbrough, "A lot of things you have to do in business and in many fields, things that are sound business practices, sometimes hurt people. So this is sort of the conflict of being a fiction writer. If you're going to shut out all your experiences and those of people you know, you won't be left with much to write about."

There are undoubtedly instances in which you should probably back off, but I'll leave that to your own sense of ethics. When I was in graduate school at Iowa, a friend told me of a terribly traumatic occurrence that had happened to her in the not-too-distant past. Unfortunately, she told several people in the workshop about this traumatic event, confiding in them, getting it off her chest. Most of the people she told were trustworthy. I, for one, never even *thought* of writing about it. Written as fiction, it probably would come out seamy and melodramatic, a chunk of indigestible six o'clock news. But one of our number, a man who was widely considered one of the worst writers in the workshop, thought it would make a marvelous story and told her he was going to write about it. She asked him not to, and reluctantly, he agreed he wouldn't. But he lied. So my friend went to the same man Jenny Fields had complained to. He told her pretty much the same thing: there's nothing you can do about it, and you shouldn't worry because it probably won't be published anyway. Of course, the book was published, and much to the amazement of everyone in the workshop, the writer got the biggest advance for that book that any of us had ever seen. Our first lesson: Trash sells. This experience upset my friend, and I don't blame her, but I have mixed feelings. I think it was unethical of the writer to tell her that he wasn't writing the story based on her life when he, in fact, was. But I also think that no one outside the workshop ever knew this story was based on my friend. It caused her psychic damage, but you should know to whom you're telling your stories, whom you can trust.

Writers generally respect each other's turf, like wary gang members. But you can't always count on that, either. Remember, writers with Faulkner's attitude (if not his talent) abound, and many of them tend to believe their self-appointed genius justifies any cruelty. At Iowa, we used to make little copyright marks in the air with our fingers when we told an anecdote. If someone steals from me, I remember what Barry Hannah once told me when he was my teacher at Iowa: If you have only one idea as a writer, you can't be much of one.

I always run into people who have good stories to tell, but they're afraid what will happen if their crazy aunt or dying mother or best friend reads the piece. I don't know why they tell *me* their stories. I might not steal from your life, but I think it's bad luck to talk about your work before you write it. Your subconscious won't differentiate between an oral or a written telling of the story, and if you tell it to me, you might just lose interest in the subject. Your desire to tell your story might slip away. Usually, I tell people to write their stories about their crazy aunts or insane friends and worry about it later. If your story means something to you, if it's important to you, write it, transform it as much as possible, and decide what to do with it later. Sometimes we feel too much guilt about these things. If you write the story sensitively, if you care about the subject matter, maybe you'll turn out something beautiful, a celebration and questioning of life in all its complexity, something that you and all your crazy friends can identify with.

▼
Stories Appended

▼

Installations

by Robin Hemley

> *One of the first things the group did was to engage its film*
> *maker-associate Ken Kobland to shoot the beautiful surreal-*
> *istic movie that concludes the piece. In the film, Mr. Vawter,*
> *outfitted in Arabic-bohemian garb, prods the flesh of an elderly*
> *dead woman with his walking stick.*
>
> —Stephen Holden in the *New York Times*

Finding things. That's what I love most about my job. Over the last ten years, I've found money, rings, wallets, knives, a couple of guns, umbrellas, pens, watches. Weird little statues. I have three Buddhas sitting at home, and a big African ebony thing with an hourglass in the middle.

A lot of things you wouldn't believe. A piece or two of men's or women's underwear almost every week, sometimes fresh, more often soiled. At 2 A.M., a cigarette lighter made out of a hand grenade rolls around in the middle of the car. No one even notices, or if they do, they just think, "Someone's dumb idea of a joke," and go back to sleep or look out the window, daring the thing to explode. After all, these people ride the El every day. They've been around the block a few times. So have I. Some people would pull the emergency brake and yell, "Run for the hills!" But you can't faze *me.* Instead, I pick up the pineapple, see it's just a lighter, and stow it in my conductor's jacket. Now it sits on my coffee table at home.

Of course, I'm not supposed to keep anything I find. Regulations state you're supposed to turn everything in to Lost and Found.

Yeah, right.

At rush hour, a guy wearing polyester pants with a pattern that looks like chain mail steps into my car. A frilly straw hat covers his head, but I notice him because he's plastered with kooky buttons all over his chest like some Soviet field marshal. The buttons have sayings on them: "Are We Having

Fun Yet?" "Instant Asshole . . . Just Add Alcohol," "Wake Me Up, I'm A Lot Of Fun," "Trust Me, I'm A Doctor," "Dain Bramaged," "Hallucination Now In Progress. Please Stand By." "Ask Me If I Care," "I'm The Person Your Mother Warned You About," and "Born Again Pagan."

A little guy with half yellow and half black hair accompanies the button man. An army poncho hangs from his shoulder and a cigarette sits behind his ear. He looks faithful but bored, like the bodyguard of a low-level dignitary, and carries a book with a strange title, *Utopia TV Store*.

"It took me thirty-five years to overcome my disease," the button man tells me, "but I did it."

"That's good," I say. No big surprise that he wants to talk to me. I come from a family of authority figures. My uncle Jerry's a priest and you can see my brother Ted on billboards all over the 'burbs. He's the model for Captain Safety Belt, wearing a hat like mine and two seat belts criss-crossed like bandoliers on his chest. I've dealt with plenty of people like the button man, people who latch onto the conductor because he's the Cardinal Bernardin of the rush-hour chaos. They're always holding forth to me about something or other. The camera that follows them around their apartment. Or how they saw the Holy Ghost pissing on the station escalators.

"I learned how to make buttons all by myself," says the man. "No one showed me how."

"That's nice," I say.

I lean into the intercom and announce, "No smoking, littering, or radio playing allowed. Clark and Division will be next. Clark and Division." I run those words together, and emphasize the "Vision" so it becomes ClarkandiVISION, like I'm announcing some spectacular new movie technique. Filmed in Technicolor, Panavision, and introducing . . . ClarkandiVISION. What does it look like? Narrow and dark. The way things look when you're speeding through a tunnel. A couple of loons get on, you say, "Roll 'em." The doors close, the loons leave, you say, "Cut, that's a wrap."

The commuters stand in their defense stances, like people in a kung fu movie waiting for the hero to unleash his awesome power. They eye the button man warily while holding onto the seats and bars to keep from falling.

I'm sure in the next ten minutes I'll learn all about the button man's life, how he's overcome his disease and found sanctuary in the world of buttons.

"I'm a writer," the button man tells me. "I'm writing a novel right now about my experience, and I've also got a hundred poems about my disease. My novel's going to be called, *In It To Win*. That's because I stayed in it for thirty-five years and now I'm winning."

"That's nice," I say. The guy looks his age, which is remarkable for a loon. Most of them look about twice their actual age. Yesterday, a guy told me the Shriners had vowed to make an example of him before his twenty-first birthday. (I've dealt with other people who think The Mooses, The Elks, or The Lions Club are trying to hunt them down. I wonder if they freak out every time they see a donation box by a cash register.) The kid looked to be late thirties, but then I saw he was still a teenager like he said, that the lines in his face were from lack of sleep, not age.

I'm younger than the button man, but I look almost forty. My hairline is eroding faster than the beach in front of some North Shore condo. My mustache is turning grey. My voice is losing its authority, becoming thinner. And my toenails have curled and yellowed like old people's. A couple of weeks ago, I found something on my big toe, and two of my friends told me it was a bunion. A bunion! I didn't think the word even entered your vocabulary until you were eighty. Presidents aren't the only ones who age in office. Conductors, too.

As we make the brake-screeching turn to Clark and Division, the button man's yellow-and-black-haired friend drops his book at my feet. I wait for him to retrieve it, but he acts like it's just some litter he's not going to bother with.

"A movie company is going to interview me tomorrow," the button man says. "They want to do a video on me. In a little while the *Sun-Times* is going to do a story about me and my disease. Maybe not today or tomorrow, but soon. I'm that confident. I'm hot. Isn't that right, Gus?" and he nudges his buddy. "The *Sun-Times* is going to do a story on me."

"That's right," says Gus.

"He always agrees with me," says the button man and laughs.

We unload some people at Clark and Division and head off.

"It took thirty-five years out of my life."

"That's too bad," I say.

The button man starts making funny noises. "Coo Coo Coodle Coo," he sings.

After a few choruses, the button man stops abruptly, looks out the window, and shouts, "We're talking schizophrenia here." The commuters near him scoot away and look down their chests.

"This wasn't a good idea to take the El," the button man tells his friend. "Remind me never to take it again. It's too claustrophobic. It's counterproductive and you know how I feel about things that are counterproductive."

"That's right," says his friend.

"Let's get some more buttons, Gus," the button man tells his friend. "I feel like some more buttons. How 'bout you, Gus?"

"Whatever you say," says Gus, and they both get off the car at Fullerton.

I'm a little sorry to see them go. People like them make the job interesting. I try my best to sympathize. You have to make these people feel appreciated. They lead rough lives, and besides, they're the CTA's most frequent riders.

We start up again. Gus has left his book behind. Each page has a little paragraph with titles like, "Kill Yourself with an Objet d'Art" and "A Vegetable Emergency." I try figuring out a few paragraphs, but they don't make any sense. I'll turn it in to the Lost and Found.

Then, at Belmont, a girl about twenty flings herself at me and yells, "A prose poem fan. A kindred spirit."

At first, I'm thinking, "Great, another live one." She starts jabbering about the book in my hand. I'm about to tell her I just found it on the floor, but then I figure there's no harm in letting her talk. She's a runt: skinny with no hips and nubby breasts. Her hair's black, short, and tufted like a boy's. But she's quick to smile and laugh, and she locks her eyes on me. A uniform freak, I figure.

Her name is Ivy, and she's from a small town about ten miles south of Beloit, Wisconsin. "Cody, Illinois," she says. "The Beefalo capital of the Midwest." She's twenty-one, a student at the Art Institute, where she's studying performance art.

"You mean like musicals?"

She laughs and says, "I mean like the Wooster Group, or Michael Meyers or Ethel Eichelberger or David Cale or John Kelly—"

"Never heard of them," I say and get up to announce the next station and open the doors.

When I return, she says, "Then you've probably heard of—" She pauses, puts a hand to her chest, and leans forward. "Laurie Anderson." She says this as though she's really saying, "Hemorrhoids." "Personally," she continues, "I'd rather see *Beatlemania* or a strobe light flickering for forty-eight hours."

If you know what she's talking about, you've got me beat. But I pretend to understand her anyway, just like I did with the button man.

Ivy leans forward again. "Don't you think the El would be an ingenious place for an installation?"

"Yeah, right," I say, "but not until they fix the air conditioners."

We sit across from each other. Ivy huddles close to me, her eyes bright, and says, "I can be your accomplice."

"Sounds great," I say.

She tells me one weird story after another. A man and a woman are tied together by a three-foot rope for a year. By choice. They have to follow each other everywhere. Even to the john. And they hardly knew each other before they tied the knot, so to speak. Of course, I know people who get into that sort of thing. Bondage. But Ivy shakes her head and says, "You're completely wrong and absolutely right. It's bondage of a different sort. They're making a statement about the bondage of male/female role-playing. And on the positive side, they're saying that the male and female parts of everyone are inextricably bound. The more we try to escape from the Other, the closer he/she follows."

Yeah, right.

When my shift is up, Ivy gets off with me at my stop. She seems completely oblivious to the fact that we've gotten off the train. She just keeps walking beside me and talking. Asking questions. Most of them she answers herself. I haven't figured her game yet, but I don't mind her tagging along.

I live in Wrigleyville, on Cornelia, a block from the Friendly Confines. That's my favorite neighborhood in the city. The best thing is summer. Sometimes I walk out on my back porch, and hear the national anthem shimmering from the park. You can't help but feel you're in a dream when you're doing something really ordinary, like taking a load of laundry down to the laundry room, and all of a sudden there's "The Star-Spangled Banner." Not to mention when you're sitting on the pot and a cheer of thirty thousand people comes out of nowhere. It makes you tingle. You feel like you're a part of something. Sometimes, when I hear the anthem or a cheer I drop whatever I'm doing, head over to Wrigley Field, and see if the scalpers have an extra bleacher ticket. Then I zone out in the right-field bleachers for the rest of the day, drinking Old Style, getting a red nose from the sun, and yelling and screaming at the left-field bleachers, "Left field sucks! Left field sucks!" One day, the Mets are in town, and Strawberry rocks one right to me. Naturally, I want to make this part of my memorabilia collection, but no way with the animals around me. "Throw it back! Throw it back!" they chant, and when I hesitate, someone sloshes beer on me. So I plop the ball back on the field, and Dawson picks it up and tosses it to the side. Everyone around me cheers and the guy next to me gives me a nudge and belches. At that moment I feel like Strawberry's homer isn't worth diddly-squat.

At my apartment, Ivy won't stay in one spot for more than five seconds. The place is a sty, but she insists on checking out every room.

"You looking for something?" I say. "You want something to drink? I've got Cuervo Gold and Old Style."

"I don't drink alcohol," she says, momentarily appearing in my bedroom door before crossing to the bathroom.

"Then all's I got is Tahitian Treat," I say, peering at the plastic liter bottle in my fridge. The only other thing to eat or drink is a two-foot-long summer sausage from Hickory Farms that my mom bought me for my birthday. All the way in the back is my jar for Cubs tickets. I keep them there so that if the apartment burns up, it won't be a total loss. Right now, I have a ticket in the jar for Cubs Umbrella Day. It's a Dodgers game with Valenzuela pitching, but half of the reason I'm going is the free umbrella. I already have a Cubs AM/FM radio from Radio Day, a Cubs cooler from Cooler Day, and a Cubs briefcase from Briefcase Day.

"Tahitian Treat sounds luscious," she says.

I bring the drinks into the living room and start flipping through my records for something to play.

"What kind of music do you like?"

"You have any Sinatra?" she says.

"Does the Pope shit in the woods?"

I put on the album with "Witchcraft."

Ivy emerges from the bathroom and says, "I grew up with Sinatra," and walks to the couch and stands on top of it. She steps behind me to the end of the couch. I take a sip of Old Style. Ivy plops down and picks up her glass of red pop. She holds this out in front of her and says, "I never would have guessed Tahitian Treat looked like this. I've never seen anything so red, have you? Where do you think they get it from? Do you think there's a red-dye mine in Tahiti? I bet the native miners have to wear dark goggles in the Treat mines."

"I guess so." I take another sip of Old Style.

"You've got a great view from your bathroom," she says.

"It's just the wall of the next building."

"You ever go to Exit or the Cubby Bear?" she says.

"No."

"You know, Vacant Yellow's at the Cubby Bear on Saturday. Vacant Yellow's a group of ex-cabbies from Boston. I saw an interview with them in the *Face* this month. Can you believe Metro advertises in the *Face*? I don't go there often. Too much techno-funk. But sometimes if you just want to bop around, it's all right. If you're tired of staring into the abyss. I was in there last weekend with a whole crowd from London. They must have seen the ad in the *Face*."

Ivy takes a sip of her Tahitian Treat, and I nod. I imagine Ivy and the London crowd bopping around in the abyss.

She puts down her glass and sits back on the couch with me.

"You have an eclectic soul, don't you?" she says. "And old."

I've just finished my shift. I'm tired. I still have my uniform on. "Old King Cole was a merry old soul and a merry old soul was he," I manage.

Apparently, that's the wrong thing. Ivy slides away and gets up from the couch. She makes a slow circuit of the room. I pick up my grenade lighter from the coffee table and toss it from one hand to another for a while. Ivy ends up by my mantel and looks at me as though she's going to start a speech. I just watch her and finish my beer.

Then she picks up one of my Cuervo Gold bottles and turns it over. I have about a hundred and eighty empty Cuervo bottles around the house, fifty of them on my mantel. "What's this?" she says. "It says, 'Cicero. Sally and Mary Siriani, July 19, 1987.'"

"My Cuervo collection. It's something I started doing about five years back. Every time I finish one, I put the date I drank the bottle, and who I shared it with."

She picks up another one and reads, "Sally and Mary Siriani. Wrigleyville. July 20, 1987."

"The Sirianis and me go all the way back to kindergarten."

She picks up another one and reads, "Sally and Mary. In the gutter. July 21, 1987."

Ivy puts the bottle down, wanders back to the couch, and sits down next to me again. She sits with her hands crossed on her lap and her head tilted like a tourist listening to directions.

"Tell me about them," she says.

"There's not much to tell," I say. "They're sort of the party type. Sort of wild."

"Are you sort of wild?" Ivy says.

I half shrug. "Yeah, sort of sort of," I say. "Let me tell you how I found that hand-grenade lighter. It's quite a story."

Ivy grabs my hand-grenade lighter. She knocks over the glass of Tahitian Treat. Crazily, she whips the lighter across the room.

"Duck!" she yells and buries herself in my lap.

The grenade slashes through the middle of my Cuervo collection, bounces off the mantel, and thuds twice. Two of the bottles shatter right off, glass spraying everywhere. Five others topple off the mantel, three bursting on the hardwood floor. Frank coughs into a new song. The two unbroken bottles roll toward me, one stopping against a leg of the coffee table.

Ivy stays in my lap, hands over her head.

Slowly, she raises her head and opens her eyes. She looks around the room like someone emerging from a bomb shelter.

"Sort of sort of," she says.

Sometimes I believe that people aren't nearly as bizarre as they let on. I imagine a date with the button man.

I reach for my can of Old Style on the coffee table and tilt it to my mouth. Empty. One warm drop, as refreshing as sweat, trickles onto my tongue.

I'm not easy to faze, but I don't expect this kind of behavior from a girl I invite over. Not that I invited her over.

I feel like I've just spent an afternoon in the bleachers. The way you get when you've been drinking beer in the sun for three hours. Bleached out. Completely in-between. Up for anything. That's how I feel right now, watching Tahitian Treat drip down the leg of the coffee table and onto an empty Cuervo bottle.

I'm not sure exactly how this happens, but we wind up slow-dancing in the middle of the living room, which is a mess. We dance around the debris.

In bed, her breath catches when I touch her, so I take my hand away. Ivy goes to sleep right off, but I lie there for a couple of hours before stammering into a rush-hour dream. Too many people stand in the small space in between the cars, and I can't get near enough to latch the safety chains. One by one, they fall off as we round the corners.

The next day, Ivy starts bringing stuff into the apartment. She says she's been staying in Wicker Park with some junkie friends of Phil, her ex-boyfriend. A pan of beef stroganoff she made disappeared and turned up a week later under a pile of clothes in one of her roommates' closets. And Phil stabbed her with a fork. She rolls up a sleeve and shows me four red marks, closely spaced. "Phil's a tag artist," she tells me. "A good one, too. But he's awfully volatile. Besides, the landlord showed up today with a cop, and the two of them started putting our furniture on the front steps. I asked Gem what was going on. 'What happened to the rent money I gave you?' I said. 'I don't know,' she said. 'I been paying him every month. Maybe he don't remember.' I figured I could stay with you a couple of days."

Within thirty-six hours of our meeting, Ivy's completely installed herself in my apartment. I'm just a bystander. I don't say yes and I don't say no. But I'm curious.

We pass through a white curtain into this scene: a darkened room with a naked man and woman, thirtyish, lying like two sticks of old butter in the middle of the room. Either they're dead or mannequins. The music in the room sounds like the part in *The Wizard of Oz* where Dorothy and her boyfriends are looking at the witch's castle, and the soldiers march around singing: "O-li-eyohhh-oh."

Ivy takes my hand and we approach the couple on the floor. A dozen other people saunter around as though nothing special's going on. We can't get any closer than five feet. The couple on the floor are surrounded by hundreds of apples in the shape of a cross. A ragged bat hangs above them, its ribbed wings stretching six feet. A sideways neon eight sways between the wings and glows pale blue.

This is what Ivy calls an installation. This is what I call a fun house.

Up close, I see their chests moving slightly, a small tremor from one of the woman's fingers touching the man's hand, a flickering eyelid. I study them and wonder if I've ever seen them on the El. I wonder if the woman's parents know this is what she does for a living.

"The man looks a little like the button man without his buttons."

Candles burn on their chests. Luckily the candles are in jars, or the wax would be excruciating. Still, the heat must get to them. Not that I can tell. They're not exactly your liveliest couple. I can imagine showing up at Angel's Shortstop, my neighborhood bar, with them stiff as corpses on the bar stools, the candles still stuck on their chests. Angel would serve them up a couple of Old Styles, and squint at me and say, "They friends of yours?"

Yeah, they're installations.

We take the El back to Belmont and walk over to Clark Street. Everything seems strange tonight: a man waiting in the window of a tattoo parlor, the moan coming out of a storefront church.

Ivy asks me what I think about the installations. I don't know. I haven't thought about it. What are you supposed to think about a naked man and woman with candles on their chests?

"Everything," she says. "Adam and Eve lying in suspended animation beneath death and infinity. Christ figures surrounded by the forbidden fruit."

Yeah, well, I guess.

We turn the corner of Clark and Belmont, and two kids, one black and one white, not more than nine years old, slam into us as they tear through the parking lot of Dunkin' Donuts.

"Hey, watch where you're going," I say, touching the white one lightly on the shoulder.

"You watch where you're going, you fag," the kid tells me.

The black kid has a pizza box in his hands. He smiles and says, "You want some pizza?"

"Yeah, you want some pizza?" says the white kid.

The black kid opens up the box. Inside is a squirrel, its head smashed, its legs stretched out, its belly split open. At least a hundred cars have run over it. As flat as a pizza. A circle of dried tomato paste surrounds the carcass.

Before I can react, the kids run off shouting and laughing. They block one pedestrian after another yelling, "Hey, you want some pizza? Free pizza."

Ivy picks up a soft-drink cup from the sidewalk and throws it after them. The cup, plastic lid and straw still attached, falls to the ground three feet away.

"You brats," she screams. "Come back here."

Ivy takes off. The white kid trips. She chases the other one. I can't make out much through the distance and pedestrians. A few minutes later, she comes smiling back with the pizza box in her hands, the lid closed.

"What do you want *that* for?" I say.

"Stealing is the most sincere form of flattery," she says. "Picasso did it. Every great artist does it."

"Throw it away."

"Are you kidding?"

"Throw it away."

"Don't give me orders. I had to fight them for it."

I don't say a word. I'm tired of her. I was curious before, but now I'm just tired. I head for Angel's Shortstop and Ivy tags along. I figure it's Ivy's turn to feel out-of-place. Not many out-of-place people ever wander into Angel's. If they do, they wander back out again in a hurry. The crowd at Angel's is as tight as a VFW post.

Ignoring Ivy, I sit down on a stool at the bar. There isn't one for her, so she stands in between my stool and the next guy's, and places her pizza box on the counter. Angel gives her a look. Then she looks at me. I order a couple shots of Cuervo with Old Style chasers.

"I'll have to tap a new keg," says Angel. "How 'bout something else in the meantime?"

"How 'bout a mug of beefalo swill?" I say. "Come on, Angel. I'm talking brand loyalty."

"I'll go tap a new keg," she says. Angel is about sixty years old and has a white bubble hair-do. She comes to Chicago via the coal mines of Kentucky, and her husband's long-gone with black lung. Angel's jukebox has only the thickest country-and-western songs, with three exceptions: "A Cub Fan's Dying Prayer," Sinatra's version of "Chicago," and "Angel of the Morning." She's always pumping quarters painted with red fingernail polish into the jukebox and pushing those three tunes. I can't count the number of times I've come into the Shortstop and heard her belting, "Just call me angel of the morning, baby. Just one more kiss before you leave me, angel." She thinks of the Shortstop as a family establishment, even though I'd fall off my stool if I ever saw a family walk through the door. Maybe a family of cockroaches or sewer-bred alligators. Definitely not a family of mammals.

When Angel returns with the Old Styles, Ivy pushes hers away and says, "I don't drink alcohol."

"Angel, this is Ivy," I say. "She comes from Cody, Illinois, the beefalo capital of the Midwest. It's ten miles south of Beloit."

"Blech!" says Ivy.

"What?"

"Beloit. I grew up with the name. It sounds like a quarter being dropped in a toilet. Beloit . . . Besides, I live in Chicago now."

"Yeah, she's a performance artist," I tell Angel.

"Pleased to meet you," she says.

"You want some pizza?" Ivy says.

"No, she doesn't want any pizza," I say, and put my hand on the lid.

"Domino's?" Angel says.

"It's not pizza," I say. "It's a squirrel."

"A squirrel."

"Yeah, a dead one."

"Pepperoni," Ivy says. "You want to see it, Angel?"

"Sure, why not?"

"No, you don't want to see it," I say. My hand is still on the lid.

Ivy looks sideways and gives me a half smile, a dare. Her look says "What's the big deal?" She's right. After all, Angel's not my mother.

With my job and all, I'm not easy to faze, but Ivy definitely fazes me. Not only her actions, but the way she dresses. An orange scarf as big as window drapes. Black fishnet stockings and metallic silver lipstick. Usually my life is pretty dull, but around Ivy, I feel the way I do when I'm sitting on the pot and I hear the fans cheer in Wrigley Field.

"You ever had squirrel?" says Angel. "Tastes just like chicken. Of course, there ain't as much meat on a squirrel."

"Do you always believe what you see, Angel?" Ivy says.

"Almost never," says Angel, leaning toward her, a look of concentration on her face. "A fella come in here the other day selling key chains. He had a metal man and a metal woman on the key chain, and when he wiggled a lever they started doing things. He said he had a whole trunkful in his car, and did I want to sell some on a card behind the counter? I said, 'Look around, this is a family place.' He said, 'You'd be surprised. People just love them. I've seen grandmas and young girls go crazy over them.' 'Yeah, well this is a gay bar, buddy,' I said. 'That's fine,' he said. 'I can take off the woman and put on another man. I already did that with one gay establishment. I'll put on dogs. I'll put on a man and a horse. Even two Japanese girls and a rhinoceros if that's what you want. Whatever turns you on.' Some people just want to shock you. I could have called the cops, but I ignored him. Eventually, he just slithered back under his rock."

"You want some pizza?" Ivy says.

"Yeah, why not?" says Angel.

I take my hand off the lid and wait for Ivy to open up the box, but she doesn't move. What's she waiting for? I wonder if I'm going nuts. If Ivy's brainwashing me. I've known her two days, and suddenly I want to show Angel the dead squirrel in the pizza box.

"One object can have many functions," Ivy says. "Consider this pizza box. For you and me, it signifies food. For Rocky the squirrel, it's his final resting place. When you put the two together, it's repulsive. Why? Because food and death are opposites, right? No, not at all. Food and death go hand in hand, but our escapist society allows us to blithely ignore that fact. Hold the mayo, hold the lettuce, special orders don't upset us. Right, Angel? Next time you go to an open-casket funeral, don't be surprised if you see a pizza with the works lying there."

I have a strange feeling in my mouth. My tongue seems to be getting bigger. I've gone through my whole life barely noticing my tongue, and now, all of a sudden, it seems humongous. I can't figure out where to place it. I try to settle it down by my cheek. I stick it between my teeth.

Angel tucks her chin into her neck.

My tongue has swollen to the size of a blimp.

Still, I manage to say to Angel, "Ya wa thom peetha?"

"Sure, why not?" she says.

I open up the box and Angel shrinks back.

She gives me a look and I can already tell that she's canceled me out as a regular. Now, I'm just another bar story: "You remember Rick? He came in here with a squirrel in a pizza box. Yeah, it was dead."

Ivy shows up at work with me the next day. All she does is read poetry between stops, take notes, and draw sketches of the commuters. She's sort of nuts, but I like the way she looks at things. To her, everything's art. You can spit on the sidewalk and that's art. The commuters at rush hour are art, too. The way they crane their heads over the platform to see the train coming. They bob out as far as they can without sprawling onto the tracks. I've seen this sight every day for ten years, but now Ivy tells me it's beautiful. Up and down the line, they wait, sticking their necks out. Ivy says they look like a bunch of pigeons jostling for breadcrumbs. All I see are some cranky people ready to be home.

When the doors open, they cram onto the car. At Washington, a couple more shove their way inside. At the next stop, Grand Ave., no one else can possibly fit, but a few try anyway, and the doors won't close. The button man and his friend are trying to jam on. He looks like he's added some buttons. Now they cover not only his chest, but his back, too. Over the intercom I say, "Clear the doors on car number five. Get in or get out and wait for the next train." Of course, no one except me has any idea which car's number five. But the button man and his friend are the ones who get off. As the doors close, I read some of his new buttons: "I Drink To Make Other People More Interesting," "No One Is Ugly After 2 A.M.," "It's Been Monday All Week," "Welcome To The Zoo," "The More People I Meet, The More I Like My Dog," "Beam Me Up Scotty . . . There Are No Virgins Left," "Only Visiting This Planet," "Art May Imitate Life, But Life Imitates Television," and "Time Flies When You Don't Know What You're Doing."

Ivy yells in my ear. "Now there's an artist! A walking circus."

"Yeah, a walking circus," I say, and laugh. "Las Vegas on a stick."

"That's perfect," she says, giving me a small hug. She puts what I just said into a notebook, writing in the tiniest print I've ever seen.

According to Ivy, my apartment is art, too. Or, at least she'd like it to be. I'm not so sure, but I give her the run of the place anyway. I figure it can use some straightening, but Ivy goes a little overboard. She spends one whole weekend rummaging through the apartment, throwing out some things and rearranging others. Half of my memorabilia collection gets the boot. I hate getting rid of this stuff.

"What about these?" I say, showing her my three Buddha statues that I found on the El. She points to the largest of the Buddhas and says, "That's a keeper." She's sitting in the middle of the living-room floor sorting through my memorabilia. In the throwaway pile is my African ebony hourglass, my Cubs briefcase, my AM/FM radio, and my Cubs cooler.

"I kind of think this is artistic, don't you?" I say, picking up my Cubs briefcase.

"It's up to you," she says. "I'm just making suggestions."

She looks so disappointed.

Later, I put the throwaway pile in a box and set it downstairs by the trash bin with a sign that reads, "Free."

I still haven't got the hang of all this.

Ivy starts taking me to different installations. At one gallery a man toasts dozens of Pop Tarts while reading the Constitution. At another, a guy sits in the fetal position inside a three-foot-tall box. Outside is a video screen that shows him sitting there. After that, a woman in black pajamas lectures on nuclear war while pelting us with eggs. Then there's the Mystery Installation. No one knows where it is, who's the artist, or what's supposed to happen. Only the date. The flyer says simply "Coming April 17."

One night, we're sitting in the living room taking target practice at my Cuervo collection with my hand-grenade lighter. I've given up drinking, and now we shatter a few bottles every night before turning in. I'm down to about a hundred.

The phone rings and I answer. "Is Ivy there?" a man's voice says hesitantly.

I point to Ivy, and she points to herself. "Who is it?" Ivy says. In the five weeks that Ivy's been with me, no one's called her. She doesn't seem to have any friends. Only acquaintances. People in galleries who don't even seem to know her name, hug her, and ask, "Where have you been hiding?" and move on before she has a chance to answer. Around most people Ivy acts stiff and angry, like she expects to be insulted. Only around me does she loosen up, though I'm not sure why. Sometimes I think we're pretty compatible, but sometimes I think she just needs a place to stay.

"Can I tell her who's calling?" I say to the man.

"Tell Ivy it's her parents," says the man. "We'd like to speak with her."

"Ivy, it's your parents."

"I have nothing to say to them," she says.

"Ivy, it's your parents," I repeat. "I can't tell them that."

Ivy shrugs. "Tell them I've turned into a dragonfly. When they learn to speak dragonfly I'll talk with them."

"We'd just like to speak with her, that's all," says her father. "Is she all right?"

"Yes, yes," I say. "She's fine." I put the receiver to my chest and say, "Ivy, please. Speak with your folks. You can't not speak with your folks."

"Okay," she yells and leaps up from the couch. She rips the phone away from me and puts it to her ear. "Okay," she says to the phone.

After that she doesn't say anything for a minute.

"Okay, I won't hang up," she says finally.

She stands there holding the phone about six inches from her ear, like a snake dancer with a coiled rattler.

As we're lying in bed that night, Ivy says, "I hope you're not too happy. I hope you're not enjoying yourself too much."

"Not in the least," I tell her. "I'm in agony. Don't touch me there. It's too agonizing."

Ivy takes her hand away.

"I was just kidding," I say. "I like a little agony from time to time."

One thing about this girl. She takes everything literally.

"The secret is staying off-balance," she says. "Whenever I start seeing someone, I immediately think of how we're going to break up. Then I'm happy. If I imagine the worst, then I can relax and enjoy myself."

"Here," I say, taking her hand. "Put your hand back there. I was just kidding."

"My parents think that it's wrong to cut yourself off from the people you've grown close to," she says, looking up at the ceiling and absentmind-edly stroking me. "To me, it's just moving on, shedding skin."

"Yes, that's it," I say. "Yes. There. That feels good. No, I mean bad. It's right in between."

I start to give Ivy a hand with her installations. The first one's small, un-planned, but not quite spur-of-the-moment. We head for the Loop on a warm Sunday afternoon with a Lady Remington razor. I shave Ivy's head on the steps of the Art Institute. Then she shaves my head. This is one of the parts I hadn't planned. At first I'm thinking, "Wait a second," but then I see the surprised faces of the spectators: commuters every one of them. *I'm* doing something crazy now. Let someone else be the authority figure this time.

We gather our hair and arrange it around the head of one of the stone lions in front of the museum. Our goal is to transform the lion into Moe of the Stooges, but it's harder to get loose hair to stay in place than you might think. The bangs are the most difficult. Unfortunately, before we can get the head in shape, the wind scatters our clippings.

We've got a pretty good-sized crowd around us, maybe twenty people. A puppeteer, with not nearly as many onlookers, stands jealously on the steps by the other stone lion. We ignore him as he goes through his routine with his marionettes. He swivels them around, and the two puppets point and jeer at us. They're not the only ones. The crowd is on the ugly side. "There are better ways to get attention," one marionette yells. "Why do you do such disgusting things?" the other says. Most people just walk by without look-ing at us. Ivy says they're the ones who worry her the most, the people who don't notice.

———————

Sometimes Ivy starts shivering when it's not even cold. When I touch her, she says, "You're always touching. I feel like bruised fruit. So I stop touch-ing and she says, "You're so distant. You're the worst lover I've ever had. I've been having a lot of dreams about women lately." I try touching her again, but she's restless.

"What's going to make you happy?" I say. "Sacrificing a beefalo? A vat of putrefying squirrels?"

She's alert again and smiling. I meant the question as an insult, but she looks like she expected it.

"Commuting at the speed of art," she says like this is the only possible answer.

It's hard to tell the audience from the passengers tonight. They're all audi-ence, I guess. I'm off-duty, but I'm wearing my conductor's uniform. I go up to the real conductor, a guy named Fred, and explain what we're doing. He just twists his mouth and stares at me. I ask him what his problem is, and he says, "What happened to your hair? Didn't you used to have hair?"

"I shaved it for an installation," I tell him.

He twists his mouth again.

"Never mind," I say. "Here's twenty bucks. Just leave us alone for half an hour, okay?"

"Okay," he says. "But I still got to know what it is. I could lose my job. So could you."

"It's just art," I tell him. "Nothing to worry about."

"Well, okay then," and he walks off with the twenty I've handed him.

The train's moving steady at about 30 mph. I keep my hand on the back of one of the seats as we rock back and forth. We round a corner and sparks shoot up from our wheels.

I get on the intercom and announce, "Hello, you miserable commuters. This is Jason, your conductor from hell. No smoking, littering, or radio playing allowed."

About twenty of the passengers smile at me. The other ten keep their eyes in front of them as though they're soldiers in foxholes waiting for an assault. Good, I've got their attention. Now I can tell who the audience is and who the real commuters are. One young child balances in the middle of the aisle. "Carlos, *ven aca!*" his mother yells from three seats back. She's got four other children gathered in two seats around her. She's about seven months pregnant and wears a blue T-shirt with dark smears on it. The T-shirt has a picture of a bulldog and reads, "YALE."

Carlos doesn't hear his mother or doesn't want to obey. He bends down and picks up something invisible from the floor. Then he rubs it while squatting and rocking to the rhythm of the train.

"Carlos!" the woman yells again and darts out into the aisle and snatches the kid. She dangles him by an arm and swats him loudly.

Then she gives me a look like I was the one who made Carlos disobey. Like I want Carlos to be a juvenile delinquent. Like I was the one who just smacked him.

A little late, Ivy enters the car from the door at the other end. She looks as pregnant as the woman with the Yale T-shirt. She's carrying two shopping bags, and she wears a platinum blond wig with a huge patch torn out of the scalp. Ivy closes the door behind her and starts waddling down the center aisle. Most of the passengers turn around and watch.

When she's halfway up the aisle, she squirms in her dress and moans. She reaches into one of her bags, takes out a turkey baster, and squirts it at the person sitting in the seat nearest her. A stream of milk trickles onto the man's crotch. The man looks at her and barks twice. Most likely he's one of the people she invited to the installation, but it's hard to tell. I've seen regular passengers bark before.

"Excuse me, miss," I yell down the aisle. "No smoking, littering, or radio playing allowed. No turkey basting."

The woman in the Yale T-shirt cranes her neck into the aisle and looks at Ivy. Then she puts her arms around her two closest children.

Ivy sticks her turkey baster back into her shopping bag and keeps walking up the aisle.

After she's gone about five feet, she moans again and starts rubbing her pregnant-looking belly. "Oh my," she yells. "I feel it! I think I feel it!"

She takes another step and something slips between her legs and plops with a wet slap onto the floor.

Ivy steps back and reveals a slab of uncooked liver lying at her feet. Quickly, she snatches it up. "Get back here, you little rascal. You ain't incubated long enough yet." She stuffs the slab of liver back into her dress.

"Miss," I yell, "No smoking, littering, radio playing, turkey basting, or liver deliveries allowed."

The train approaches the station. As it slows down, the woman in the Yale T-shirt gathers her children around her. She pushes the five of them in front of her, her arms sweeping them along, her eyes fixed on Ivy.

Ivy stands in her way. The woman, frantically trying to get around her as the train stops, knocks into Ivy, who loses her balance momentarily and staggers backwards as the train lurches to a standstill.

With a sucking sound, the rest of Ivy's fake pregnancy slithers out of her dress. The whole mess slops on the floor. Chicken gizzards and bloody cow and pig entrails. Ivy looks as surprised as anyone because this was supposed to happen gradually.

The doors open, but the woman stands there a moment looking straight at Ivy and spits, *"Puta!"*

Then she herds her children out the doors. About five other people push through the doors with her. Undaunted, Ivy chases them off the train by squirting them in the back with her turkey baster.

Fred, in the next car, closes the doors and we start up again.

I hear someone pounding on the doors. The woman in the T-shirt raps with her knuckles, her face twisted, her mouth open, her eyes pleading.

"What is it?" I say.

We gather speed, and she falls away from the door like someone being hooked off a stage. As she crumples, I hear her scream. "Carlos!" she yells.

I turn around and see Carlos kneeling, playing with the fallen gizzards. He looks up and displays his hands to me as though I'm his father and he's just washed up for dinner. He's covered with chicken and beef blood. The boy puts his fingers in his mouth and giggles.

Ivy thinks it's funny and stupid that someone would forget her own kid on the train. Ivy's friends think it's part of the installation. I take a minute to react, but then I pull the emergency cord. The brakes echo the mother's scream. I run to get Fred and tell him to head back. He starts yelling and says he's going to report me, that I'm definitely going to lose my job.

After we reunite Carlos with his mother, Ivy and her friends traipse off to Angel's Shortstop for after-installation drinks. "You'll love this place," Ivy tells her friends. Poor Angel.

I'm left alone on the platform with the woman and her kids. The woman yells while her kids look up at me in awe. I listen even though I can't under-stand a word she's saying. I just stand there while she yells. She keeps this up for longer than is possible for one person to yell at another. The train leaves. Ten minutes later another train pulls into the station. She keeps yelling. But I stand here and take it. Finally, she herds her kids away and leaves me.

I stand alone on the platform at Addison for a while, facing Wrigley Field. I start pacing back and forth. I walk to the edge of the platform, where it narrows into a point and signs warn of the danger of electrocuting yourself. My life is ruined. In an alley below me a black dog trots between the garbage cans. Past the alley and before Wrigley Field, there's a large parking lot. A couple of apartment buildings stand on either side. A poster on one of the buildings shows Harry Caray with his butterball head, thick glasses, and uncontained joy, leaping through space. His arm is raised as though he's about to lead the crowd at Wrigley Field during the seventh-inning stretch: "Okay now, let's hear it! Take me out to the ballgame!" Bold letters below him pronounce: "CUB FAN, BUD MAN"

A boy about ten, who's drunk or pretending to be, staggers down

Sheffield, grabbing a lamp post and twirling around. He does a strange limbery Watusi down the sidewalk. No one else is around and he doesn't know I'm watching. Who does he think he's doing this dance for?

"Hey! You!" I yell, but he doesn't hear, or pretends not to.

In a minute he's turned the corner and is gone.

A cannon burst, a sonic boom. Then the sound of thousands of wind chimes buffeted in a typhoon.

Glass is flying all over the parking lot from the building with the Harry Caray poster. It takes me a second to realize what's going on, but then I see the windows of the building have been blown out. A gas explosion, a bomb factory, a huge shotgun blast. Who knows?

A group of teenagers dashes out of the building and into the lot.

Someone runs from the building on the other side of the lot and yells, "Hey, is everything cool? Is everything cool?"

A man clambers out of a window by Harry Caray's knee. He swims, two quick overhead strokes before he hits the ground. Two kids climb over the fence at the back of the building. All over the parking lot, people are running around yelling, "What happened? Is everything cool?"

I hear a laugh, or maybe it's a cry. It comes from the building, and someone's yelling, "Did you call them? Are they coming?"

I feel so clear-headed as they run around. I look out toward the lakefront with its apartment complexes all lit up, and what am I thinking about? Water. A drop of it falling on the third rail. Worlds within worlds sizzling within that drop. A black dog trotting between cans, living off garbage. A drunken boy doing a strange Watusi. Harry Caray leaping joyfully through the abyss. This clear agony I'm feeling. I'm thinking about Ivy touching me, the rash she's given me, the skin I've shed. I feel like a tunnel with wind rushing through it. I feel like an underground test, a needle pointing to a zone past measurement.

I turn around again and lean over the railing of the El. Below me stands a cluster of kids, watching an orange flame bend a window.

"Hey. Hey you!" I yell.

All of them turn around at once and stare. They're looking up at me so expectantly, their eyes wide, their faces ready to receive.

"Did you see that?" I yell down to them. "Did you SEE that?"

▼

Risk

by Charles Dickinson

Owen is the host tonight. Washing glasses, he flips them in the air until they are just winks in the light. Catching them again takes his breath away.

Frank is the first to arrive. Then Nolan. Frank wore dirty clothes that afternoon when he took his laundry down to the big machines in the basement of his apartment building; with the load in the washer, soap measured, and coins slotted, he added the clothes he was wearing and made the long walk back upstairs to his apartment naked. He paused to read the fine print on the fire extinguisher. Noises in the building set birds loose in his heart. Frank takes the red armies when they gather to play the game of world conquest.

They hear Alice arrive in a storm of gravel. She has moved herself stoned across twenty-two miles of back roads in just under twenty minutes. She lives with a man she has known for seven months, in a rented farmhouse on a hundred acres of land. The man is good with a garden and with his hands, a warmhearted, full-bearded man who plays the banjo professionally, an amicable host when the game is at their house. He loves Alice, but still she meets another man on the sly. Half her appointments and reasons for being away from home are fabrications. This other man treats her like a child, making fun of the gaps in her knowledge, hurting her feelings, which she perversely enjoys. It is a counterpoint to the sweet man at home. Alice plays black.

The world is arranged on Owen's kitchen table. A strong yellow light shines down through the night's first gauzy sheets of smoke. The game's six continents—North and South America, Africa, Asia, Europe, and Australia— are not entirely faithful to the earth's geography. Each continent is formed from territories, and between these territories war will soon be waged with armies and dice.

Owen pours Frank a beer. Owen hosts as often as possible; he would play three or four times a week if he could. The gathering of his friends soothes him and fills dark spaces in the house. The smoke softens edges. He tries to get Eileen, his wife, to play, but she refuses. She remains in the other rooms. None of the players press on this point of awkwardness.

Owen shuffles through the game cards, a glass of beer at his elbow, a cigarette in an ashtray. Alice comes into the kitchen and shades her glassy eyes. "Hi," she says.

"Speak for yourself," Frank says.

Nolan, who has arrived in a sour mood, says, "The nation's motorists are safe for a few hours."

Alice hangs her coat on the tree by the door. She takes her makings out of her purse and carefully arranges them by her place at the board.

"Wine in the fridge," Owen says. "I'll get it for you in a second." He shakes the white dice and throws them across the face of the world. A pair of fives and a six.

"Oo," Alice says. "Hot."

"I'll take that all night."

Frank asks, "Who's late again?"

Les is late again; he makes a point of it. He never offers to host, nor does he ever bring beer or food. He feels that his presence is sufficient. Les always rolls good dice. It is something he demands of himself. He wins more often than the other players. From early March to early December, he drives a 1,000-cc motorcycle without a helmet. The others allow him to continue to play despite his cheap habits because he is so good; to bar him would be cowardly. But Frank has dreamed of Les hitting ice on his cycle, his unprotected head bouncing sweetly on the highway.

Les and Pam arrive at the same time, though not together. Les's hair is swept back like Mercury's wings. Where Les is allowed to play because he is the best player, Pam, the worst, is invited back because she is so generous and so good-looking. She has large green eyes, long curly pale-red hair, and heavy breasts tucked into a loose sweater. She is usually the last to arrive and the first to lose all her armies and be eliminated. She has been playing for a year and still does not have a handle on the game. She tries to have a sense of humor about this. She always brings a large bag of pretzels and two six-packs of Dutch beer. She is always welcome. She plays pink.

Pam is in love with Nolan. She tries to catch his eye from across the room as she hands Owen her sack of food and beer. She has been with Nolan just that afternoon. It is stitched in her memory in dim light. The run through stinging branches to his basement, their time there, their almost being caught by his wife. They met at one of these gatherings and have known each other a year; Nolan's presence kept her coming back after she learned that she was not very good at the game and probably never would be. She liked his lean frame and dark-blue eyes and the clever look his glasses gave him. But he is married, to a woman named Beth. Pam has met her once, a shy, tall woman with a plain face—she played the game a half-dozen times, even winning once.

Pam knew from the first she appealed to Nolan. She learned long ago she appeals to most men. They had a cup of coffee out in the open, later a lunch in the shadows, then a drink that afternoon and a sly sneaking into his house from the rear basement door. She takes her seat at the table. Nolan won't look at her. Her head swims in dates and half-remembered cycles. She had thought she was between lovers and was using no contraception. Her calculations told her she was safe, but she is not absolutely sure.

Getting settled, Owen shakes the dice, sips his beer, smokes, observes. Frank has his twenty red armies in five neat rows of four. Alice has rolled a joint thick as her little finger and touched a match lovingly to one twisted end. Blue smoke flows upward. A seed explodes and Pam jumps, laughs. Nolan grimaces.

Les counts out his twenty green armies. He is serene. The night, so clean and cold out on the highway, has purpose. He won the previous two times they played. He smiles idly around at those soon to fall. He asks Owen, "Did you buy that stock I told you about?"

"I don't have the money, Les."

"Get it. I went in at three and a half and it's seven already." He pauses to decline the joint Alice offers. "It's a great place for your money."

"I like banks," Frank says.

Les proclaims, "Banks are for suckers."

"They're insured," Frank says.

"So? You've got to go for the big return in this economy. Most people aren't chickenshit like you, Frank."

Owen, who as host strives for player equanimity, says mildly, "I still don't have the money."

Les shrugs. He can only do so much. He says, "Let's get this carnage under way."

Two red dice go around the table, each player rolling to see who goes first. With six players, the world's forty-two territories will be divided evenly. But the player who starts will be the first to have three cards (a card earned each turn if a territory is conquered), which he or she might be able to cash for extra armies. Nolan's throw of ten is tops. Owen smiles and deals out the cards. They diverge from the rules in allotting territories. Each card represents a territory that a player will soon occupy with armies. Luck is involved, and time is saved. The players bring the cards up off the table, fan them in their hands, try to plot.

Les has been dealt New Guinea, and that is toehold enough for him on the continent of Australia. He deposits every available army there.

"A clear signal from Down Under," Nolan says. "Les is going for his continent early."

Les smiles beatifically.

Alice's seven territories are spread all over the world. She smokes her joint and studies her options. She knows that with six players, one or two will be eliminated early. A player without a firm base will be picked off a little at a time. Four of her territories are in Asia, which is much too large to try to hold as a continent. As she thinks, she feels herself float out of her seat; she feels her heels tap the chair seat as she rises clear. When she is on the ceiling, she lets out a laugh that is like taking on weight and drifts back down. Nobody has witnessed her brief ascension. They are too engrossed in the coming war. She sips wine and comes to a decision. She doesn't like Les very much when they play, and she owns Siam. It is the doorway to Asia from Australia, which Les will inevitably control. She puts all her armies in Siam.

Les looks over at her. She loves it when she makes his eyes go mean and flat. Les has green eyes, not as green as the color he plays, but green like dirty dollar bills. His eyes are always so cool and rich and calculating. He expects to win; this attitude rankles Alice no end. He may win tonight, but first he will have to fight through her.

Nolan has been splitting his armies between Central America and Greenland, preparatory to a run at North America. Seeing Alice's troop placement, he announces, "A bloodbath on the horizon in Siam."

Alice says, "I'm ready." Les drinks his wine.

"Les may want to invest in body bags," Frank says.

"I'm ready," Alice repeats.

Through all this, the only thing Owen hears is his wife moving in the room next to the kitchen. She has gone in there to get a book or the night's paper. She makes soft flutterings like a bird caught in the wall. He wishes she would come in, watch the game, have a glass of wine or a beer. An hour before the players arrived, they talked about having another baby. More than a year had passed, they were both in their early thirties, a better time would not arrive. But she could not give him an answer. Her willingness and her sadness remained locked together inside her.

Through the crack beneath the door he sees the light in the next room go out. He hears Eileen move deeper into the house, away from him; he thinks he hears her moving away long after the sounds have been hidden by the war around him.

Owen has Egypt, North Africa, and Madagascar, and he is delighted. He will soon control the continent of Africa. He won't be one of the first players eliminated, the host forced to sit and top off drinks and think.

Frank says cheerfully, "It's a gas to have the Middle East," and loads it full of his armies. He has nowhere else to go. His other armies are scattered in every continent, and worthless. He says, "The Middle East is the territory around which the world revolves."

"Frank's trying to sell himself a bill of goods," Les says.

"The poor jerk has nothing *but* the Middle East," Alice says.

Frank replies, "It's oily yet."

Pam owns Brazil and Venezuela, the doors in and out of the continent of South America. She divides her armies between the two territories.

"A bold move," Nolan announces. She looks to see if he is making fun of her, but his eyes trip away from hers.

The world is full of colored armies soon to contend. Nolan begins. After placing his three free armies, he attacks Les's lone army in the Northwest Territory, loses an army before advancing, then loses another getting Owen out of Alaska.

"It's never easy," Nolan says. But he now controls the three routes in and out of North America. He takes his card. The game moves to Frank.

"Am I in danger?" Owen asks.

"Possibly," Frank says. He puts his three free armies in the Middle East.

"Because I want to go to the john."

"I just want to go for a card," Frank replies.

Owen leaves the kitchen. Let them wait for him if he can't get a straight answer. Eileen is in their bedroom. She sits against the headboard reading; she looks up almost warily when her husband appears.

"Who's winning?" she asks.

"Just started. Why don't you come out and say hello? Have a little wine."

His wife shakes her head. Her hair is a thick caramel wave that runs in and out of the light like surf. Her face is delicate and oval-shaped. He reads in her eyes that she expects the worst possible news at any moment. "I'd have to get dressed all over again," she explains. She's ready for sleep, in a flannel nightgown buttoned up the front and tied with a ribbon at the base of her throat. He kisses this spot, then uses the bathroom before returning to the game. Making his way down the shadowed hall, he glances into his house's second bedroom, but forces himself to think about getting hold of Africa instead.

Frank has darted into Southern Europe, taken his card, regrouped back in the Middle East, and stopped. Les has taken Australia. His armies wait in a clot in Indonesia, across a strait of blue-green water from Alice's Siamese force.

"The world is taking shape," Owen notes.

"Les suggests everyone invest in philatelic devices," Frank says.

"They're illegal in this state," Alice says.

Owen says nothing. He won't sit down just yet; not until it is his turn. He is unable to lose himself in the game. This has never been a problem. Tonight, though, he is itchy.

While he gets wine and beer and opens Pam's pretzels and pours them into a bowl, hosting the event in all earnestness, Pam takes South America. She and Les have continents, though they are the two continents easiest to win and hold, and hence worth only two bonus armies per turn. Still, they are continents. Les and Pam won't drift rootless over the world.

Alice's three free armies go into Siam. She looks at Les, her left eyebrow cocked, a question asked. He meets her look blankly. She sees that he has pushed his anger down. His cash-green eyes have reclaimed their arrogance.

Not yet, she decides. She attacks Nolan in India for her card, then pulls back into Siam.

"Buy body bags," Frank urges one and all. "Buy stock in the Red Cross."

Now Owen takes his seat. "Who has hot dice?" he asks.

"Nobody, really," Nolan reports. "Still too early. I think Alice should go after Les before his heat up."

"Les suggests we invest in numismatic tools," Frank says.

Owen rolls the dice against Pam and takes the Congo. His armies advance down through South Africa and up into East Africa. Just like that, Africa is his. He is spread too thin to hold it, he supposes, but he has a continent.

Nolan's turn again, and he can't remember what he wants to do next. Beth's face swims up to him, fitted on Pam's lush body. He stirs in his seat and tries to concentrate. He must fortify North America. One minute he was having a beer with Pam and the next he had come to this dangerous decision and they were parking her car a block over from his house. Cutting through the lawns, the darkening spaces between the houses, he could think only of the lack of cover. All the leaves were fallen; this was an affair meant for summer. He pulled the girl along by the hand. They went into the basement by the back door and undressed in the failing light. She tasted of flat beer when he kissed her for the first time. Chimes went off upstairs; he counted with them to five as he kissed her belly—an hour before Beth was due.

"Whose turn is it?" Les asks pointedly. Nolan's attention jerks back to the game. The world spreads before him. The girl keeps looking at him; she will give him away if she isn't careful. He is playing blue. Her sexual presence hit him the first time he saw her: a chemical lust. She never had to open her mouth. In fact, he preferred that she didn't. The peeling back of layers of existence that was life with Beth was never a factor with Pam. She was not very good at the game, and he knew nothing about her life otherwise. At their early meetings he filled the silent spaces talking about himself. He never thought about Beth at those times; she existed on a different plane. He found it remarkably easy to ask Pam to make that run to the basement with him. It would be the extent of what he wanted to know about her. Only when they were out in the open and on the run did it strike him what a wild chance he was taking.

And after they had been in the basement only twenty minutes, as they were finished and sitting in an awkward envelope of silence, a door opened above them and Beth's heels cracked smartly on the floor over their heads.

"Nolan," Les snarls, "it's too early in the game for such long thoughts."

Frank says, "It will be the rumination of your soul."

Nolan looks at Pam, then his eyes fly past. She waited with him in his basement like a canny burglar. Her ripe body had become an unwieldy burden he must transfer out of there for his own safety. His wife moved about upstairs, and the sky outside darkened. Then they slipped out the basement door and back to her car. She drove him to where he had left his car. They did not say a word, moving on those dark streets, as though his wife might yet hear. He took deep breaths to calm himself. Leaving, he had looked back up at the house, and in the rectangle of light of the upstairs bedroom window he had thought he saw a woman looking out. But he had lost his glasses in the rush of adultery. He was flying blind. He had to be careful driving. At home he put on a spare pair and made a quick, surreptitious inspection of the basement. Nothing. No glasses. They were buried somewhere like a land mine. He might step on them at any moment and blow himself up. Beth, happy to see him, undressed and pulled him into bed with her. He said he didn't have time but she insisted; he noted no strangeness in her behavior, no knowledge of what he had done, of what he had become.

Owen gravely says, "As host, I'll have to rule you either move immediately, Nolan, or forfeit your turn."

Nolan slaps his three free armies down in Alaska. He conquers Les in Quebec from Greenland, then takes his card and sits back. Pam is a little disappointed. After such long consideration, she had expected something grand from Nolan.

"Bold," Les sneers.

"Jam it."

Frank drops more armies into the Middle East. Les says, "You can't let Owen keep Africa."

"Always fomenting trouble," Owen says good-naturedly. The possibility of attack hurries his blood, though. Frank moving on Egypt or East Africa is strategically sound. By the next turn, Owen will be better fortified. If he survives here, Africa will be his, probably for the entire game, with its three bonus armies per turn. Frank has the manpower at the moment and Owen's dice are rarely better than fair.

Frank attacks Owen in East Africa. Africa falls in six rolls of the dice. Les says, stirring more trouble, "You're poised to cut across North Africa and take South America away from Pam."

"No, thanks," Frank says. Too many armies wait in North Africa and Brazil. There is nothing in it for him. "I am content, not contentious," he says, and moves half his force back into the Middle East.

Les shakes Alice's shoulder, pretending she has fallen asleep. "You with us?" he asks in a loud voice. "Enough brain cells still alive to finish the game?"

She purses her lips as if to kiss and blows blue smoke in his face.

"I am ready," she says carefully, from the ceiling. These three words falling down to Les pull her after them like anchors. She wraps her leg around a leg of the table for balance and the table leg convulses. Les shrieks theatrically, "God! She's trying to get me sexually aroused so I'll go easy on her in Siam. But it won't work!"

He untangles his leg from Alice's. She grabs the table edge lest she float away again. A balloon of nausea rises in her. She puts her hand to her mouth and concentrates.

"Looking pale," Les says to the others, pointing at Alice.

"No fair throwing up on the world," Frank warns. "If you don't like your situation, be a man and live with it."

Les puts three armies in Indonesia, two in the Ukraine. He decides he is in no hurry. Let things build. He rolls the dice and there is a six. He gets a card from another point on the globe.

"Uh-oh," Frank says.

"Very efficient use of that six."

"Thank you," Les says modestly.

Alice smiles at them all. "It's early yet."

The world comes to Owen and it goes away. He is a fine host, and breaks out corn chips and roast-beef sandwiches, empties ashtrays, opens beers, pours wine. He spills liquids into the oceans and across the plains of Asia. The players groan and protest. A whale dives in the Mid-Atlantic. To the south, a tall ship moves under sail. He excuses himself. The light is out in their bedroom. It is 1:00 A.M., and Eileen sleeps in blankets wrapped tight as a premium cigar.

He passes the second bedroom going back and decides to go in. The crib had been dismantled right away. Even a year later the four indentations remain in the carpet where the casters pressed, stake holes for a precise parcel of ground. The baby had been so weightless, and home for such a short time; he is always amazed that she could mark the room so indelibly.

A night light remains in the wall socket. His wife might have overlooked it when she was cleaning out the room. She might have been afraid to look down. He kneels by it and snaps it on. A mouse's head, a glowing white face, round black ears, cartoon-rodent eyes. It's kind of unnerving: the head of a tiny ghost floating above the floor. Not the sort of thing for a baby girl. Had she been scared to death?

Owen returns to the game. Without Africa he is nothing, and the game has become a chore. He will be eliminated soon. Frank is gone already. Les took him out with the force he built in the Ukraine, using this secondary force to win cards and let some of the steam out of the situation brewing between Siam and Indonesia. Frank waited too long to take this Ukraine army seriously, and now he has gone outside; nobody knows what has happened to him.

Pam is pinned in South America. Owen's last armies block her in North Africa. Nolan has a major force in Central America. He will march on her in Venezuela.

The bloodbath between Alice and Les approaches. "You've got to come through me pretty soon," Alice taunts. "Nolan's getting too strong."

"This is a fact," Owen says. He desires resolution of this conflict so he can send his guests away.

The door opens and Frank is back.

"Where you been?"

"Standing naked in the dark," Frank says.

No one pays any attention. Nolan is attacking Pam. He goes after her in Venezuela, because it is the sound move at that point in the game, and also because he wants her gone. She usually leaves after she has been eliminated. Nights past, he was sorry to see her go. Now she embarrasses him. He expects her to slip up and start crying. She keeps looking at him.

Nolan rolls the dice and Pam waits. If he would look at her they might reach some understanding, but his eyes are fixed to that spot on the board where her dice will fall.

"Come on, come on," he says impatiently.

She rolls and loses two armies. Alice says, "Don't let him badger you."

"It's OK," Pam says softly. She thinks she will cry. Everything is wrong.

"Would you roll the dice?" he asks sharply.

She flings the dice across the board. She keeps them in sight through filmed eyes and sees sixes come up, which on closer inspection are really fours. Her tears make the pits shiver and drift. But fours are enough to win a pair of armies from Nolan, who rolls nothing higher than a three.

"Get him," Alice cheers.

But they are only dice; only Les has learned to tap their souls. Nolan's superior forces pick implacably away at Pam. Her armies fall like threads in a garment until they are all gone and she feels naked and stupid. Out of the game again. She turns her cards over to Nolan. He cashes them for extra armies and moves without a word against Owen in Africa. Pam watches this action blankly. She could open her mouth and tell everyone of the time she spent with Nolan in the recent past. She wields this knowledge like an ax on her tongue and is larger within herself for not using it.

She takes her empty glass and washes it out in the sink. At her back, Nolan eliminates Owen.

"You'll pardon me if I don't stay for the end," she says.

Owen stands, wipes his palms on his trousers. "I don't blame you for leaving," he says. "I'm bored myself."

"The pitiable whine of the previously conquered," Les observes dryly.

Owen smiles and takes Pam's coat off the tree and helps her into it. He walks her out to her car.

"Thanks for coming," he says. He likes being outside, away from the smoke and the bloodlust. The white gravel of his driveway gleams. The air feels like it wants to snow. He takes Pam's keys gallantly, and after she shows him the one, he unlocks her car door. Owen leans in and kisses her good night. She hands him a pair of glasses.

"They belong to the guy playing blue," she says. "I saw him downtown today and we had coffee together and he left them with me by mistake."

These words break over Owen in a rush; he can only say, "OK."

He stays outside after Pam is gone. Nolan's car is unlocked; he puts the glasses on the dash. He has no interest in the truth of their coming into Pam's possession. He returns to his house through the front door. He hears the voices of the players in the kitchen, the labored buzz of an old digital clock turning a minute over. Through the dark passages of the house, moving with a freedom bestowed by his guests' believing he is still outside, Owen glides into the bedroom. His wife lies wrapped and asleep. He understands now why the night's game offered him nothing; it was an event out of order of importance. Eileen comes half awake at the way he pulls the covers and makes a space for himself in the loose, warm cylinder. He gets her nightgown unbuttoned and untied and fights through the clumsy hands she throws in his path. He plants a long kiss on her sour mouth. She utters a word into his mouth that he ignores. She will kill his desire if he lets her.

"Where are your friends?" she whispers, warm in his ear.

"In the kitchen. The world will fall soon."

"You aren't being a good host." He is stirred unimaginably to hear teasing in her voice. Her hands have opened against his back.

"They think I'm outside," he whispers. "This way, I can be two places at once."

She kisses him on the neck. They move on together, Owen careful of dark chasms of memory he must transport his wife over. She proceeds along a fine edge that her husband slowly widens.

Les says, "Siam from China."

"Hand me the bones, please," Alice says. Frank gives her the white dice. "Like skulls," she says, "with twenty-one lance holes."

"Siam from China," Les repeats.

"Pincer movement," Nolan announces.

"Pinch her movement and she'll follow you anywhere," says Frank.

Les has swept his second force into China so he can attack Alice's Siamese armies from both north and south. He rolls dice the same way from first to last: three shakes of his left fist, then a gentle, coddling tipping of the dice out onto the board, as though they might bruise. It is his secret that he treats the dice well so they will reciprocate. He once revealed this secret while drunk and voluble, and seven straight games of cold dice followed as punishment.

He beats on Alice from China: a softening action. Alice is poised for defeat. He can see in her slack face that she has had enough: enough grass, enough of their company, enough of this game. She is tired and anxious to go home.

"Where's Owen?" Nolan asks.

"He walked Pam to her car," Frank says.

"That was a half-hour ago."

"So?" Les asks, impatient at this break in his concentration. "Go look for him if you're so concerned. But shut up."

"Gee, Les, you're such a charming guy," Frank says.

"Eat it."

"Come on, Les," Alice complains. "Roll the dice. I wanna go home."

"The night is breaking up in a sea of bad juices," Frank says. "Why does it always have to be this way? Like love."

"Shut up, Frank."

Nolan is at the window, cupping hands around his eyes to see through the light reflected on the glass. Chrome winks from the handlebars of Les's motorcycle. He can see Alice's car, his car, Frank's car. Not Pam's car, though.

"They left together," he says.

"Who did?" Frank asks.

"Pam and Owen."

"No way," Alice says.

"Intriguing, though," Les admits.

"Her car is gone. So is Owen. You put it together."

"He's married," Frank says.

"Frank, you're such an innocent," Alice says.

Frank says, "And his wife is in the other room. Who'd have the nerve to go off with another woman under those conditions?"

Nolan says, "Maybe she's asleep. Maybe he figures she figures he's still out here. She never checks on him. Maybe he figured it was worth the gamble."

"Are we still playing?" Alice asks Les. He is startled; he has been thinking about Pam. The dice feel funny in his hand, as though the corners have been shaved fractionally, or the pits rearranged. They feel cool at being ignored in the midst of their performance for him. He is afraid to roll, and when he does it's all ones and twos. He rolls cold for the next five minutes, losing armies, losing confidence. In time his China force is wiped out, and Alice still exists firmly in Siam. Outnumbered, she nonetheless has the hot dice that ordinarily are his province, as though they have taken another lover. Fives and sixes roll languorously from her hand. Alice licks her lips, wide awake now. Hot dice get everyone's attention. Les awaits her exclamation of disbelief in her good fortune, which will drive the dice spitefully back to him. But it does not come. He loses armies in pairs. By and by, they are evenly matched, Siam and Indonesia, and Les stalls to count armies, trying to cool her dice this way.

Nolan says, "I feel uncomfortable without a host." He opens himself a fresh beer. He begins to look through bills that Owen keeps stacked on the counter next to the telephone.

"Jesus, Owen has $1,108 on his Visa," he informs the others.

"Stop that," Alice scolds.

Les likes this unexpected turn; Nolan's rude exploration has taken Alice's mind off the game.

"Many people are faced with serious and potentially catastrophic debt," Les says.

Nolan goes on. "A phone bill for $79.21."

"What if Owen comes back and finds you doing that?" Alice asks. When her head is turned away from Les, he blows gently toward the dice in her hand to cool them.

"He's with Pam," Nolan says. Saying this makes it a fact; makes him feel released.

"Roll the dice," Les orders. "I want to get out of here before daylight." He is certain that the dice have come back to him. Alice has lingered too long between throws. She has lost favor by ignoring the good fortune that the dice were eager to bestow. He reminds her, "I'm still attacking."

Alice rolls, thinking of Owen. He had telephoned her when the baby died, the phone seeming to explode with compressed tragedy in the middle of the night. To this day, she can't talk to Eileen without seeing grief encasing her like an invisible jar. Only lately has Alice seen her smile. Would Owen go off with Pam at just such a time?

Les wins two armies. Then two more.

Nolan says, "A bill for $177.44 from People's Gas."

Alice wishes Owen would return and discover Nolan and banish him forever. But the house is silent except for the click of dice. Maybe Owen *has* left with Pam; maybe it is the only response to this time in history. The man Alice meets on the sly is married to a sweet woman who he claims has nothing of interest to say. And Alice has never considered herself fascinating. The man she shares the farmhouse with had a marriage end years ago when he was caught in a hammock with another woman. She thinks this might make her safe, that he might understand if he ever catches her.

Les rolls and Alice falls. He was right: the dice have come back. When he clears her out of Siam, he still has ten armies in Indonesia. He takes the four cards Alice holds, and with the cards already in his hand cashes twice for forty-five armies, a huge green force he places with care to battle Nolan while his dice are running hot. It takes another hour to finish the game.

The dice are at home in Les's loosely cupped fist and at two minutes to four o'clock in the morning he is the winner for the third consecutive time. Alice and Frank sit quietly and watch.

"Dear Les," Alice says, standing and stretching. "You do go on."

"And on ... and on," Frank says. "Like a fungus." He shakes Les's hand. He folds Owen's board, puts the cards away, puts the armies in their containers.

Nolan asks, "Did Owen take his key?"

"I couldn't tell you," Les says.

"If we lock the door," Frank says, "and he has to knock to get in, we could be inadvertently exposing him to exposure. Or exposure. A guy like Owen could die of exposure."

"He should've thought of that," Nolan says.

"He can just say he forgot it," Les says. "He could say he went to breakfast after the game and forgot it."

Alice puts the wine in the refrigerator and washes out the glasses. She leaves a small light on over the stove.

Birds stir outside, though it is still dark. The four of them stand, corners of a square, in the driveway.

"Somebody mentioned breakfast," Nolan says.

Frank pats his pockets. "I'm broke."

"I'll buy," Nolan says. "The vanquished will buy with the reparations they receive from the victors."

"Ha! You'll get nothing from me," Les says.

"I'll still buy."

"I think I'll pass," Alice says.

"You'll pass on a free meal?"

"I don't feel so hot."

"Suit yourself," Frank says.

The other three turn from her and make their plans. She does not want to be alone just then, though a sleeping man who loves her awaits at the end of the drive home. Nolan and Frank start their cars and drive off and she is left standing there with Les. He sits astride his motorcycle, pulling on his gloves and watching her.

"Come with us," he urges.

She moves to his side. "I'm tired of Nolan and Frank." She kisses Les. "Can't we go somewhere?"

He laughs. "That might be difficult to explain. I've been coming and going at awfully odd hours. She thinks I play this game at all hours of the day and night."

"Coward."

Owen is awakened by Les's motorcycle starting. Unwinding himself from Eileen, he feels her stir. She loops an arm around his waist when he sits up on the edge of the bed. His friends will be going for breakfast at this early hour. It is a tradition of the game. The night's war will be replayed. Stories will be told, rumors will be spread. Owen would love to go with them, but he doesn't dare.

▼

Nada

by Judith Ortiz Cofer

Almost as soon as Doña Ernestina got the telegram about her son's having been killed in Vietnam, she started giving her possessions away. At first we didn't realize what she was doing. By the time we did, it was too late.

The army people had comforted Doña Ernestina with the news that her son's "remains" would have to be "collected and shipped" back to New Jersey at some later date, since other "personnel" had also been lost on the same day. In other words, she would have to wait until Tony's body could be processed.

Processed. Doña Ernestina spoke that word like a curse when she told us. We were all down in El Basement—that's what we called the cellar of our apartment building: no windows for light, boilers making such a racket that you could scream and almost no one would hear you. Some of us had started meeting here on Saturday mornings—as much to talk as to wash our clothes—and over the years it became a sort of women's club where we could catch up on a week's worth of gossip. That Saturday, however, I had dreaded going down the cement steps. All of us had just heard the news about Tony the night before.

I should have known the minute I saw her, holding court in her widow's costume, that something had cracked inside Doña Ernestina. She was in full luto—black from head to toe, including a mantilla. In contrast, Lydia and Isabelita were both in rollers and bathrobes: our customary uniform for these Saturday-morning gatherings—maybe our way of saying "No Men Allowed." As I approached them, Lydia stared at me with a scared-rabbit look in her eyes.

Doña Ernestina simply waited for me to join the other two leaning against the machines before she continued explaining what had happened when the news of Tony had arrived at her door the day before. She spoke calmly, a haughty expression on her face, looking like an offended duchess in her beautiful black dress. She was pale, pale, but she had a wild look in her eyes. The officer had told her that—when the time came—they would bury Tony with "full military honors"; for now they were sending her the medal and a flag. But she had said, "No, *gracias,*" to the funeral, and she sent the flag and medals back marked *Ya no vive aquí:* Does not live here anymore. "Tell the Mr. President of the United States what I say: No gracias."

Then she waited for our response.

Lydia shook her head, indicating that she was speechless. And Elenita looked pointedly at me, forcing me to be the one to speak the words of sympathy for all of us, to reassure Doña Ernestina that she had done exactly what any of us would have done in her place: yes, we would have all said *No gracias,* to any president who had actually tried to pay for a son's life with a few trinkets and a folded flag.

Doña Ernestina nodded gravely. Then she picked up the stack of neatly folded men's shirts from the sofa (a discard we had salvaged from the sidewalk) and walked regally out of El Basement.

Lydia, who had gone to high school with Tony, burst into tears as soon as Doña Ernestina was out of sight. Elenita and I sat her down between us on the sofa and held her until she had let most of it out. Lydia is still young—a woman who has not yet been visited to often by *la muerte.* Her husband of six months has just gotten his draft notice, and they have been trying for a baby—trying very hard. The walls of El Building are thin enough so that it has become a secret joke (kept only from Lydia and Roberto) that he is far more likely to escape the draft due to acute exhaustion than by becoming a father.

"Doesn't Doña Ernestina feel *anything?*" Lydia asked in between sobs. "Did you see her, dressed up like an actress in a play—and not one tear for her son?"

"We all have different ways of grieving," I said, though I couldn't help thinking that there *was* a strangeness to Doña Ernestina and that Lydia was right when she said that the woman seemed to be acting out a part. "I think we should wait and see what she is going to do."

"Maybe," said Elenita. "Did you get a visit from *el padre* yesterday?"

We nodded, not surprised to learn that all of us had gotten personal calls from Padre Álvaro, our painfully shy priest, after Doña Ernestina had frightened him away. Apparently el padre had come to her apartment immediately after hearing about Tony, expecting to comfort the woman as he had when Don Antonio died suddenly a year ago. Her grief then had been understandable in its immensity, for she had been burying not only her husband but also the dream shared by many of the barrio woman her age—that of returning with her man to the Island after retirement, of buying a *casita* in the old pueblo, and of being buried on native ground alongside *la familia.* People *my* age—those of us born or raised here—have had our mothers drill this fantasy into our brains all of our lives. So when Don Antonio dropped his head on the domino table, scattering the ivory pieces of the best game of the year, and when he was laid out in his best black suit at Ramírez's Funeral Home, all of us knew how to talk to the grieving widow.

That was the last time we saw both her men. Tony was there, too—home on a two-day pass from basic training—and he cried like a little boy over his father's handsome face, calling him Papi, Papi. Doña Ernestina had had a full mother's duty then, taking care of the hysterical boy. It was a normal chain of grief, the strongest taking care of the weakest. We buried Don Antonio at Garden State Memorial Park, where there are probably more Puerto Ricans than on the Island. Padre Álvaro said his sermon in a soft, trembling voice that was barely audible over the cries of the boy being supported on one side by his mother, impressive in her quiet strength and dignity, and on the other by Cheo, owner of the bodega where Don Antonio had played dominoes with other barrio men of his age for over twenty years.

Just about everyone from El Building had attended that funeral, and it had been done right. Doña Ernestina had sent her son off to fight for America and then had started collecting her widow's pension. Some of us asked Doña Iris (who knew how to read cards) about Doña Ernestina's future, and Doña Iris had said: "A long journey within a year"—which fit with what we had thought would happen next: Doña Ernestina would move back to the Island and wait with her relatives for Tony to come home from the war. Some older women actually went home when they started collecting social security or pensions, but that was rare. Usually, it seemed to me, somebody had to die before the island dream would come true for women like Doña Ernestina. As for my friends and me, we talked about "vacations" in the Caribbean. But we knew that if life was hard for us in this barrio, it would be worse in a pueblo where no one knew us (and had maybe only heard of our parents before they came to *Los Estados Unidos de América,* where most of us had been brought as children).

When Padre Álvaro had knocked softly on my door, I had yanked it open, thinking it was that ex-husband of mine asking for a second chance again. (That's just the way Miguel knocks when he's sorry for leaving me—about once a week—when he wants a loan.) So I was wearing my go-to-hell face when I threw open the door, and the poor priest nearly jumped out of his skin. I saw him take a couple of deep breaths before he asked me in his slow way—he tries to hide his stutter by dragging out his words—if I knew whether Doña Ernestina was ill. After I said, "No, not that I know," Padre Álvaro just stood there, looking pitiful, until I asked him if he cared to come in. I had been sleeping on the sofa and watching TV all afternoon, and I really didn't want him to see the mess, but I had nothing to fear. The poor man actually took one step back at my invitation. No, he was in a hurry, he had a few other parishoners to visit, etc. These were difficult times, he said, so-so-so many young people lost to drugs or dying in the wa-wa-war. I asked him if *he* thought Doña Ernestina was sick, but he just shook his head. The man looked like an orphan at my door with those sad, brown eyes. He was actually appealing in a homely way: that long nose nearly touched the tip of his chin when he smiled, and his big crooked teeth broke my heart.

"She does not want to speak to me," Padre Álvaro said as he caressed a large silver crucifix that hung on a thick chain around his neck. He seemed to be dragged down by its weight, stoop-shouldered and skinny as he was.

I felt a strong impulse to feed him some of my chicken soup, still warm on the stove from my supper. Contrary to what Lydia says about me behind my back, I like living by myself. And I could not have been happier to have that mama's boy Miguel back where he belonged—with his mother, who thought that he was still her baby. But this scraggly thing at my door needed home cooking and maybe even something more than a hot meal to bring a little spark into his life. (I mentally asked God to forgive me for having thoughts like these about one of his priests. *Ay bendito,* but they too are made of flesh and blood.)

"Maybe she just needs a little more time, Padre," I said in as comforting a voice as I could manage. Unlike the other women in El Building, I am not convinced that priests are truly necessary—or even much help—in times of crisis.

"Sí, Hija, perhaps you're right," he muttered sadly—calling me "daughter" even though I'm pretty sure I'm five or six years older. (Padre Álvaro seems so "untouched" that it's hard to tell his age. I mean, when you live, it shows. He looks hungry or love, starving himself by choice.) I promised him that I would look in on Doña Ernestina. Without another word, he made the sign of the cross in the air between us and turned away. As I heard his slow steps descending the creaky stairs, I asked myself: what do priests dream about?

When el padre's name came up again during that Saturday meeting in El Basement, I asked my friends what *they* thought a priest dreamed about. It was a fertile subject, so much so that we spent the rest of our laundry time coming up with scenarios. Before the last dryer stopped, we all agreed that we could not receive communion the next day at mass unless we went to confession that afternoon and told another priest, not Álvaro, about our "unclean thoughts."

As for Doña Ernestina's situation, we agreed that we should be there for her if she called, but the decent thing to do, we decided, was give her a little more time alone. Lydia kept repeating, in that childish way of hers, "Something is wrong with the woman," but she didn't volunteer to go see what it was that was making Doña Ernestina act so strangely. Instead she complained that she and Roberto had heard pots and pans banging and things being moved around for hours in 4-D last night—they had hardly been able to sleep. Isabelita winked at me behind Lydia's back. Lydia and Roberto still had not caught on: if they could hear what was going on in 4-D, the rest of us could also get an earful of what went on in 4-A. They were just kids who thought they had invented sex: I tell you, a telenovela could be made from the stories in El Building.

On Sunday, Doña Ernestina was not at the Spanish mass and I avoided Padre Álvaro so he would not ask me about her. But I was worried. Doña Ernestina was a church cucaracha—a devout Catholic who, like many of us, did not always do what the priests and the Pope ordered but who knew where God lived. Only a serious illness or tragedy could keep her from attending mass, so afterward I went straight to her apartment and knocked on her door. There was no answer, although I had heard scraping and dragging noises, like furniture being moved around. At least she was on her feet and active. Maybe housework was what she needed to snap out of her shock. I decided to try again the next day.

As I went by Lydia's apartment, the young woman opened her door—I knew she had been watching me through the peephole—to tell me about more noises from across the hall during the night. Lydia was in her baby-doll pajamas. Although she stuck only her nose out, I could see Roberto in his Jockey underwear doing something in the kitchen. I couldn't help thinking about Miguel and me when we had first gotten together. We were an explosive combination. After a night of passionate lovemaking, I would walk around thinking: Do not light cigarettes around me. No open flames. Highly combustible materials being transported. But when his mama showed up at our door, the man of fire turned into a heap of ashes at her feet.

"Let's wait and see what happens," I told Lydia again.

We did not have to wait for long. On Monday Doña Ernestina called to invite us to a wake for Tony, a *velorio,* in her apartment. The word spread fast. Everyone wanted to do something for her. Cheo donated fresh chickens and island produce of all kinds. Several of us got together and made arroz con pollo, also flan for dessert. And Doña Iris made two dozen *pasteles* and wrapped the meat pies in banana leaves that she had been saving in her freezer for her famous Christmas parties. We women carried in our steaming plates, while the men brought in their bottles of Palo Viejo rum for themselves and candy-sweet Manischewitz wine for us. We came ready to spend the night saying our rosaries and praying for Tony's soul.

Doña Ernestina met us at the door and led us into her living room, where the lights were off. A photograph of Tony and one of her deceased husband Don Antonio were sitting on top of a table, surrounded by at least a dozen candles. It was a spooky sight that caused several of the older women to cross themselves. Doña Ernestina had arranged folding chairs in front of this table and told us to sit down. She did not ask us to take our food and drinks to the kitchen. She just looked at each of us individually, as if she were taking attendance in a class, and then said: "I have asked you here to say good-bye to my husband Antonio and my son Tony. You have been my friends and neighbors for twenty years, but they were my life. Now that they are gone, I have nada. Nada. Nada."

I tell you, that word is like a drain that sucks everything down. Hearing her say *nada* over and over made me feel as if I were being yanked into a dark pit. I could feel the others getting nervous around me too, but here was a woman deep into her pain: we had to give her a little space. She looked around the room, then walked out without saying another word.

As we sat there in silence, stealing looks at each other, we began to hear the sounds of things being moved around in other rooms. One of the older women took charge then, and soon the drinks were poured, the food served—all this while the strange sounds kept coming from different rooms in the apartment. Nobody said much, except once when we heard something like a dish fall and break. Doña Iris pointed her index finger at her ear and made a couple of circles—and out of nervousness, I guess, some of us giggled like schoolchildren.

It was a long while before Doña Ernestina came back out to us. By then we were gathering our dishes and purses, having come to the conclusion that it was time to leave. Holding two huge Sears shopping bags, one in each hand, Doña Ernestina took her place at the front door as if she were a society hostess in a receiving line. Some of us women hung back to see what was going on. But Tito, the building's super, had had enough and tried to get past her. She took his hand, putting in it a small ceramic poodle with a gold chain around its neck. Tito gave the poodle a funny look, then glanced at Doña Ernestina as though he were scared and hurried away with the dog in his hand.

We were let out of her place one by one, but not until she had forced one of her possessions on each of us. She grabbed without looking from her bags. Out came her prized *miniaturas,* knickknacks that take a woman a lifetime to collect. Out came ceramic and porcelain items of all kinds, including vases and ashtrays; out came kitchen utensils, dishes, forks, knives, spoons; out came old calendars and every small item that she had touched or been touched by in the last twenty years. Out came a bronzed baby shoe—and I got that.

As we left the apartment, Doña Iris said "Psst" to some of us, so we followed her down the hallway. "Doña Ernestina's faculties are temporarily out of order," she said very seriously. "It is due to the shock of her son's death."

We all said "Sí" and nodded our heads.

"But what can we do?" Lydia said, her voice cracking a little. "What should I do with this?" She was holding one of Tony's baseball trophies in her hand: 1968 Most Valuable Player, for the Pocos Locos, our barrio's team.

Doña Iris said, "Let us keep her things safe for her until she recovers her senses. And let her mourn in peace. These things take time. If she needs us, she will call us." Doña Iris shrugged her shoulders. "*Así es la vida, hijas:* that's the way life is."

As I passed Tito on the stairs, he shook his head while looking up at Doña Ernestina's door: "I say she needs a shrink. I think somebody should call the social worker." He did not look at me when he mumbled these things. By "somebody" he meant one of us women. He didn't want trouble in his building, and he expected one of us to get rid of the problems. I just ignored him.

In my bed I prayed to the Holy Mother that she would find peace for Doña Ernestina's troubled spirit, but things got worse. All that week Lydia saw strange things happening through the peephole on her door. Every time people came to Doña Ernestina's apartment—to deliver flowers, or telegrams from the Island, or anything—the woman would force something on them. She pleaded with them to take this or that; if they hesitated, she commanded them with those tragic eyes to accept a token of her life.

And they did, walking out of our apartment building, carrying cushions, lamps, doilies, clothing, shoes, umbrellas, wastebaskets, schoolbooks, and notebooks: things of value and things of no worth at all to anyone but the person who had owned them. Eventually winos and street people got the news of the great giveaway in 4-D, and soon there was a line down the stairs and out the door. Nobody went home empty-handed; it was like a soup kitchen. Lydia was afraid to step out of her place because of all the dangerous-looking characters hanging out on that floor. And the smell! Entering our building was like coming into a cheap bar and public urinal combined.

Isabelita, living alone with her two little children and fearing for their safety, was the one who finally called a meeting of the residents. Only the women attended, since the men were truly afraid of Doña Ernestina. It isn't unusual for men to be frightened when they see a woman go crazy. If they are not the cause of her madness, then they act as if they don't understand it and usually leave us alone to deal with our "woman's problems." This is just as well.

Maybe I *am* just bitter because of Miguel—I know what is said behind my back. But this is a fact: when a woman is in trouble, a man calls in her mama, her sisters, or her friends, and then he makes himself scarce until it's all over. This happens again and again. At how many bedsides of women have I sat? How many times have I made the doctor's appointment, taken care of the children, and fed the husbands of my friends in the barrio? It is not that the men can't do these things; it's just that they know how much women help each other. Maybe the men even suspect that we know one another better than they know their own wives. As I said, it is just as well that they stay out of our way when there is trouble. It makes things simpler for us.

At the meeting, Isabelita said right away that we should go up to 4-D and try to reason with *la pobre* Doña Ernestina. Maybe we could get her to give us a relative's address in Puerto Rico—the woman obviously needed to be taken care of. What she was doing was putting us all in a very difficult situation. There were no dissenters this time. We voted to go as a group to talk to Doña Ernestina the next morning.

But that night we were all awakened by crashing noises on the street. In the light of the full moon, I could see that the air was raining household goods: kitchen chairs, stools, a small TV, a nightstand, pieces of a bed frame. Everything was splintering as it landed on the pavement. People were running for cover and yelling up at our building. The problem, I knew instantly, was in apartment 4-D.

Putting on my bathrobe and slippers, I stepped out into the hallway. Lydia and Roberto were rushing down the stairs, but on the flight above my landing, I caught up with Doña Iris and Isabelita, heading toward 4-D. Out of breath, we stood in the fourth-floor hallway, listening to police sirens approaching our building in front. We could hear the slamming of car doors and yelling—in both Spanish and English. Then we tried the door to 4-D. It was unlocked.

We came into a room virtually empty. Even the pictures had been taken down from the walls; all that was left were the nail holes and the lighter places on the paint where the framed photographs had been for years. We took a few seconds to spot Doña Ernestina: she was curled up in the farthest corner of the living room, naked.

"Cómo salió a este mundo," said Doña Iris, crossing herself.

Just as she had come into the world. Wearing nothing. Nothing around her except a clean, empty room. Nada. She had left nothing behind—except the bottles of pills, the ones the doctors give to ease the pain, to numb you, to make you feel nothing when someone dies.

The bottles were empty too, and the policemen took them. But we didn't let them take Doña Ernestina until we each had brought up some of our own best clothes and dressed her like the decent woman that she was. *La decencia.* Nothing can ever change that—not even la muerte. This is the way life is. *Así es la vida.*

▼

Death in the Woods

by Sherwood Anderson

I

She was an old woman and lived on a farm near the town in which I lived. All country and small-town people have seen such old women, but no one knows much about them. Such an old woman comes into town driving an old worn-out horse or she comes afoot carrying a basket. She may own a few hens and have eggs to sell. She brings them in a basket and takes them to a grocer. There she trades them in. She gets some salt pork and some beans. Then she gets a pound or two of sugar and some flour.

Afterwards she goes to the butcher's and asks for some dog-meat. She may spend ten or fifteen cents, but when she does she asks for something. Formerly the butchers gave liver to anyone one who wanted to carry it away. In our family we were always having it. Once one of my brothers got a whole cow's liver at the slaughter-house near the fairgrounds in our town. We had it until we were sick of it. It never cost a cent. I have hated the thought of it ever since.

The old farm woman got some liver and a soup-bone. She never visited with anyone, and as soon as she got what she wanted she lit out for home. It made quite a load for such an old body. No one gave her a lift. People drive right down a road and never notice an old woman like that.

There was such an old woman who used to come into town past our house one Summer and Fall when I was a young boy and was sick with what was called inflammatory rheumatism. She went home later carrying a heavy pack on her back. Two or three large gaunt-looking dogs followed at her heels.

The old woman was nothing special. She was one of the nameless ones that hardly anyone knows, but she got into my thoughts. I have just suddenly now, after all these years, remembered her and what happened. It is a story. Her name was Grimes, and she lived with her husband and son in a small unpainted house on the bank of a small creek four miles from town.

The husband and son were a tough lot. Although the son was but twenty-one, he had already served a term in jail. It was whispered about that the woman's husband stole horses and ran them off to some other county. Now and then, when a horse turned up missing, the man had also disappeared. No one ever caught him. Once, when I was loafing at Tom Whitehead's livery-barn, the man came there and sat on the bench in front. Two or three other men were there, but no one spoke to him. He sat for a few minutes and then got up and went away. When he was leaving he turned around and stared at the men. There was a look of defiance in his eyes. "Well, I have tried to be friendly. You don't want to talk to me. It has been so wherever I have gone in this town. If, some day, one of your fine horses turns up missing, well, then what?" He did not say anything actually. "I'd like to bust one of you on the jaw," was about what his eyes said. I remember how the look in his eyes made me shiver.

The old man belonged to a family that had had money once. His name was Jake Grimes. It all comes back clearly now. His father, John Grimes, had owned a sawmill when the country was new, and had made money. Then he got to drinking and running after women. When he died there wasn't much left.

Jake blew in the rest. Pretty soon there wasn't any more lumber to cut and his land was nearly all gone.

He got his wife off a German farmer, for whom he went to work one June day in the wheat harvest. She was a young thing then and scared to death. You see, the farmer was up to something with the girl—she was, I think, a bound girl and his wife had her suspicions. She took it out on the girl when the man wasn't around. Then, when the wife had to go off to town for supplies, the farmer got after her. She told young Jake that nothing really ever happened, but he didn't know whether to believe it or not.

He got her pretty easy himself, the first time he was out with her. He wouldn't have married her if the German farmer hadn't tried to tell him where to get off. He got her to go riding with him in his buggy one night when he was threshing on the place, and then he came for her the next Sunday night.

She managed to get out of the house without her employer's seeing, but when she was getting into the buggy he showed up. It was almost dark, and he just popped up suddenly at the horse's head. He grabbed the horse by the bridle and Jake got out his buggy-whip.

They had it out all right! The German was a tough one. Maybe he didn't care whether his wife knew or not. Jake hit him over the face and shoulders with the buggy-whip, but the horse got to acting up and he had to get out.

Then the two men went for it. The girl didn't see it. The horse started to run away and went nearly a mile down the road before the girl got him stopped. Then she managed to tie him to a tree beside the road. (I wonder how I know all this. It must have stuck in my mind from small-town tales when I was a boy.) Jake found her there after he got through with the German. She was huddled up in the buggy seat, crying, scared to death. She told Jake a lot of stuff, how the German had tried to get her, how he chased her once into the barn, how another time, when they happened to be alone in the house together, he tore her dress open clear down the front. The German, she said, might have got her that time if he hadn't heard his old woman drive in at the gate. She had been off to town for supplies. Well, she would be putting the horse in the barn. The German managed to sneak off to the fields without his wife seeing. He told the girl he would kill her if she told. What could she do? She told a lie about ripping her dress in the barn when she was feeding the stock. I remember now that she was a bound girl and did not know where her father and mother were. Maybe she did not have any father. You know what I mean.

Such bound children were often enough cruelly treated. They were children who had no parents, slaves really. There were very few orphan homes then. They were legally bound into some home. It was a matter of pure luck how it came out.

II

She married Jake and had a son and daughter, but the daughter died.

Then she settled down to feed stock. That was her job. At the German's place she had cooked the food for the German and his wife. The wife was a strong woman with big hips and worked most of the time in the fields with her husband. She fed them and fed the cows in the barn, fed the pigs, the horses and the chickens. Every moment of every day, as a young girl, was spent feeding something.

Then she married Jake Grimes and he had to be fed. She was a slight thing, and when she had been married for three or four years, and after the two children were born, her slender shoulders became stooped.

Jake always had a lot of big dogs around the house, that stood near the unused sawmill near the creek. He was always trading horses when he wasn't stealing something and had a lot of poor bony ones about. Also he kept three or four pigs and a cow. They were all pastured in the few acres left of the Grimes place and Jake did little enough work.

He went into debt for a threshing outfit and ran it for several years, but it did not pay. People did not trust him. They were afraid he would steal the grain at night. He had to go a long way off to get work and it cost too much to get there. In the Winter he hunted and cut a little firewood, to be sold in some nearby town. When the son grew up he was just like the father. They got drunk together. If there wasn't anything to eat in the house when they came home the old man gave his old woman a cut over the head. She had a few chickens of her own and had to kill one of them in a hurry. When they were all killed she wouldn't have any eggs to sell when she went to town, and then what would she do?

She had to scheme all her life about getting things fed, getting the pigs fed so they would grow fat and could be butchered in the Fall. When they were butchered her husband took most of the meat off to town and sold it. If he did not do it first the boy did. They fought sometimes and when they fought the old woman stood aside trembling.

She had got into the habit of silence anyway—that was fixed. Sometimes, when she began to look old—she wasn't forty yet—and when the husband and son were both off, trading horses or drinking or hunting or stealing, she went around the house and the barnyard muttering to herself.

How was she going to get everything fed?—that was her problem. The dogs had to be fed. There wasn't enough hay in the barn for the horses and the cow. If she didn't feed the chickens how could they lay eggs? Without eggs to sell how could she get things in town, things she had to have to keep the life of the farm going? Thank heaven, she did not have to feed her husband—in a certain way. That hadn't lasted long after their marriage and after the babies came. Where he went on his long trips she did not know. Sometimes he was gone from home for weeks, and after the boy grew up they went off together.

They left everything at home for her to manage and she had no money. She knew no one. No one ever talked to her in town. When it was Winter she had to gather sticks of wood for her fire, had to try to keep the stock fed with very little grain.

The stock in the barn cried to her hungrily, the dogs followed her about. In the Winter the hens laid few enough eggs. They huddled in the corners of the barn and she kept watching them. If a hen lays an egg in the barn in the Winter and you do not find it, it freezes and breaks.

One day in Winter the old woman went off to town with a few eggs and the dogs followed her. She did not get started until nearly three o'clock and the snow was heavy. She hadn't been feeling very well for several days and so she went muttering along, scantily clad, her shoulders stooped. She had an old grain bag in which she carried her eggs, tucked away down in the bottom. There weren't many of them, but in Winter the price of eggs is up. She would get a little meat in exchange for the eggs, some salt pork, a little sugar, and some coffee perhaps. It might be the butcher would give her a piece of liver.

When she had got to town and was trading in her eggs the dogs lay by the door outside. She did pretty well, got the things she needed, more than she had hoped. Then she went to the butcher and he gave her some liver and some dog-meat.

It was the first time anyone had spoken to her in a friendly way for a long time. The butcher was alone in his shop when she came in and was annoyed by the thought of such a sick-looking old woman out on such a day. It was bitter cold and the snow, that had let up during the afternoon, was falling again. The butcher said something about her husband and her son, swore at them, and the old woman stared at him, a look of mild surprise in her eyes as he talked. He said that if either the husband or the son were going to get any of the liver or the heavy bones with scraps of meat hanging to them that he had put into the grain bag, he'd see him starve first.

Starve, eh? Well, things had to be fed. Men had to be fed , and the horses that weren't any good but maybe could be traded off, and the poor thin cow that hadn't given any milk for three months.

Horses, cows, pigs, dogs, men.

III

The old woman had to get back before darkness came if she could. The dogs followed at her heels, sniffing at the heavy grain bag she had fastened on her back. When she got to the edge of town she stopped by a fence and tied the bag on her back with a piece of rope she had carried in her dress-pocket for just that purpose. That was an easier way to carry it. Her arms ached. It was hard when she had to crawl over fences and once she fell over and landed in the snow. The dogs went frisking about. She had to struggle to get to her feet again, but she made it. The point of climbing over the fences was that there was a short cut over a hill and through a woods. She might have gone around by the road, but it was a mile farther that way. She was afraid she couldn't make it. And then, besides, the stock had to be fed. There was a little hay left and a little corn. Perhaps her husband and son would bring some home when they came. They had driven off in the only buggy the Grimes family had, a rickety thing, a rickety horse hitched to the buggy, two other rickety horses led by halters. They were going to trade horses, get a little money if they could. They might come home drunk. It would be well to have something in the house when they came back.

The son had an affair on with a woman at the county seat, fifteen miles away. She was a rough enough woman, a tough one. Once, in the Summer, the son had brought her to the house. Both she and the son had been drinking. Jake Grimes was away and the son and his woman ordered the old woman about like a servant. She didn't mind much; she was used to it. Whatever happened she never said anything. That was her way of getting along. She had managed that way when she was a young girl at the German's and ever since she had married Jake. That time her son brought his woman to the house they stayed all night, sleeping together just as though they were married. It hadn't shocked the old woman, not much. She had got past being shocked early in life.

With the pack on her back she went painfully along across an open field, wading in the deep snow, and got into the woods.

There was a path, but it was hard to follow. Just beyond the top of the hill, where the woods was thickest, there was a small clearing. Had some one once thought of building a house there? The clearing was as large as a building lot in town, large enough for a house and a garden. The path ran along the side of the clearing, and when she got there the old woman sat down to rest at the foot of a tree.

It was a foolish thing to do. When she got herself placed, the pack against the tree's trunk, it was nice, but what about getting up again? She worried about that for a moment and then quietly closed her eyes.

She must have slept for a time. When you are about so cold you can't get any colder. The afternoon grew a little warmer and the snow came thicker than ever. Then after a time the weather cleared. The moon even came out.

There were four Grimes dogs that had followed Mrs. Grimes into town, all tall gaunt fellows. Such men as Jake Grimes and his son always keep just such dogs. They kick and abuse them, but they stay. The Grimes dogs, in order to keep from starving, had to do a lot of foraging for themselves, and they had been at it while the old woman slept with her back to the tree at the side of the clearing. They had been chasing rabbits in the woods and in adjoining fields and in their ranging had picked up three other farm dogs.

After a time all the dogs came back to the clearing. They were excited about something. Such nights, cold and clear and with a moon, do things to dogs. It may be that some old instinct, come down from the time when they were wolves and ranged the woods in packs on Winter nights, comes back into them.

The dogs in the clearing, before the old woman, had caught two or three rabbits and their immediate hunger had been satisfied. They began to play, running in circles in the clearing. Round and round they ran, each dog's nose at the tail of the next dog. In the clearing, under the snow-laden trees and under the wintry moon they made a strange picture, running thus silently, in a circle their running had beaten in the soft snow. The dogs made no sound. They ran around and around in the circle.

It may have been that the old woman saw them doing that before she died. She may have awakened once or twice and looked at the strange sight with dim old eyes.

She wouldn't be very cold now, just drowsy. Life hangs on a long time. Perhaps the old woman was out of her head. She may have dreamed of her girlhood, at the German's, and before that, when she was a child and before her mother lit out and left her.

Her dreams couldn't have been very pleasant. Not many pleasant things had happened to her. Now and then one of the Grimes dogs left the running circle and came to stand before her. The dog thrust his face close to her face. His red tongue was hanging out.

The running of the dogs may have been a kind of death ceremony. It may have been that the primitive instinct of the wolf, having been aroused in the dogs by the night and the running, made them somehow afraid.

"Now we are no longer wolves. We are dogs, the servants of men. Keep alive, man! When man dies we become wolves again."

When one of the dogs came to where the old woman sat with her back against the tree and thrust his nose close to her face he seemed satisfied and went back to run with the pack. All the Grimes dogs did it at some time during the evening, before she died. I knew all about it afterward, when I grew to be a man, because once in a woods in Illinois, on another Winter night, I saw a pack of dogs act just like that. The dogs were waiting for me to die as they had waited for the old woman that night when I was a child, but when it happened to me I was a young man and had no intention whatever of dying.

The old woman died softly and quietly. When she was dead and when one of the Grimes dogs had come to her and had found her dead all the dogs stopped running.

They gathered about her.

Well, she was dead now. She had fed the Grimes dogs when she was alive, what about now?

There was the pack on her back, the grain bag containing the piece of salt pork, the liver the butcher had given her, the dog-meat, the soup bones. The butcher in town, having been suddenly overcome with a feeling of pity, had loaded her grain bag heavily. It had been a big haul for the old woman.

It was a big haul for the dogs now.

IV

One of the Grimes dogs sprang suddenly out from among the others and began worrying the pack on the old woman's back. Had the dogs really been wolves that one would have been the leader of the pack. What he did, all the others did.

All of them sank their teeth into the grain bag the old woman had fastened with ropes to her back.

They dragged the old woman's body out into the open clearing. The worn-out dress was quickly torn from her shoulders. When she was found, a day or two later, the dress had been torn from her body clear to the hips, but the dogs had not touched her body. They had got the meat out of the grain bag, that was all. Her body was frozen stiff when it was found, and the shoulders were so narrow and the body so slight that in death it looked like the body of some charming young girl.

Such things happened in towns of the Middle West, on farms near town, when I was a boy. A hunter out after rabbits found the old woman's body and did not touch it. Something, the beaten round path in the little snow-covered clearing, the silence of the place, the place where the dogs had worried the body trying to pull the grain bag away or tear it open—something startled the man and he hurried off to town.

I was in Main Street with one of my brothers who was the town newsboy and who was taking the afternoon papers to the stores. It was almost night.

The hunter came into a grocery and told his story. Then he went to a hardware-shop and into a drugstore. Men began to gather on the sidewalks. Then they started out along the road to the place in the woods.

My brother should have gone on about his business of distributing papers but he didn't. Every one was going to the woods. The undertaker went and the town marshal. Several men got on a dray and rode out to where the path left the road and went into the woods, but the horses weren't very sharply shod and slid about on the slippery roads. They made no better time than those of us who walked.

The town marshal was a large man whose leg had been injured in the Civil War. He carried a heavy cane and limped rapidly along the road. My brother and I followed at his heels, and as we went other men and boys joined the crowd.

It had grown dark by the time we got to where the old woman had left the road but the moon had come out. The marshal was thinking there might have been a murder. He kept asking the hunter questions. The hunter went along with his gun across his shoulders, a dog following at his heels. It isn't often a rabbit hunter has a chance to be so conspicuous. He was taking full advantage of it, leading the procession with the town marshal. "I didn't see any wounds. She was a beautiful young girl. Her face was buried in the snow. No, I didn't know her." As a matter of fact, the hunter had not looked closely at the body. He had been frightened. She might have been murdered and some one might spring out from behind a tree and murder him. In a woods, in the late afternoon, when the trees are all bare and there is white snow on the ground, when all is silent, something creepy steals over the mind and body. If something strange or uncanny has happened in the neighborhood all you think about is getting away from there as fast as you can.

The crowd of men and boys had got to where the old woman had crossed the field and went, following the marshal and the hunter, up the slight incline and into the woods.

My brother and I were silent. He had his bundle of papers in a bag slung across his shoulder. When he got back to town he would have to go on distributing his papers before he went home to supper. If I went along, as he had no doubt already determined I should, we would both be late. Either mother or our older sister would have to warm our supper.

Well, we would have something to tell. A boy did not get such a chance very often. It was lucky we just happened to go into the grocery when the hunter came in. The hunter was a country fellow. Neither of us had ever seen him before.

Now the crowd of men and boys had got to the clearing. Darkness comes quickly on such Winter nights, but the full moon made everything clear. My brother and I stood near the tree, beneath which the old woman had died.

She did not look old, lying there in that light, frozen and still. One of the men turned her over in the snow and I saw everything. My body trembled with some strange mystical feeling and so did my brother's. It might have been the cold.

Neither of us had ever seen a woman's body before. It may have been the snow, clinging to the frozen flesh, that made it look so white and lovely, so like marble. No woman had come with the party from town; but one of the men, he was the town blacksmith, took off his overcoat and spread it over her. Then he gathered her into his arms and started off to town, all the others following silently. At that time no one knew who she was.

V

I had seen everything, had seen the oval in the snow, like a miniature racetrack, where the dogs had run, had seen how the men were mystified, had seen the white bare young-looking shoulders, had heard the whispered comments of the men.

The men were simply mystified. They took the body to the undertaker's, and when the blacksmith, the hunter, the marshal and several others had got inside they closed the door. If father had been there perhaps he could have got in, but we boys couldn't.

I went with my brother to distribute the rest of his papers and when we got home it was my brother who told the story.

I kept silent and went to bed early. It may have been I was not satisfied with the way he told it.

Later, in the town, I must have heard other fragments of the old woman's story. She was recognized the next day and there was an investigation.

The husband and son were found somewhere and brought to town and there was an attempt to connect them with the woman's death, but it did not work. They had perfect enough alibis.

However, the town was against them. They had to get out. Where they went I never heard.

I remember only the picture there in the forest, the men standing about, the naked girlish-looking figure, face down in the snow, the tracks made by the running dogs and the clear cold Winter sky above. White fragments of clouds were drifting across the sky. They went racing across the little open space among the trees.

The scene in the forest had become for me, without my knowing it, the foundation for the real story I am now trying to tell. The fragments, you see, had to be picked up slowly, long afterwards.

Things happened. When I was a young man I worked on the farm of a German. The hired-girl was afraid of her employer. The farmer's wife hated her.

I saw things at that place. Once later, I had a half-uncanny, mystical adventure with dogs in an Illinois forest on a clear, moon-lit Winter night. When I was a schoolboy, and on a Summer day, I went with a boy friend out along a creek some miles from town and came to the house where the old woman had lived. No one had lived in the house since her death. The doors were broken from the hinges; the window lights were all broken. As the boy and I stood in the road outside, two dogs, just roving farm dogs no doubt, came running around the corner of the house.

The dogs were tall, gaunt fellows and came down to the fence and glared through at us, standing in the road.

The whole thing, the story of the old woman's death, was to me as I grew older like music heard from far off. The notes had to be picked up slowly one at a time. Something had to be understood.

The woman who died was one destined to feed animal life. Anyway, that is all she ever did. She was feeding animal life before she was born, as a child, as a young woman working on the farm of the German, after she married, when she grew old and when she died. She fed animal life in cows, in chickens, in pigs, in horses, in dogs, in men. Her daughter had died in childhood and with her one son she had no articulate relations. On the night when she died she was hurrying homeward, bearing on her body food for animal life.

She died in the clearing in the woods and even after her death continued feeding animal life.

You see it is likely that, when my brother told the story, that night when we got home and mother and sister sat listening, I did not think he got the point. He was too young and so was I. A thing so complete has its own beauty.

I shall not try to emphasize the point. I am only explaining why I was dissatisfied then and have been ever since. I speak of that only that you may understand why I have been impelled to try to tell the simple story over again.

▾

If You Step on a Crack

by Sharon Solwitz

Her first and only husband sat on the couch in front of the pre-game inter-view, his attention flicking back and forth between her and the set. From four doors south across Waveland Avenue the lights of Wrigley Field cast their salmon glow on his long-sleeved shirt and the wall behind him. Three stories down, the steps of Cub and Cardinal fans crunched along the alley, a steady sound overlaid by occasional spates of mild, ritualized jeering. Blue and red caps glimmered in the September twilight as they bobbed toward the bleacher entrance. "Come let's cheer them on to ignominy," said Andy, to whom she had been married longer than any of her friends to their hus-bands. He held out his hand.

She had been watching with more than mild irritation a golden-haired boy of twenty or so take a whizz in the alley. "What fun," she said, to either, to both.

He laughed. "You have to think like a Cub fan. It's not victory we're after. It's watching them play almost well enough to win, then making fun of them and yourself for getting sucked in to hoping!" He laughed again. A high school vice principal, he was in his heart the Cubs play by play man. He'd call the games just ahead of Brennan and Harry Caray with patter at times identical to theirs. Tonight, though, she couldn't appreciate his gift.

"That's my back door," she called out the window. "Why don't you go smell up your own neighborhood?"

The boy turned up a face hauntingly beautiful in the manufactured twi-light. "Wanna zip me up, lady?"

"I'm calling the police!"

"Like I'm scared," he said.

"I'm boiling the oil," she shouted, "so why don't you stay right here under my window with your thing hanging out—"

"Maya," Andy said, "he's a Cardinal fan. That's how they're raised in St. Louis."

She turned, saw her five-year-old twins at the doorway, their identical mouths open in the same little O. "Guys, come here, I want to show you what not to turn into."

"Maya."

"I want to help speed you to an early death in which your body parts erode slowly," she whispered into the dusk. Her sons were dancing on tiptoe at her elbow, her husband, massaging the back of her neck, but she felt alone on an island. Last week at the mammogram follow-up she'd read upside down the last line of a paragraph on the print-out on Ahranjani's desk: *The possibility of tumor cannot be ruled out.*

—What are the chances either way? she'd asked him. Coolly, she thought.

—Fifty-fifty, I'd say. The calcifications bother me.

—Why do they bother you?

—They don't follow the line of the vein.

—But *calcifications*— They sound so *innocent!*

—Maya, get hold of yourself.

At the door of Andy's study trying to recall the tremor or whatever it was in her voice that Ahranjani had responded to, she'd felt her knees go weak. But Andy had processed the information so quickly she wasn't sure he'd absorbed it. "Fifty-fifty? Well— we'll think about the good fifty!"

She hadn't wanted to distress him. She'd wanted to bear her apprehension with grace and courage. But his optimism seemed empty and vague.

"Maya, honey, you'll know tomorrow. The worst part's the uncertainty."

"*I'll* know?" she said, the words coming from between her teeth. "What do you mean *I'll* know? Am I the only one who'll know?"

"Of course I'll know too," he said, more confused than wounded.

She did not say that the worst part was not at all the uncertainty but the chance of pain and disfigurement and early death. A woman she taught with was fighting lung cancer. Her friend Gail, four years younger, had just had a lumpectomy. Her mother had died from something that started with a bad mammogram. Her childhood heroine was Edith Cavell, an English nurse and member of the anti-German underground who, facing the firing squad, had refused a blindfold. Maya imagined Edith with her back to the bloody wall, a corner of her cotton gown rippling in the wind, her open eyes boring deep into the mouths of the muskets that would end her life. But she didn't want to be Edith Cavell. She didn't want to be caught and shot. "Let's make water balloons," she said to Seth and Simon. "When the enemy comes we have to be ready."

Because now everything meant something.

It was like twenty years ago when she swallowed a whole tab of acid when everyone else was doing half and got stuck in that quivery space right after the luminous ascent. Objects unfurled and refurled, into and out of whatever they were made of, threatening to freeze at the point of terrifying ugliness.

Then, it was dangerous to speak with friends you didn't absolutely trust or look too long at your face in the mirror. Now, for the past week, she ate only brown rice and vegetables high in vitamins A and C. She watched films from the forties with their classic, unambiguous lines of comedy or heroism. She tried to visualize the troops of her white blood cells marshalling their protective force at given parts of her body. But still her mind or whatever was attempting the control could not fully manage itself. She saw herself bald and then weak, sick, dead, mourned for—Andy bereft, then marrying again, Seth and Simon confused by her absence, then used to it, till she was a fragment of memory only a shrink could call up, a sweet, blurry face in a photograph.

Twenty years ago before husband, children, house, job, tripping on dare-devil acid in women's lock-up she had kept panic in check by meditating on the worst life could present her—poverty, shame, imprisonment for up to five years (the maximum penalty for possession of a shopping bag-ful of marijuana). She'd imagined herself ugly and old on a park bench, sans family and friends, a filthy blanket, a few torn paperbacks—all she owned—in a bag at her feet, and her mind, infused with the Zen she was practicing those days, had, gasping, managed to say, I can take it! When her boyfriend's family's lawyer came to lower her bond she was calm and remote, amused, almost, which annoyed, she could see, even her boyfriend. But now, tonight, testing each possible downward step in her current potential tragedy to see if it could bear her weight, she couldn't get as far, even, as "bald." She couldn't embrace for a minute the vision of her hair falling out, not one coarse, wavy red strand. So although she had come to the point as a Cubs fan of being able to recognize Andre Dawson on the street and to impress her husband's friends with her recall of, say, the number of homeruns he'd hit his first year as a Cub (49), she couldn't watch the Cubs on TV with Andy tonight. If she stepped on a crack she'd break her mother's back. When someone peed on their aluminum siding it eroded her small store of good luck. If the Chicago Cubs lost to the St. Louis Cardinals tonight, her body's immune system would be overwhelmed, her T cells helpless in the face of the dark area in the X ray of her right breast, a spot that was to be removed tomorrow morning and biopsied. And the Cubs were a game below five hundred, their hitting the second worst in baseball.

Her sister called. "Maya," she said, "I had *three* and they were all negative!" Her voice was loud and bright, thrumming with her own medical good fortune.

"I know," Maya said.

"You sound on top of it," her sister said. "I was a basket case the first time. I kept thinking about—you know. The last time wasn't so great either, I thought three strikes and you're out—"

"Call no man happy till he be dead," Maya said. "Sophocles said that. Or was it Aeschylus?"

"You're showing off, Maya."

"Janice," she said, "I have to put the kids to bed."

"Frankly," Janice said cheerfully, "I think it's just a matter of time. Sometimes I think I should get a *preventive* mastectomy."

"Janice, the kids are screaming for me."

"Janice drives me crazy," she said to Andy.

"Me too," he said, laughing as if he knew just what she meant. She felt none of the flow of warmth that signalled that she believed he did know.

He leaned back against the couch and stretched his legs as the Rainbow Children's Choir, all of whom had a physical or mental handicap, sang the national anthem. Her children sat on the floor with their backs to the screen, working on their Lego constructions. Seth's were always closed, perfect boxes, while Simon made vehicles bristling with flags and weapons. "The Star-Spangled Banner" rose swirling, pure and shrill into the air of the TV room. "Look, Mom," one of the boys would say from time to time, thrusting a primary-colored artifact into her hands. "Oh dear," she'd say, "will it explode?" Or, "I'd feel so safe inside!", relieved to see by their expressions of pleasure that she had not inadvertently conveyed her self-concern.

Once, the sound of crunch signalled footsteps in the alley. She and the boys leaned out the window, giggling frantically, juggling the wobbly balloons they'd filled with water. But so far no one else had tried to urinate. "It's a beautiful night here at Wrigley Field," Andy said.

"It's a beautiful night," said Harry Caray, "as the Cubs fight to hold onto third place."

Her father called with tears in his voice.

"Dad," she said, "I'm not dead yet."

On the other end of the line she felt him adjust his mood. "You always were a tough one," he said.

"That's correct," she said.

By the time the children's lights were out it was the top of the third, and the Cubs were already two down. She thumbed through the paper on the kitchen table, gazed at the first of the four words to unjumble on the Dear Abby/mindgame page—FLONE. She tried *elfon; fenol;* arriving at *felon,* staring till it too looked wrong. She wandered from room to room, adjusting pillows, returning small bright plastic figures to bright plastic tubs. She settled across the sofa from Andy, stretching her bare feet toward his lap.

He began to massage the arch of her foot, kneading deliciously just short of pain. He slipped a finger between two of her toes, a gesture as exquisitely sexual as junior high school, that sometimes liquefied the lower half of her body. But now her skin felt numb to the sixth or seventh layer. On the screen the Cubs pitcher walked two men in a row. His next pitch was so low the catcher collapsed on it, searched for it under his knees as the men went to second and third. "Here's the pitch. Ball three low. Wilkins had to pick it out of the dirt," Andy said.

"Wilkins made a great stop," said Harry Caray. "Looks like Morgan's having a little control problem."

Maya saw and heard but did not absorb, gauging the depth and the parameters of her isolation. It had been there last year at the cabin they rented in Door County, amid the pines, the mosquito repellent, Andy and the boys' obvious joy. It had been there the year before over expensive food at the Drake on their fifteenth wedding anniversary. In their current lovemaking she sometimes counted her husband's eyes one, two, three, four, or rode into orgasm on a fantasy of cinema and leather in which he played no part.

She returned to the kitchen, unscrambled the rest of the words without a pause, STORN (snort), DAWTOR (toward), SPOCER (corpse), angry with the *Jumble* editors for selecting the last word with all its unpleasant associations. As she tried to stave off the ugly picture it pulled the first three words into a declarative sentence: *Felon snort toward corpse*—she who had been accused but not convicted of being a *felon* (possession of marijuana in 1972) *snort*ing (cocaine, with an orthopedic surgeon she'd dated just before meeting Andy) *toward* her destiny as a *corpse*—a splash of verbal tea leaves pointing toward tomorrow's denouement? She stuffed the paper in the wastebasket.

There had once been between her and Andy something that could stop her thought. She remembered an airport good-bye, and tears in his eyes as he bent to pick up his suitcase. And the taste of his breath, the light prickle of the hairs on his arms; the entire week of his absence she slept with her cheek to the T-shirt he'd left at her apartment. When she'd had the twins at thirty-eight she had started to believe all over again that nothing was too late, they could have everything after all, if they worked hard enough. But the euphoria was gone, and that sense of visceral, passionate connection so remote it was less a feeling than a remembered idea—not through anyone's viciousness, just the normal erosion of intensity over time. If things turned out well tomorrow she would be happy, and perhaps happy with Andy, but some time not very far away, she felt sure, they would separate.

The Cubs tied it up in the bottom of the third, and Maya returned to the TV room. Andy held out his arms. She sat down beside him.

"Feeling better?" he said.

Blandly handsome Ryne Sandberg, who'd just gotten a double, took a step out from the base. In the on-deck circle Andre Dawson swung three bats around and around his head. Mark Grace, who looked to her like a cartoon athlete, grounded out to the pitcher. "I'm trying not to think about it," she said.

He nodded approval. "For the best."

A flash of white streaked before her eyes. She said in a light, conversational voice that hurt her ears, "You know, the real problem with illness and death is how alone you are."

"Maya," he said, "I do not believe you're ill. In fact, you look terrific tonight."

The sexual desire in his voice made something harsh rise to the back of her throat. "I'm trying to behave," she said. "I don't seem to be doing very well."

"You're doing fine," he said. She folded her hands in her lap, watched Dawson fly out to end the inning.

"This is how it's been," Andy said. "They are just not executing!"

"They look tuckered out," Harry Caray said cheerfully.

Steve Stone said, "They look bored. For 43 million you'd think they'd put out a little!"

To ease her sudden, irrational anger, which filled the air around her head with a kind of black dust, she tried to direct her breath in one nostril and out the other, a meditation she'd last practiced with her legs crossed on the bare metal bunk in women's lock-up. But she hadn't done anything like this in twenty years, she was assailed by the image of herself in a beauty chair, asking the operator, please, to weave the long thick curls she was shaving from her head into a wig that wouldn't look like a wig. Wearing the imaginary cunningly fashioned natural-hair wig that still looked like a wig, she saw the shock in the eyes of her friends as they said words of admiration or consolation and turned away, just as she had turned away from the blue cotton-knit turban her friend Gail had worn over her own balding head. Blue is restorative.

Unable to erase or alter the mental picture she worked to embrace it. Envisioned her face without the mane of hair that even now, in her forties, strangers would comment on. Imagined her features sans the aureole of her hair, small and ordinary-looking below the chemotherapy turban. Imagined her hair growing back under the turban, thicker and curlier than before, just as her mother's had, miraculously, without a trace of gray; in her coffin she had looked young and tragically beautiful, like Snow White. Standing before the firing squad, Edith Cavell had shaken her head at the proffered blindfold. Maya said the word "brave" to herself, a cup of tea to hold in her hands. Andy sat with his arm stretched out toward her on the back of the couch. Shyly, almost, he touched her shoulder. She inhaled through her left nostril, observed the stream of air passing out through her right, though her breaths were coming so hard her throat hurt trying to slow them down. "I keep thinking about my mother," she said.

He lowered the volume on the set. "That was ten years ago. Detection is better now."

"I can't remember what they called the bad stuff on her X ray. Was it calcifications?"

"Maya, you're going to drive yourself crazy."

"Do you want me to read Norman Cousins?"

"I don't know!"

She picked up one of the water balloons that were laid out on a towel under the window. She jiggled it in her hand. "The problem," she said, "is you have no capacity for flashforward."

"Would you like to make love?"

"No!" Her voice was pure and high to her ears, soundless as a dog whistle. "I would like to throw this water balloon at you."

"Go ahead," he said.

"That's the problem."

"What? That I won't fight with you?"

"You skitter over the surface of things. Your feelings have no substance." She shifted the heavy balloon from hand to hand, a little bomb; a breast. Within such frail walls its unexpected weight made it seem surreal, as if it came from a place with laws different from hers.

"Maya," he said, "I know why you're doing this."

He explained that she, like most people, revised history in the light of present good or bad fortune. If you're happy, then everything that's ever happened seems a rung in the ladder that has brought you there; and vice versa. "Mostly you like me, Maya. Try to remember that."

"Jesus," she almost shouted, "don't go rational on me. If I disappeared, you'd grieve for a day, then onward."

"That's idiotic!"

Her throat hurt where the words had emerged but there was more to say. "If someone accosted me on the street, you'd smile politely. You'd say, I wish you'd stop that, young man."

She squeezed the balloon tight, daring it to burst, and felt at the same time a twinge in her breast. Cancer doesn't hurt, she said to herself automatically. "I hate Norman Cousins," she said more lightly. "How can you tell someone to lower stress? Doesn't it create stress, working to lower stress?"

When she looked up, his face had gone rubbery. It was as if she had entered a mosque without covering her head or said something in English that turned out to be, in the local language, an obscenity. He gazed at the screen; didn't seem to hear the phone when it rang.

It was her best girlfriend Alice. "I won't keep you. I just want you to know I'm thinking about you, girl."

"Alice."

"Oh, dear," Alice said. "Do you want me to come over?"

The words Maya wanted to say were lodged behind some obstruction at the back of her throat.

"Where's Andy?" Alice said. "Listen, I'm coming over right now."

"No," Maya said. "I'm okay. I'm fine."

"You don't sound fine."

Maya swallowed. "I feel like murdering my husband. Although he is and has been a perfectly nice, caring person. But rational being that I still am, I know that my feelings might very well change tomorrow. So I will not murder my husband. At least not tonight. You can call me tomorrow night."

"Maya, I don't like to leave you like this."

"You're sweet, Alice. This helped. Really."

"Maya, I love you."

She opened the refrigerator, gazed at the covered bowls, the row of clean-wiped condiments in the door compartment.

She walked into the living room, raised the blind, gazed out on the dark garden. A roar from the crowd came in the window, crescendoed, stopped abruptly, a long fly ball caught on the warning track or rocketed into the stands just below the foul pole.

She ran down the hall to the children's partially open door, her eyes following the crack of hall light across Simon's blanket. She tiptoed into the room, lay down on the floor beside his futon. He breathed softly, evenly, in and out. His neck smelled sweet.

She returned to the living room. Outside, the pink-purple air hummed with the sounds of Wrigley Field, the rise and fall of fan pleasures and disappointments, a net of normality to catch her if she fell. She raised the screen, leaned out as far as she could, drinking in the warm, noisy summer air. If she believed in God, she might have resorted to bargaining: Give me good news tomorrow, and I'll plant an acre of trees in Israel, I'll give a tenth of my income to the JNF. But her offer, she was sure, was too paltry and trite for a God with real power over life and death, and even if the Eternal would have agreed to such a specifically Jewish, unimaginative pledge, she would have had to preface it with, "Excuse me, I know you haven't heard from me in a while, and I know it's wrong to come to you just when I need some-thing, and I'm not sure even now, talking, if someone is listening out there," her words dying into the silence of embarrassment and shyness.

"Don't jump," Andy said.

She pulled her head in, turned politely around.

"You were awful to me," he said.

"I know. I'm sorry." Although close enough to touch, he seemed small to her, as if she were looking at him through the wrong end of a telescope. "I don't think I love you, Andy."

"You don't mean that."

She fixed on the fine black mesh of the screen above the open mouth of the window, wanting to suck her words back into wherever they had come from. As a teenager her first uttered *I love you* had made something like flowers leap from her skin, melded the jumble of joy and terror and weak-ness in her limbs into a single emotion that felt eternal. Certain words, she had always known, had an alchemical creative force. She gave him a look of terrified apology.

"It's not true," he said. "Why do you say it if it's not true?"

Her eyes bored into his eyes, she cocked her head to the same side and at the same angle as his, trying to become better than she was. "I'm a bad yogi. I can't make the journey all by myself to the end of pain."

He embraced her, kissed her neck, kissed down the top of her chest to where her bra began.

"Here's a Zen story," she said. "A monk is being chased by a tiger to the edge of a cliff. He starts to climb down the cliff, but there's another tiger below, looking up hungrily. As the ledge he's on starts to crumble he sees a flower growing out of a rock, and smiles at the flower. And receives instan-taneous and perfect enlightenment."

"And so?"

"I don't feel like smiling at flowers."

"Maybe you need more tigers in your life."

He unhooked her bra, kissed a circle around her right, her questionable breast.

He said, "Don't you want me to do this?"

She wanted to want him to do this, their perhaps last lovemaking with her body intact. But the idea made her shudder. Her skin was a layer of dead whitish cells, dry and tight over her bones; she could not suffer the opening and entry into her body like Edith Cavell. She turned to one side, shielding her chest with her upper arm. "Okay," he said. "All right."

He returned to the TV room. She walked downstairs, out to the front gate. South across Waveland the heads of the top row of bleacher fans bobbed and swayed against the purple sky. Behind her their own white-sided build-ing glowed a ghostly amethyst, insubstantial as a storybook house. The air shimmered with the silence of a mass of people waiting for something to happen. There came a loud cheer; someone had done something good. But lots of Cardinal fans had come to the game. She couldn't see the scoreboard, didn't know whether to be pleased or concerned.

The wind rose slightly, a cool September breeze. Turning to go back in, she saw at her feet, glowing salmon-pink like everything else, a crumpled McDonald's carryout bag. Inside were the remains of a Big Mac and an empty Batman cup, recently tossed over the chain-link fence that encircled their yard. Holding the bag between thumb and forefinger she felt her way along the narrow passage between her house and a neighbor's, unlocked the wooden gate to the alley.

She had just dropped the bag into one of the alley trash bins when foot-steps she hadn't registered made her aware of them as they abruptly ceased. Less than ten feet away a man stood with his back to her. She watched a dark spot form between his legs at the base of her house. A puddle gathered at his feet. He danced out of the way, resnapping his pants, giving her a smile of somewhat inebriated complicity. Blond, with small, exquisite features, he might have been the man she had screamed at earlier that night.

"You seem to like our facilities," she said.

He gazed at her, his smile drying on his face. He shrugged and walked away. She stared at his retreating back, the triangular narrowing from shoul-der to hip of a well-built young man. She called out, "You know, you're not that well hung."

He stopped, turned. "What's that, ma'am?"

"Did your mother bring you up to be a disgusting pig? Where are your manners and your brains?"

"Shit," he said.

She stood her ground, inured to pain like a yogi, like someone who knows no matter what that she will die tomorrow. "You have an itsy-bitsy teeny-weeny dick. I want you to think about that next time you want to pull your pants down where you're not supposed to. What, are you going to sock me? There's a brave lad."

He took a step toward her, a hand upraised. His handsome boyish face looked red, though it might have been the lights of Wrigley. Part of her wanted to run but her legs were stiff; she didn't move even when he was close enough for her to smell the beer on his breath. But when he grabbed her shoulder so hard the little bones crunched together, she was astonished to find herself doing what had been forbidden so many years ago she couldn't remember ever having had the impulse: She bit the back of his hand. As he fell back, drawing his hurt hand to his mouth, she felt on her tongue the little hairs on his skin, the oddly metallic taste of his blood, and she fled inside the gate and upstairs, locking doors.

From the TV-room window she and Andy tossed out water balloons, watched the young man vanish into the shadows at the end of the alley. They gave each other a high five. She was trembling, he, unnerved by what she had just done, laughing wildly. He put his arms around her; they sank to the floor. She looked at his face, wondering whether or not she honestly wanted to kiss him, when a small, blurred but unmistakeable jolt ran through her body along her spine to the bones of her skull. It was the physical equivalent of a dream she sometimes had of falling out of bed. She jumped up, noticing that one of the children's Lego constructions had fallen off its shelf. Andy shouted out the window, "Stop that!" She felt another jolt. The TV rocked on its stand. "It's your friend," he said.

Down in the alley an old white convertible backed up three or four feet till it banged the garage on the other side. In the driver's seat was a blond-haired, red-faced, handsome young man. Head down, shoulders hunched like a football player, he slammed his car at a corner of their building. There was a distinct crack.

"Our back gate," he said.

In the purple light the man's wet hair looked pink, his head smaller than before. He backed up again. She dialed 911, but as she gave their address she was thrown to the floor. "Andy honey, he's trying to knock our house down!"

"We should have built out of brick," he said.

"That's really funny."

"We're taking things into our own hands," he said, raising the window as high as it would go. He took out the screen. "Let's hear it for Bernard Goetz. Give me a hand with the TV, darling."

Together they lifted the heavy set to the windowsill, balancing it on the edge. "When he makes his next move, just let go," he said. "Let's hear it for Bernard and Mrs. Goetz. Your Honor, sir, I was protecting my family. Aim for the windshield. I hope we don't kill him."

"Andy, are you sure you want to take the chance—"

Her words trailed off. She stood at the window beside him, burning with a fury so pure and unfettered it was almost love, the two of them, husband and wife together holding their relatively new 24-inch Sony portable television set against the ravaging hordes. There was a siren, a flashing blue light. Startled, she let go of her side of the load. To compensate, Andy pulled back on his side, then to stop the set from falling on him, he sent it forward and out the window. It dented the trunk of the big white car speeding off down the alley, then smashed into its elemental shards of glass and pressboard.

The police car screamed away after the convertible and for a moment there was silence. Then came a roar, at first tentative, then crescendoing, sustaining itself. They ran to the living room, turned on the radio to learn that Mark Grace had just crossed the plate. He had blasted a ball out onto Waveland Avenue. With a man on. Bottom of the seventh, Cubs 4, Cardinals 2.

She sat down on the floor beside Andy, leaning back against the sofa. "The floor feels sloped. Does it feel sloped to you?"

"It's always been sloped."

"We should inspect." She tried to get up.

"Tomorrow."

"I'm busy tomorrow," she said. "That's supposed to be funny!"

She broke away from him, saw tears in his eyes, sat down. "What's the matter, Andy? The Cubs might win this one."

He kissed her forehead.

"Andy," she said, "tell me why you're crying."

He wouldn't look at her.

"Andy," she said, "I know why."

He took her hand, kissed it. His cheeks were damp.

"This is what I wanted." She kissed his mouth. Her lips felt warm and larger than usual, she loved kissing him. "To know you're in this too."

"Of course, I'm in it!" he said. "Where else have I been?!"

"But now I *feel* it. Before, I couldn't feel it."

"I don't see why you couldn't feel it!"

He seemed a little angry with her but she was kissing his face, his hands. They made love on the floor like teenagers, wild and mindless of consequences. When at last they rolled onto their separate backs on the rug, he said, "So from now on I can only have you when there's a war going on outside?"

"That's right. If I know you're concerned about it."

"I don't know if I can take it." He laid his head against the base of the sofa, gazing out at the salmon-gray night.

"You'd better," she said. She watched him absorb the top of the ninth. There was one out. According to Steve Stone, Assenmacher (4 saves) was keeping the ball low. "You'd better," she said, but without urgency. The voices of the announcers seemed preternaturally sharp, almost luminous. Balls crackled like lightning into the catcher's mitt. She felt whole, well, immortal as a teenager. "I have this nice feeling," she said, her lips to the top of his arm.

"It'll go away," he said.

"But it's here now," she said, licking his arm, savoring the sharp, sour taste of salt.

▼

Apple

by Josip Novakovich

One snowless winter morning before going to school, I collected sawdust in baskets in Father's clog shop and dumped it out in the yard next to a walnut tree. The circular saw was running in his shop, yet I saw no father behind it. I found him in a corner, behind a pile of wooden soles, prostrate, praying. I was terrified of his praying.

Late that evening as Father drank warm milk and chewed dark bread, he told our grandmother how he'd heard someone calling him—the way Samuel was called—and yet he could see nobody. It was an angel of God calling him to prayer. That afternoon he had also felt someone touch him on the shoulder, and when he had turned around there was nobody. An angel of God had been there to strengthen him.

Grandmother said that she was glad to hear it, and then she coughed. When she didn't cough, her bronchial wheezing had a soothing rhythm to it, and I listened to it more than to my father's stories, which went on all evening.

The next morning, Father walked around the town and begged everybody for forgiveness "in the name of Christ" for all the wrongs that he had wittingly and unwittingly committed. He gave his former assistant, who now had his own shop, two bales of ox-hide. Earlier my father had sold him a rotten bale, creating a bad reputation for the assistant's new business.

Father brought home an astonished old peasant, forcing him to take a large sum of money because, several years before, Father had forced the peasant to sell him wood too cheaply—the peasant had wept, to no avail, that he and his children could not make it through the winter on so little money.

The following Sunday, even though it was my father preaching in our Baptist church, I was bored, and made deep creases between the grains of the soft bench wood with my thumbnails, each crease representing one year—that's how long it seemed that the sermon lasted. Stealthily, I read a chapter from *A Journey to the Center of the Earth,* which I had stored in the Bible. A retired electrician and distant relative, who sat behind me, tapped me on the shoulder to make me stop. My father preached Christ's giving up His ghost on the cross, and in the middle of the sermon he wept.

Father had played the bass in the church orchestra and sang with the deepest voice in the choir. When he shouted at home, the whole household, including the cat, ran out into the yard. When he missed shaving for just one day, his chin was black; he often rubbed his raspy cheeks against mine, laughing—if he had pressed harder, he would have swept off my skin. The same man now cried in front of more than a hundred people. I blushed.

But at home, as if aware that I was ashamed of him, he said to me, "If you understood God's grace, you would have to weep." He took me out into the moonless night, and from the apple-scented garden he pointed to the stars swimming in moist, dizzying blackness. "See, God created the stars. It takes millions of years for the light to reach our eyes, and God's thought is everywhere in no time at all. God's thoughts are right here with us."

"I can't feel it," I said.

"You are lucky you can't. Moses could see God's radiance only from behind as It passed. We would die if we saw nearly as much. You cannot be close to God and live!"

It was January 6th, and snow stormed outdoors, slantedly. When I looked through the window, I had the feeling that the household floated into heaven sideways. The big patches of snow resembled the down of a huge, slain celestial bird, whose one wing covered our whole valley, and the spasmodic wing must have been flapping, because it was windy. As soon as the snow touched the ground, it melted.

After a day in the clog-making shop, Father stepped into the living room, solemn and luminous. Ivo read comic books. Father said to him, "Don't blaspheme against God by reading trash. Why don't you read the Bible, or study math?"

"I don't feel like it," said Ivo.

The cat, who was sleeping on the roof of a large clay stove, stretched herself and blinked, her pupils contracting in vertical slits, coiled her tail as if scared Father would deliver her a blow, and jumped off the stove. Usually she rushed to sit in his lap. Now she sat on the Bible on the chair next to my bed and licked her paws, now and then looking at him mistrustfully.

"And you," he addressed me, "how can you allow this dirty animal to sit on the Bible?" As if to punctuate his question, the cat twisted her body and licked the root of her tail. I chased her off the somber book. Mother's slow, heavy steps resounded in the corridor, against the cement, louder and louder. She walked in with a basketful of wood and, breathing heavily, knelt in front of the stove and stirred the thin ashen embers with her bare fingers in such a quick way that she did not burn herself. Her method of doing it always disturbed me.

"Sons, why do you let Mother carry the wood? Why don't you help her?"

We made no reply.

He addressed me, "Yozzo, bring me an apple from the attic."

I went to the attic over the creaky wooden steps, and the flashlight didn't work. I was scared of the dark. I knew the attic very well, so I found the apples and pressed them with my thumb to find a large one, neither hard nor soft, but crunchy. Taking the red apple with his large hand from mine, he said, "I didn't know we had such beautiful apples—you surely can choose! I hope you choose your wife so well, so you won't look at other women and sin in your heart. Hum, there's nothing more joyous in this life than the beauty of a woman."

My mother said, "That's no way to talk to a child!" He replied, "It is."

"Will I ever be able to speak in tongues?" I asked him. "He can do it"— I pointed at Ivo—"though he reads garbage!"

"Though I speak with the tongues of men and of angels, and have not charity, I am become as sounding brass, or a tinkling cymbal. And though I have the gifts of prophecy, and understand all mysteries . . . and though I have all faith, so that I could remove mountains, and I have not charity, I am nothing. Don't worry about the tongues, son."

"But if I spoke in tongues, then I'd be sure to go to heaven."

"He who wants to save his life, will lose it, and he who loses it for my sake, will gain it. Don't worry about salvation."

He looked at me for a long time. Then he dug his teeth, some of them made of gold, into the apple, his gray mustache spreading like a brush on the red skin of the fruit while he was biting. Saliva collected in my mouth as if he had chewed a lemon. He ate one half slowly and left the rest on the plate. A haze of brown soon covered the white crystal apple meat. His face suddenly lost color, turning ashen gray, and he said, "I don't feel well."

"Let's go to the doctor's, then!" said my mother.

"No, I don't want to go there."

"Let me go fetch him."

"No. Maybe I'll go there tomorrow, if God wills."

"You speak strangely, let me go."

"No, it's no big deal—everything will happen the way God wills it."

My mother didn't look pleased at his conversation and she left for the bedroom. In the doorway as he was leaving the living room, he looked long, sadly, at Ivo, who continued reading the comic books, and at me, as I patted the purring heathen goddess. He closed the door quietly.

In *The Secrets of Paris* I read about drunks and wondered what it was like to be so drunk in a cellar that you sing without noticing that you are doing it. I fell asleep, the book sliding out of my hands.

Late at night I heard a scream. Ivo was shaking me violently, "Father's dying!" he shrieked.

It was pitch black in the room. I sprang out of bed, and both of us ran to the bedroom of our parents. "Where's Mother?"

"Gone to get the doctor."

There was a feeble light from the night table casting an orange hue over our father; the corners of the room stayed dark. In the double marital bed, two beds put together, he lay in his striped blue and gray pajamas. His gray chest hair stuck out through the unbuttoned top of his pajama shirt. He was propped up on a pillow. His eyes were closed and he breathed slowly, inarticulate sounds coming from his throat. Above the bed was a photograph, framed in wood: he—in military uniform—and my mother at their wedding, cheek against cheek, both of them handsome and unsmiling.

His breath was partly a snore, partly a sort of choking. His face was pale, and as he hadn't shaved that day, his chin was blue and gray. Ivo and I were so terrified that we couldn't go to his side of the bed; we went to our mother's side. We started screaming prayers, whatever came to our minds, to the Heavenly Father, to let our earthly father live. We had been taught to keep our eyes closed when praying. So I was closing my eyes to pray, and opening them to see how our father was. His gurgling noises came from his throat, as if he were using a mouthwash. White foam appeared on his lips, and began to trickle down his chin from one corner of his mouth. We shrieked.

"God, don't kill him!" I yelled.

"God, let it be your will to let him live! We cannot change your will, but make it your will, if . . ." Ivo shouted.

A drop of blood trickled from our father's nose, onto his mustache, and from it onto his chin, and it dropped onto the hair of his chest. A loud breath came out of him, and it lasted long, without him drawing in another, and when the body was silent, again, some more air wheezed out of his throat and red foam appeared in the corners of his lips. His head dropped forward. Ivo and I grabbed his left hand. He had taught us where to find the pulse, hoping we would wish to become doctors in order to find all about the ways of the heart. I pushed Ivo's fingers away, so I could feel, he pushed mine, so he could feel. No pulse. His hand was cool and swollen. Ivo, green in face, pressed his palm against Father's chest, kneeling on the empty side of the bed.

"Nothing! His heart's stopped!" he shouted. "It's finished."

I looked at the clock next to the preserved cherries and blackberries on the dark brown cupboard—grains slanting into trapezoid forms. The large hand of the clock covered the small hand.

"Midnight!" I shouted. "And it's the midnight between the sixth and seventh days of the month! Isn't six the number of man, and seven the number of God?"

"Yes! Yes! That means he went to God!" Ivo said. "That's a sign!" We stared at his face. It bore no expression, neither joy nor sadness, neither peace nor war; he looked as if he were listening to something attentively with his eyes closed, like an icon in which ears and not eyes see you.

Ivo said, "Look!" and pointed at a piece of paper—Father's handwriting was on it, in blue ink. "In his last hour, when Mother had gone to the doctor's, he called me and asked for a piece of paper. He wrote down his will calmly. See, his handwriting is no different from usual—just read, see how clear his mind was!

"Then he said, 'Look, I will die very soon. Don't forget to love God with all your heart, mind, and soul, don't ever forget that, and all else will come from it. Let us pray.' We began to pray, he prayed for all of us, except for himself. Then he grew quiet and closed his eyes and began to breathe heavily. I began to pray for him aloud. He opened his eyes, and said, 'Not for me, pray for yourself! You are remaining on earth, and now leave me in peace, I must breathe out my soul to God.' Then he lay back on the pillow, like now."

My body trembled and my teeth chattered. I looked around as if to find a getaway, but the windows and the door could not do. There was no way out.

"So I prayed again to God to spare him," said Ivo. "He opened his eyes once more, and said, 'I am going!' He meant he was going to heaven. He said it with certainty." Ivo's face was yellow green and his eyes slanted, as if he had changed his race to Mongolian. "What will become of us?" he asked me. Our father lay no longer a man but a corpse on the bed; blackness of the night was seeping in through the windows. The clock ticked like a time bomb.

We went into the living room, turned on the lights, and didn't dare to leave the room. I prayed to God to revive my father as He did Lazarus—I would serve Him all my life then. Yet I was scared that Father would indeed be brought back to life, but not be the same as he used to be; instead, he might have something heavenly in him, something that would kill me on the spot as soon as I beheld it, turning me into ashes.

The doors opened. Mother, wet from snow, came in with the doctor. Ivo and I stood in the middle of the room in our long spacious flannel pajamas, with broad blue vertical stripes, in the fashion of Turkish soldiers from an old picture book. With the doctor came in the stink of tobacco and booze. "Where is he?" he asked without breaking his stride.

"He's dead," I said.

"But where is he?"

"He is in heaven!" said Ivo. "You won't find him anymore."

"Oh, my God," cried our mother in an unearthly chilling way. And she ran with the doctor following her into the bedroom. We watched from the door. The doctor listened with his stethoscope, searching for sounds on the chest of our father. "It's too late!" he said.

Our pale mother said, "My God, what will I do with these ones?" and looked at us. Besides being terrified, I was scared, if that makes sense, that aside from a big fear of death, I had a smaller fear, of the future. How would we live? The doctor walked out, his chin on his chest, and several men walked in.

The man who used to help my father make clogs, Nenad, opened his mouth as if he would say something, but he said nothing. The uncle, a hefty man, breathed heavily, went to see the corpse and stayed there for a long time. He came back and grunted, as though he were asleep and snoring.

He lifted me onto his knee and rocked me up and down thoughtfully. His whole chest rising and falling, he said, "One thing is the other life, and another this life, and we don't have him anymore."

When Ivo and I went to our bedroom, Ivo switched off the lights, and I switched them back on. "Why do you want the lights on? You can't sleep with the lights on."

"I'd be scared of the dark," I said.

"What more is there to be scared of?" he snarled.

"I want the lights on," I said, and he let me have my way. Soon he was wheezing, asleep. I couldn't sleep. What if I die too? I couldn't breathe well. Maybe I am dying? No, children don't die just like that, unless they have a high fever. I touched my forehead, and it felt cool, but feelings could lie. But why should fever be dangerous? Fever should be healthy, the farthest away from death—death is cold. I shivered under my covers. I looked at the window—a big blue-black square in the wall. I propped myself up in bed, realizing I wouldn't be able to sleep, realizing my father had died in this position. I lay on my side, but the black windows behind my back disturbed me; when I faced them, they disturbed me even more.

What if God doesn't exist, and here we are almost envying our father for having died a holy death? I looked at Ivo with envy. See, he's a good Christian, he has peace. He has seen the whole death, and I missed it. When I came in, Father was no longer conscious; maybe he was already dead, or in the last stretch of dying; perhaps he would have told me something, the way Jacob told his son Joseph.

Still, the way it was it seemed it had to be. I felt ill in my stomach, and didn't dare to move out of my bed, lest I should injure the holy balance of reality, its finality.

I heard firm boot steps on the staircase, and then in the corridor. My older brother Vlado, who had been serving as a physician in the army in Novi Sad, stepped into the room, and said: "I heard it. Don't be afraid, everything will be all right. Why don't you switch off the lights, it's daybreak?"

"Look how dark it is." I pointed at the black square in the wall.

"No, it isn't, look!" He switched off the lights, and the square changed into light gray-blue. "And if I turn the lights back on, it'll look dark outside, but it isn't." He was in a green uniform, a cap with a red star on his head. He had a benevolent, encouraging expression on his face. Then our mother came in and said, "You know, that lout of a doctor, Slivich, was not at the hospital when he was supposed to be. He had left a message that he was at the Happy Cellar but went instead to the Last Paradise on Earth. By the time I found him, drinking and gambling, Father was already dead." She pointed in the direction of the bedroom with the corpse, tears in her nose. "Cerebral hemorrhage, he said."

Vlado went to see the corpse. He came back and said that it was a heart attack, and that Father could have been saved with a timely injection of adrenaline.

"But he didn't want me to get the doctor," she said. "Everything that happens is His will, he said, and not a single hair falls out without His will. Maybe it's better this way. He had ruined his health—two years in the army before the war, five in the war in the rain, sleet, snow, and sun ruined his kidneys. He had taken so many medications for kidneys, high blood pressure—his heart loomed so large on X rays that it always astonished doctors. And then the religious seizure—he did not even sleep, he prayed and prayed for the last two months!"

"He could have lived on—a large heart is not necessarily a terrible thing," said Vlado.

Now it was bright outdoors and we switched off the lights. The sun began to shine.

I walked out of the house and sat on a felled tree trunk—and with my thumbnails I peeled the rugged bark. The windows on the house loomed black. My mother called me in for breakfast. Nauseated, I put my finger on my tongue.

A friend of Ivo's, Zoran, walked into the yard and sat next to me on the trunk and peeled the bark. "Now we are the same!" He seemed to be glad—now we could be real friends. His father had been killed while defending a woman from a rapist, who had shoved a bayonet through his chest. Zoran had grown up without a father, without any recollection of him whatsoever. Often in the middle of shooting arrows at trees, playing Robin Hood—he was Will Scarlet; I, Little John; Ivo, Robin Hood—he'd asked me, "How is it to have a father?"

"I don't know how to tell you—I don't know how it is not to have a father."

Now I said, "Yes, now we are the same."

"You'll find out how it is to live without a father," he said.

"Yes."

"But I still won't be able to find out how it is to have a father, and you know that," he said.

"Yes, now I'll know nearly everything I wanted to know," I said.

"So we are not exactly the same." He tore a thorn from a roseless rosebush, and cleaned his teeth, pushing the thorn between them, and he did it so violently that he spat blood.

"So we are not exactly the same," I said.

Several hours later more than a dozen relatives in the living room discussed the dead man. My sister-in-law said, "When we saw him last at the train station, he waved to us for a long time, as if he knew he wouldn't see us again. He had joked wittily, played with his granddaughter"—a blond little brat who at the moment dug her fingers into the soil of a flowerpot, and began to knead it into a cake—"and lifted her onto his shoulders. I thought, What a healthy man!" Everybody evoked their last images of him aloud and it was all said in a tone of regret, amazement, and, at the same time, admiration for the integrity of his death. I thought I could contribute. "Ivo shook me out of sleep in the back room. He screamed, 'Father's dying!' I leaped out of bed, and there he was, purple foam trickling down his chin, gurgling noises coming through his throat, and then he choked, and the blood trickled from his nose. . . . "

Everyone in the room frowned. I became quiet. There was silence. I thought I had said something wrong; I put my right shoulder over my chin, to hide my mouth. Yes, they didn't like hearing anything from me; I wanted to impress them with how much I'd suffered and with how much my father had! I should have told them something uplifting, like Ivo when he tells them the religious stuff, like "I am going," and that stuff about the midnight between the sixth and the seventh days.

During the day, my mother washed the corpse and changed it from pajamas into a suit, his Sunday best, which he had worn on the way to the church to preach about the death of Christ. Now, however, he had no hat on his head. His swollen chubby hands with two purple nails (from hammer misses in work) were intertwined as if in prayer, though when he was dying he had lain at his sides. Maybe the hat should be put over the hands, I thought. He lay in a casket on the dining table where he used to sing, joke, and play the guitar as well as tell us Biblical stories, adding to them things I couldn't find in the Bible, like more and more adventures of Jonah. The undertaker, who had brought the casket with Father's name and age in golden letters, put some disinfecting white dust into Father's ears and nose, and then plugged the ears and nostrils with cotton—to keep the death inside.

The curtains were rolled down. Mother went to the neighbors across the road, to an old woman whose husband, also a clog-maker, had died three years before, and returned with the black flag. I went into the street to see how the house would look with the flag. Above the swallows' nests that Mother had shattered with the flagpole in the fall to prevent the swallows' return in the spring, the black flag came out between the red tiles where Father used to stick out the flag of our Socialist Federal Republic of Yugoslavia. The house looked like the tower of a missing castle, with a very simple and ominous emblem.

I recalled a dream from five years before. In the dream, Father and I sit in the living room next to Mother's casket. He says, We'll have to live without her. Can we live without her? I ask. I think so, he says. At that, I had screamed in my dream, and when I opened my eyes I was relieved that it was dawn. My mother had asked me what was wrong, and I couldn't tell her that I had dreamed she was dead, so I said that a pack of wolves was tearing me to pieces.

Hearing from my father about the prophetic powers of dreams, for years I had feared that my mother would die. And now Mother and I were sitting with Father's corpse, wondering how life without him would be.

Many people came to pay homage. Mother led them into the living room without turning on the lights. There were no candles at the side of his head. Some light came through the half-opened door and through the curtains. A strong disinfecting smell stung my eyes and nose. And what was the smell there for? To disinfect the dead one from death or from the last traces of life?

I wanted to touch my father again, but I couldn't, as if death in him would devour me too if I touched it. His cheeks were growing purple; the capillaries around his eyes were breaking open. His chin was covered with white and black stubble. Yet he still looked somehow good-natured and attentive, with his arched eyebrows and the clean parallel lines on his large forehead. His relatives and friends gathered around the casket. Some crossed themselves. Some wept. It made me glad to think that others were sad too, but

I wished they wouldn't stare like that—it was obscene, they looked at my father as if he were a new species. Ivo and I stood in the corridors all day long and asked each other, "Do you want to see him one more time?"

"I think I couldn't anymore," we would say and go back in.

The day of the burial arrived, cold and windy. "This is your last chance to see him," our mother said to us. She walked to the casket and kissed Father's purple corpse, her tears dropping onto his ear. The mortician, a dry bony man whose mustache was white on the sides and yellow beneath his nose from smoking, said, "Time to go!" He seized the casket cover, which had been leaned against the wall like some great gilt shield, and laid it atop the casket. He took a hammer and nails in his hands. Vlado snatched those away from him. As a child Vlado had worked with hammer and nails, helping with the work of nailing leather onto the wooden soles. Even Ivo and I had had to do it, and several times we had stayed up all night to meet the glass-factory deadline; we all took pride in being the best hands with hammers and nails.

Vlado hammered the nails through the yellow metal holes on the side of the cover. He hit with measure. Both the living man who was hammering and the dead man who was being hammered in must have hammered millions of nails each, the dead one more than the living one. The sound of the hammering was dull; there was no echo from the box because the box was full. Our mother wanted to take Ivo and me out of the room so we wouldn't witness this, but we wouldn't let her. I wondered why I wasn't crying. I could barely breathe, there was pressure on my chest, and my body was cold and electrified.

Four people carried the casket through the doors, down the steps of white, black-spotted stone. Masons from the Dalmatian Coast had made the steps, smoothing them out for days, and they had shown me pictures of women's pubic hair, and I hadn't believed them. I had thought women had pearls in shells there, not hair. The crowds parted before the casket like the waters of the Red Sea before Moses. The casket was carried through the varnished oak door of the house entrance into the yard, with the carriers maneuvering and panting as if with a heavy piece of furniture. There was a crowd waiting next to the thorn bushes, next to the cherry trees—no leaves—and next to the flat wall of our neighbor's house.

That wall carried no windows except a small one of the larder, with iron grates over it. People used to point their fingers at our neighbor—he had been in the wrong army during the war. Now he stood against the wall, gray, ghastly, as if waiting to be shot by a firing squad. In the midst of the yard stood a black hearse with a silvery cover. Two black horses with blinders stood in front of it, and steam rose from their backs, from the areas not covered by black satin. They did not move their tails—probably the function of tails is mostly to chase away flies, and in January there were none. They bowed their heads, as if there were grass among the wet gravel, or as if they reacted to the human emotion and gave it even better expression than the people could. The casket screeched onto the hearse. The horses moved their ears as if the noise had tickled them. The screeching brought a chalk whiteness to my sister, Nella, who had just arrived from West Germany, where she was studying to become a nurse. I used to irritate her by driving big pots over cement, because I knew that she hated the screeching of dry chalk on blackboards, and pots on the cement. Men in black, a variety of relatives, hooked green wreaths with purple tapes onto the feeble top frame of the hearse.

A procession formed. Mother, two brothers, I, and two sisters stepped behind the hearse, and behind us, three uncles and five aunts. One uncle was missing because he had loved cars so much that, as the first mechanic in town, in the middle of the winter he had lain on the ground beneath the cars and had caught pneumonia and died. I chose to walk next to Nella rather than Ivo. The procession was very slow. Now and then I turned around to see how my uncles were. They all looked thoughtful. The steadfastness of the pace held a lesson for us, some lesson anyway, as we shifted from one leg to another. Howsoever slowly we went, by howsoever many places, we could not deviate from the crooked path that led into the graveyard. We went across the railroad tracks, the casket bumping up and down. Then over a hill, past the shabby house where Father and his nine siblings had grown up. As the oldest son, he had helped his father in clog making and had attended only four grades of elementary education, though he'd been declared the best pupil of his class two years in a row, and though the school principal himself besought my grandfather to give his son a chance. "I'd be delighted to," replied my grandfather, "If you, Mr. Principal, replaced my son in the shop to feed all these children." The grandfather had died of cancer—because of his strong faith in God he had refused to go to the hospital to have a growth removed. The house had been sold a long time ago. Now in the backyard many white geese greeted the funeral with hissing. We walked around the cemetery onto a hill with three crosses in imitation of Golgotha: Jesus crucified between two robbers. Jesus was missing, somebody must have stolen him. But the robbers were on the crosses, white pigeon paint making stripes down their cheeks, as if they were weeping.

The Baptist cemetery was fenced off from the Catholic and Communist cemeteries—the Eastern Orthodox cemetery was on another hill—corresponding to our isolation in the community. Wherever we went, fingers pointed at us and hushed whispers followed us; we were called the "new-believers" in derogatory tones of voice—meaning the "wrong-believers."

The hearse got stuck in the muddy ditch between the road and the Baptist cemetery. The coachman whipped the horses with a thin leather whip to inspire them to pull the hearse, and the hearse nearly toppled over. My three uncles and a grave digger carried the casket off the hearse. The horses pulled the hearse out of the ditch. They bowed, staring at the ground, but now and then they lifted their heads and watched the burial with their large moist eyes, their foreheads contorting into sad, thoughtful expressions.

In the Baptist cemetery wooden crosses, cracked from heat, rain, and cold, tilted in the soft soil, the names erased. Others, made of old thin stone, collected moss on their northern sides, as though to protect them from the winter winds. Ivy climbed them snakily, making them resemble the emblem of medicine. Some graves did bear tombstones, but most of these had sunk half their height into the soft earth and dry weeds grew around them. Over the edge of the hill on the western slope, facing the "Whore of Babylon" (as the minister called it), Rome, the Catholic cemetery sprawled, filled with large stones, marbles, and fat little angels like Cupids—all they needed were bows and arrows. Between the graveyards from several cedar trees pigeons descended onto the ground, probably in the hope of getting crumbs of bread. I took the pigeons to be doves, and their descent a sign from God.

Beneath one cedar two fresh heaps of yellow and green soil arose like wings, and between the wings blinked no bird, but a rectangular hole, the grave. I was glad my father would be buried under an evergreen tree on the highest point of the cemetery—even better than Robin Hood beneath an oak. People gathered all over the soft cemetery, trampling old graves, sinking into them in their best shoes, totally disregarding the ones who had been dead, and paying attention only to the newcomer, or, rather, the new-leaver.

The minister stood right next to the tree, turning his back to the Catholic slope. On his left were about ten members of the church choir. They sang about death, heaven, faith, grace, and all the rest, addressing my father in his coffin. After the singing, the minister shouted a sermon, and some foam appeared over his lips, and trickled down his closely shaven round cheek, which was pink in the wind. The parallel lines of his shiny hair showed the distance between the picks of his comb. "We cannot even sing about how we miss him, because without him we don't have a good bass! We all miss him, but dear honorable citizens and comrades, brothers and sisters, I tell you, there is no point in our being sad, for this man is alive!" Saliva sprinkled out of his mouth like sparks of fire. He paused for effect. His thunderous voice echoed behind our backs from a steep hill, covered with apple orchards, beyond the cemetery.

I looked at the coffin, expecting the lid to break open.

After a hush, there was a commotion and murmur in the crowd, especially at the edges of the crowd, where the non-members of the church, including the Communists, stood.

My toes freezing, I wished the minister would stop his speech—he said we hadn't had such a good death in years, and went into the details of my father's death, nearly verbatim from Ivo's account—there was no way of stopping him. From the corners of my eyes I observed the crowd. My school classmates with our main teacher were there. A couple of girls wept, some boys looked gleeful, others nudged each other with their elbows. They were scrutinizing me and taking bets—whether I would cry or not. I learned that later from a friend. I wished I could throw stones at them. I turned round and stared at the crowds of familiar faces with animosity.

Two grave diggers, who had been waiting impatiently for the speech to be over, shifting their weight from one foot to another in soiled rubber boots, leaning their hands on the shovels, dropped the shovels, and with the help of two uncles of mine, withdrew the planks of wood from beneath the casket and began to lower the casket on ropes into the soil. The casket dropped out of my sight, and I had a sinking sensation, as if my heart had sunk into my intestines. The ropes grated against the casket, sounding like dull saws cutting into wood.

Mother and Grandmother, arm in arm, walked to the grave, and Mother leaned to the ground, picked up a chunk of soil, and handed it to the mother of my father. The old woman tossed it into the grave. A loud thump on the wood. Then Mother tossed some of the soil into the grave too. A loud thump. Great pressure in my chest. Behind my nostrils, below my eyes, it burned—it felt similar to the anesthesia for my tonsillectomy several years before. Having seen the red mesmerizing light and felt the scorching sensation on awakening I had screamed, "Am I in hell?" A doctor had had to intervene because my scream had made my throat bleed.

Vlado and Ivo threw pieces of soil, and so did my older sister Nada, tears flowing down her cheeks. Nella and I refused to throw. I walked to the grave, and Ivo wanted to stop me, pulling at my coat, so that I slid, on the edge, fighting for my balance and staring into the muddy water: atop the casket sat a bloated green frog, a beating heart.

Grave diggers avalanched soil over the casket. The thumps grew less and less loud, and more and more dull. The grave diggers sped up their work, and one of them spat into his fists—as though sealing some good agreement—to avoid getting any blisters.

From the hill you could see how the people dispersed, church-bound, or pub-bound, or home-bound. We too walked away from the grave, even though the grave had not yet been filled with soil to the top.

A warm wind lifted Nella's hair from her eyes. When I didn't watch myself, I began to skip my steps, hop. I wondered at the inappropriateness of my cheer. Nella sang "Silent Night" in German.

"Did they pray for you so you could speak in German tongues?"

"No, I learned it from tapes in a classroom."

"That's too bad. Did you see any murders in Stuttgart?"

"What a strange question!"

"I heard Germans were murderers, so I was afraid you'd never come back."

"No, they're nice."

"Impossible. Have you seen our history book? Our people hanging from the trees, houses burned, children shot to death?"

"Those were the Nazis. Modern Germans are very cultured."

"But they kill the soul in Germany and America, my teacher says. They don't believe in God, do they?"

"Most of them do, more than here."

"Uncle Pero says their bread is made of plastic foam."

She continued to sing.

In the church the minister told the congregation they should all hope to die like my father. "Who among us has prayed as much as this man had? I had a quiet minute at his side, and as I prayed for him, a voice whispered to me to stop praying and to look at his knees. I rolled up his pajamas above his knees—they were coated with a thick layer of blood crusts. So let us give praise to God for such a wonderful death. Our man is now in New Jerusalem."

As soon as the sermon turned to more general terms about the glories of heaven, I began to stick my thumbnails into the bench along the grains. The minister broke the bread, and the electrician passed it around in a small basket; wine followed in a silvery bowl resembling the Cup of Marshall Tito trophy that my favorite soccer club had won. I was glad that I couldn't participate in the ceremony—I hadn't been baptized—because I couldn't imagine salivating on the rim of the cup with a hundred old men and women. I liked the smell of wine, though.

On their way out of the church, a variety of old people stroked my hair with their dry hands—as if dipping their fingers into the sacristy, reverting to their Catholic habits—and the sacristy was my hair.

At home dozens of relatives ate the chicken paprikash and cakes Mother had somehow managed to prepare amidst all the confusion. I knew it was she who did it, because nobody else made such poppy seed cakes, cheese pies, and apple strudels. I laughed though there was no joke being told, my sister told me to stop it, and she pulled out a smooth yellow German toothbrush, and brushed the poppy seeds from between my teeth. That tickled me and made me laugh even more.

The cat, who had been outdoors for three days, scratched her back against my shin, blinked flirtingly, and purred as if everything were in the best possible order and none of us were missing. She could not count; if she had four kittens and two were taken away to be drowned, she continued purring, apparently not noticing that some of her children were missing. But if you took all of them away, for days she would moan so sorrowfully and dreadfully that you had to shudder. There were enough of us left for her. Perhaps soon I too would be used to there being one less among us, to having no father. I slipped her some white meat beneath the table when nobody was watching, and she devoured it without chewing, momentarily interrupting her purring, and continued to blink for more.

Even though Vlado, Nada, and Nella were there, Mother kept repeating that the house was empty, and I agreed—there was more echo on the staircase. "Wherever I open the door, I see him there, sitting and reading the Bible, or kneeling, or pacing around the room," she said.

Mother raised the tombstone to my father. She inscribed my father's name on it—the same as mine, to my displeasure. And to my horror, she engraved her name with the date of her birth, leaving the date of her death empty, so when she died, only one date would have to be cut in the stone. After erecting the tombstone, she walked to his grave almost every other day.

I avoided the cemetery. But willy-nilly I came to the grave a year later after drunk Uncle Pero had fallen off a barn, breaking his neck. The smooth stone, black and spotted with gray, reflected my shadow. And, as became a beekeeper, his tombstone bore a honey-colored inscription: *Death, where is thy sting?*

I feared the room where Father had died. My brother Ivo didn't. The unsmiling brown wedding picture of my parents stayed above the bed, both of them looking alert.

For years I couldn't eat apples, my father's last supper. When I did try to eat them, I choked. Every 6th of January for several years I remembered what had happened. I kept the lights on then, fearing that I myself would die.

On the first anniversary I was certain that I would die at midnight, though I knew that my belief was irrational. I put Father's Zenith watch next to my bed. I prayed, opening and closing my eyes. Thirty seconds left, ten seconds left. My heart skipped beats and pounded against my chest like a hawk in a glass cage. I was sure the glass would burst in a couple of seconds. When it was a second past midnight, jubilant, I thanked God. And so every year until my reason began to prevail.

I couldn't control dreams. Father would still be in the workshop, made of Styrofoam, lying between two chairs like a magician, without his body bending.

In one dream he appeared in his room and called me to his side. Come, Yozzo, I'll tell you something.

What will you tell me?

You are the only one who knows that I am alive.

But we buried you, you are dead.

Yes, you buried me, but I am not dead. I am about to die now.

For the second time?

For the second time. But first bring me an apple, and choose a beautiful one.

I brought him one that looked like a heart, and pressed my thumbnail into it—it was crunchy.

I walked out and wondered how we could bury him for the second time. What would the police say when we took out his second corpse? How could we hide him? Could we bury him in the garden? When I came back he was propped up on his pillow, the room stank of dead fish, and he, barely lifting his eyelids, said, Son, no rush, I'll be here for months. I am not going to die quickly like the first time.

Nobody knew that he was alive except me, and I kept him in the back room like some monster. One day I wanted to take him out for a walk, but when I touched him, his flesh fell to pieces, scattered on the white sheets, without any blood.

▼

The Lizard

[for Robin H.]

by Elaine Gottlieb Hemley

. . . A habit of observing, surmising, decorating the sky. A look under things. No, it is not a sickness in itself, though the doctors assume this need to write is an indication of abnormality. Perhaps. But not in the way they imagine. I started writing long before I could use the typewriter. It was my grand-mother's typewriter that started me, her crippled portable for which she showed an unreasonable affection, an affection she granted numerous in-animate objects. I started writing in my head, and my hearing began to fade soon afterwards. The doctors try to find a correlation. I do not believe them, but I make an attempt to remember. I see myself beside my grandmother's pool in Miami. Twenty years ago?

Perhaps I was thinking: I am a leaf, a drop of water, an instinct. I knew words like *instinct,* knew all kinds of words: tetragrammaton, analgesic, in-considerate. My mother thought it ridiculous that an eleven-year-old took the dictionary to bed with him. I would hear her laughing about it with Nat (who never read anything).

Late at night when they went out and left me alone (suspecting baby-sitters' intentions) I heard house sounds and outside sounds. As if the house were full of voices that started in the walls, trying to intrigue me with stories or plays, episodes about other people elsewhere, in which I was asked to play a leading role, though generally I declined, watching instead their hasty shadows on the ceiling. And sometimes, after they had finished their per-formance, I would hear a night bird sing my name, or call out: "Glorious . . . glorious . . . or palm fronds would rattle against my window like the low clapping of a polite audience.

When I sat alone beside my grandmother's pool I heard little things buzz about me, and other things made timid advances through the grass or in the bushes. At first, everything was green plants, water, sky, a fence, the house, what I knew, what everyone knew. Then it began to open up . . . the world within the world.

The brown one was the first. It was almost the color of the coconut palm, and it seemed to trickle down and lie in a pool of itself on a stone at the base of the tree; then it was the hue of the stone and I would not have seen it if it hadn't snapped at a grasshopper. Then, slipping through the grass, a yellow one, smaller, faintly green, almost transparent; its spine nearly visible. An orange tinge near the throat, and as if trapped by my gaze, transfixed beneath the cactus bush.

I lay with my cheek to the flagstones of the pool, alternately watching the immobilized lizards and the lacing of light through the water. I became aware of a small blue lizard, almost purple, resting near the fence. At least I supposed it rested; I couldn't see it breathe. Sometimes my mother lay as still as that on her bed, with pads over her eyes. She rested a great deal, when she was not at her receptionist job or out somewhere with Nat or having a party in our dim unfinished-looking house. The chairs were always in the middle of the floor; I don't remember anymore where they should have been. The couch was soiled and slightly worn; my mother occasionally mentioned doing something about it, but always forgot. Blinds shut us in; light seemed to disturb her. On the wall in the foyer there was a painting of a black girl lying doing, doing something I could not understand at the time, though in retrospect it appalls me. Yet even then I wondered about it. I did not want to, yet could not help looking at it. My mother had coaxed my father into leaving it there when they separated. She always told people how much it cost . . . as if she had won a bet.

In front of me the lizards seemed sunstruck, or stunned (by some exceptional news?). I touched one; it burned. But was its mind cool? Were the fluctuations of the day absorbed in its spiney shield? I went to sleep and when I awoke all the lizards had gone except one I didn't remember having seen before. It was larger than the others, green as Florida, and with muscular-looking legs. I couldn't see any ears and its eyes were lost in the mottled pattern of its skin. But as I was about to touch it the eyes flicked open, opaque, defensive. I turned over on my stomach and squinted.

I thought, had the impression, wanted to believe, was all ready to believe that I saw the lizard doing an exercise. But it wasn't like the floor touching and jogging and belt-shaking of my grandmother. It seemed more like a pose or a dance to me. I looked back because I knew that if my grandmother saw me, if she called out in her bottom-of-the-bottle voice (did all women speak to their children like that?): What are you doing there? What are you watching? . . . always suspecting something that might please me and not herself . . . I might have to show it to her. And then she would say: Why, it's just a dirty old lizard dying!

Nevertheless the lizard wasn't dying. Its legs were in the air, but that meant something else. Nor would it want to be turned right side up: it had the privilege of being on whatever side it pleased! The lizard's eyes shone golden.

Half its body was in the air; it seemed to be bringing its tail down over its head as it lay on its back, the two forelegs implanted on the ground. I tried to think where I had seen something like it; my mother's only exercises were swimming, tennis, golf. Then I remembered my aunt Sylvia, my father's sister who came to see me and take me out now and then. She was much younger than my father, still at college, studying philosophy, I adored her laugh. She told fantastic stories.

I recollected having seen her stand on her head. And turn herself into a pretzel. She had started to teach me a few things. Oga? I thought. No . . . yoga. A lizard doing yoga.

I laughed and turned on my back. Then I brought my legs over my head, too. But my stomach was full of the peanut butter and jelly sandwiches that were all, my grandmother insisted, I ever wanted to eat. It wasn't true. She just never cooked anything good.

My grandmother came out to the pool. She didn't look like a grandmother. I wondered if she ever would. She had curly blond hair and a wig just like it. Sometimes I couldn't tell which was which.

Pretending to be asleep, I could see my grandmother pussyfooting at the edge of the pool, a kerchief on her hair . . . it must have been her hair, she wouldn't have worn it over a wig. She was in her favorite tiger-striped shorts and a yellow sweater with a high neck and little sleeves. I wondered whether her neck sweated while her arms cooled.

She had pulled a deck chair out of the house and was setting it up with a frown and little impatient gestures and a look of disgust. Once, she kicked it. I was glad she thought me asleep, because she always asked me to do things before doing them herself. After settling in the chair (with a: Darn!) she went back to the house and returned with her baby-blue telephone, which had an extremely long wire that she could plug in anywhere. She seemed to be doing a dance with the wire; it coiled around her bare feet and she stepped in and out of it and twirled it around and shook it out like a lasso. Then she fell into the chair and perched the phone on her shoulder and spoke into it and typed at the same time. My grandmother wrote fashion news, edited a fashion paper. Many people knew her: they were always embracing her in stores and restaurants. Flattering her, and I knew why. So she would write something nice about them or their clothes or their restaurants. For some reason, probably because it meant free meals, she also wrote gourmet news. I couldn't bear the way she looked at those people who came out from workrooms or behind cash registers or kitchens or dressing rooms and exclaimed: Francie, you look gorgeous today! Or: Francie, you get younger every minute.... Because I could see that it wasn't true, though at the same time a tremor of pleasure would pass through my grandmother's body as she smiled her smile of absolutely young-looking, astringent, and perfectly modeled teeth. (No wonder. She was always jumping into the bathroom to brush them.)

Sometimes she would ask my opinion on the clothes she wore, as if I were the authority's authority. Or a man. Because, as she explained to me, a man's reaction to clothes was more significant than all the fashion predictions put together.

Women want to know what men think of them, she would say, as if she had worked years at this conclusion.

I liked to see her dressed up. She smiled more then, and sometimes even took me on dates. Occasionally a nightclub act might feature acrobats or animals. I loved animals.

But I tried not to notice the expression on her face when a man was with us. Because though she smiled, her eyes looked funny, as if she had caught something in them. She would glance up and down at the same time, fluttering her lashes and speaking rapidly and confusing me as to whether she was a friend or an enemy. Whatever her intention, there was a tone, a look about her that disturbed me; I preferred not to watch, or if watching were necessary, to make my mind go elsewhere. I practiced sitting still, smiling and nodding, while my thoughts reviewed something I had read the day before, or made up improbable stories. Occasionally, she caught me. Hoagy, are you there? ... Yes (but I wished I weren't). On the other hand, my mother was worse than my grandmother. Always punishing me. For not listening, not cleaning the house, not knowing what the teacher had assigned. Yet my grandmother seemed suspicious of every breath I took. I tried to be quiet and get in no one's way.

On the phone again, her voice rose. I didn't know which of her friends she was scolding, but suddenly I realized she wasn't scolding, though she spoke angrily, her throat tensed like a bow. I closed my eyes, pretending to be a lizard. Not the kind that did yoga, but still, silent, dreaming, a sun-filled lizard on a stone, dreaming it was the stone.

She spoke of a sweater, the way she only spoke of her clothes.... When women grew older, I thought, and didn't have husbands, maybe they fell in love with their clothes. Yet, how I hated the yesterday-smell of the closet, all those dresses pressed together in a conspiracy of stale talc and sweat. Why did she keep them? In her own room the closet was full of new clothes with the same body scent and perfume, though more potent, yearning.

The blue sweater, she hissed, the darling Caribbean blue that matched my eyes, made me think of all the nice things that were ever said to me.... How I loved that color! And she takes it. Rosabel. My own daughter. Always stealing!

I winced at my mother's name, even though I saw that hunter's gleam in her eyes every time she visited my grandmother. Even so. And despite the fact that nothing pleased Rosabel. She was my mother; I felt responsible for her. I wished I could unplug the phone. Slowly, so as not to distract, I let my head roll to a side. Then, slowly again, my body. The lizard, a dappled green, blinked metallic eyes. And I blinked back.

Now it pressed against the ground. Raising its head slightly, looking to one side, then the other. I thought of Sylvia doing the same. I thought I heard her tell me: Clear your mind of all but the lizard.

... It will free your spirit, she said to me.

I turned on my stomach, but too rapidly. My grandmother noticed me at once.

Hoagy! she said. Didn't I tell you to do your arithmetic? Where is your math book?

I ran through the chilly house. Looking for my math book, I passed her inflatable furniture. The previous year she had become incensed at a moving van that charged too much to deliver a small piano, had then proceeded to sell everything in the living room and substitute the inflatable, disposable, or foldable. I thought of sticking pins in the plastic or luring the dog in to try a few bites. But she only allowed the dog on the sun porch.

I found my book under the big double bed that had been my mother's when she lived there, as a girl. She was still a girl when she married. A child of sixteen, my grandmother had reminded me. Eloped, but fortunately, Francie added, with a wealthy man. Later she could not understand why anyone would give up a wealthy man (who was wild about her!)

Though it was obvious, Francie liked to add, Rosabel didn't know how to make herself interesting to men. All she ever spoke of was her job, how everyone tried to rape her. Why didn't she learn something about politics or dianetics or cybernetics?

I didn't like the bedroom. At night I would open the venetian blinds all the way so the moon and the palm trees and the smell of jasmine and oranges could enter. Then, with all forms hushed, I could forget the intrusion of the tank-shaped sauna with the radio on top ... that made me think of robots; and facing it, the vanity with its tiny drawers in which everything from snapshots the color of tea stains to lost beads and dried up raisins had been stuffed. Or next to the bed, catty-cornered (she loved catty corners) the tall dresser in which she kept a medical encyclopedia (to diagnose herself), a roll of absorbent cotton, a muddy pink toy poodle, the color of syringes, and blue satin sheets. In the bookcase built into the headrest of the bed I found children's books so old they must have been her own. All over the house there were peanut butter jars of darkening pennies that she never turned into any bank, but kept as reminders of the day when pennies were useful. As each jar filled she would tell me: It's important. It will add up someday. They'll make lots of dollars for me ... I was afraid to touch those jars. They threatened a nasty dollar-sized jangle.

And how I dreaded that dark closet where clothes at night seemed about to dislodge the door, the way a vampire, I imagined, might rise from a sewer. The door had a way of opening by itself, with a: pop! ... revealing weary dresses, boxes, dirty towels, and shoes on the floor, folded snack tables, whatnot. I trembled at the vulnerability of my own small trousers and shirts hanging with them. Was it the odor ... like an armpit ... that stifled me?

Walking circuitously to the pool, I carried my math book, notebook, and pencil. Briefly, over the telephone and above her glasses, Francie looked up; then she subsided into her work and dialed someone else.

The lizard was still there. It was actually balancing on its paws, perpendicular, tail in air. The math book fell from my hands.

Hoagy! my grandmother warned. Get that book before you kick it into the pool!

I retrieved it absently, lay on my stomach, propped the book before me, opened the notebook, and tried to start my work. But my glance kept wandering to the lizard, still balancing. It came down soporifically in the sunshine. I lifted the pencil and began a letter:

Dear Sylvia, I am looking at a lizard who I think has magic powers. . . .

—I can't get your son to do a single solitary thing he's supposed to do for school, Francie complained when my mother and her friend Nat came for me after dinner.

Oh, he's a brat, Rosabel said without altering her expression or tone of voice, while her fat white leg hung over and clung to the arm of the inflatable chair.

Nat sat on the other chair, looking as if he had driven himself through his last game of tennis. His hair fringed his forehead, and his sport shirt met his chest with a stain of geographical shape. Black hairs springing from behind the opening of his shirt shone dewily. Some of the hairs were grey. He was older than Rosabel. It seemed to me that he would have suited Francie better, despite my mother's pretty face. Actually, he had known Francie first.

Rosabel always looked cool. Even when her voice changed (like when she scolded me), her face remained serene. My grandmother, on the other hand, seemed constantly suffused by some hidden source of heat. She wriggled, grimaced, coughed, smiled aborted, nervous smiles, and had, at the same time, an expression in her eyes that made me wonder what could console her.

Nat brought to mind a Christmas ornament still hanging from a chandelier, shining its last dull shine, and about to fall down. Both Francie and Rosabel thought him handsome, despite the pneumatic waist, the oily skin, indifferent eyes.

I don't know why she doesn't let her hair down, Francie said to Nat. She has such beautiful hair. Thick, curly. Mine was never like that. All my life I've tried to make it grow; it just won't. Rosabel, why don't you let your hair down? You look forty years old.

I'm not eighteen.

She doesn't take advantage of her natural endowments. If I had hair like that, and skin, and features.... Think of the people I meet. Millionaires. But what difference does it make?

You still look pretty good, Nat grunted.

Francie thanked him without enthusiasm, adding: Forty years old ... as Rosabel got up. I looked at her hard to see what Francie meant.

Hair wouldn't make much difference, I thought, if Rosabel didn't have such a big ass. I had noticed that older women usually had big asses. Francie too, though the rest of her was slender. Slacks didn't suit either of them. My mother always wore something to half cover her ass. This time she wore a blue sweater with silky hairs swaying.

Why don't you take off your sweater? Francie asked.

Because it's mine and I don't want you to claim it, Rosabel said from inside the refrigerator door.

Hers like heck, Francie commented to Nat. She never used the real curse words with which my mother shrank the atmosphere at home.

You two girls ought to stop fighting about that sweater, Nat said in his soft, exasperated voice.

Francie, sidling up to Nat, twisted her body a little as she held her hands out with the fingers spread, and batted her eyes: Now Nat, you know you love both of us. Why don't you get Rosabel a sweater so she'll give mine back to me?

The refrigerator door banged shut and my mother came listing back to the room, a cold lamb chop in her hand. —I'm on a diet, so I get hungry, she said to the chop, turning it around daintily.

And by the way, she added, her small mouth gleaming with fat, the sweater is mine, Dad bought it.

For me! Francie exclaimed. —He promised it to me the last time I went to his office. What I really wanted was a car because I heard he bought his wife one. He never bought me a car. But I couldn't bring myself to say it. I only talked about the clothes I'd seen that day. Especially the imported sweater. He just looked out the window. Finally I cried. He never could stand me crying. So he said: OK. The sweater.

You go to his office? Nat asked.

Why not? He invites me out sometimes for a drink or dinner. We're friendly; I still get money from him. Any time he feels like it he can come back to me. He knows that. He's the only man I ever really . . . but he played around.

Yeah, said Nat. I know.

Dad delivered it to me, Rosabel asserted. You were off to Jamaica. He said I could keep it.

You're lying. Just like him.

Listen girls, said Nat, I'll buy you another.

Oh, in that case, Rosabel told Francie, you can have this thing. And she pulled it off as if she loathed it.

Francie clasped the sweater to her, adding: It has your perfume!

Rosabel went back to the refrigerator. I watched her butt swing like a buoy in a storm.

I told my grandmother the sweater looked great on her.

You're a doll! Francie grabbed me awkwardly; I didn't feel embraced. Her body seemed to have no substance. But I smiled, embarrassed. My mother saw the smile when she returned from the kitchen, with another chop. And though her voice was moderate, she frowned, which made me feel guilty. But it was Francie she accused:

Why are you always sneaking Hoagy away from me?

You're glad to get rid of him.

I was out of the house. You always come when I'm out, when you know I'll be out. Like a thief. In the afternoon.

Well, who was there to ask? Am I his grandmother or not? What about the time in St. Thomas when you kidnapped him from the hotel playground? I was frantic. You could have asked.

Me ask? I'm his mother.

I had the police out . . . Francie appealed to Nat. He shrugged as usual.

Francie let out a sigh and stood up to view herself in the mirror, caressing the hairs of her sweater. Then she asked if anyone wanted coffee.

You'll make it? Nat asked. I thought you only ate in restaurants. Where'd you take lucky Hoagy tonight?

The Italian restaurant up the street. He had spaghetti. In every gourmet place it's either spaghetti or hamburger. I don't know why I bother. Except that I can't take the time to cook anymore. Even though I was a housewife for ten years.

Come to think of it, Rosabel said.

It broke your heart to live alone with me, didn't it? Francie asked, moving toward the kitchen.

While they were drinking coffee I went outside to look at the pool in the moonlight. I told them I had left some little boats out there. But I didn't think of boats when the warm air came twining over my arms and all the sweetness of invisible blossoms approached me. I wanted to get down on my belly and scurry beneath some bush.

Where are you? I thought.

Suddenly I heard the two women shriek at each other, and at the window their shadows reached out and seemed to merge. But I knew it only seemed that way.

Mine! I heard.

Mine!

The moon, fragmented over the pool, reminded me of Sylvia's hair, how it fell on her shoulders the day we took a glass-bottomed boat. We saw the miraculous fishes then, quick as impulse, curved and flowing, in all the illusory colors of their flight.

I said to her: I'll be a sea horse.

She said to me: We'll ride the sea together.

And her laughter sounded down the fluttering depths, and up to the silver-blue, white-birded sky.

Near the cactus bush a transparent shape. I lifted it and in the moonlight saw the emptied husk of the lizard. I thought: I shall slip inside and burrow into the night.

Then I hid it behind a stone.

. . . I have no one, no one, Francie moaned as I returned to the house. . . . Nobody cares what becomes of me. Except maybe Hoagy. . . . And she rushed to lay her wet, flaky face against mine, while my mother, indissoluable, linked her arm in Nat's.

They ushered me out with the smell of Francie's tears upon me, and at my neck the urgent: I'll leave it all to you, Hoagy, everything I've got . . .

. . . I'm not sure I want it, I answered silently, looking up at the night sky, pretending not to hear, as the door closed and my mother and Nat walked ahead to the car, and I halted once, looking upward again, at miracles yet to come.

▼

Interior Design

by Philip Graham

These days I just won't get out of bed, so I lie here, idly kicking the sheets into strange patterns—a ripple of dunes, a mountain range—and I imagine I'm a peasant woman in Turkey, working alongside her husband, carving out a home from one of those cliffs of soft volcanic rock. I can see our faces and hands dusty and smeared with stone shavings and sweat, two strange creatures chipping away new rooms as we need them, and I wonder if we'll agree on every odd turning we take in the rock, every little nook or window we each wish.

All my life I've longed for something like this with a gnawing eagerness: to live among the 80 percent of the world's people who build their own homes. Unfortunately, I belong to that remaining, privileged minority: the suburbanites, who make themselves content in their cozy cubes with a narrow hall or a window's unwanted view; and the apartment dwellers, who live in rooms silently echoing with the habits of former tenants. So as an interior designer I always saw myself as a medium, helping my clients discover the house they wanted to have in the house where they already lived. I wanted to be invisible, to interfere as little as possible with my clients' desires, working within the constraints of their imaginations and the building code.

I asked, "Where would you really like to live?" and I listened to their idiosyncratic, secret dreams of home. Together we created an interior as familiar as the self, made the walls as comfortable as skin: I simply settled into someone else's mind and gave it doors and windows. There was always an urgency to my work, because I believed there's an ideal home inside each of us that slowly shrinks unless it's found.

I did my first work in the heartland, for people living in small towns who wanted their homes to counter the vast, flat spaces around them. My first clients were an elderly couple who imagined something they called Polynesian Splendor: vistas of golden beach, palm fronds, and clear tidal pools. What could be better than a home that was also a vacation, a prison that was its own parole? And that's what I gave them, though the details had to be mundane as well as exotic, because I knew these folks weren't going to leave, they just wished they could. I decided to work with local products and craftspeople, plastic palm trees from Kmart, quarry sand for the back porch. The mural painted over the indoor pool was inspired by a cheesy Dorothy Lamour movie poster, yet I made sure touches of phosphorescent paint were applied here and there, so that in the dark those tropical stars would shine, those shells glint.

Soon, the aspiring displaced sought me out, and dotted throughout miles and miles of fields were private escapes hidden in ordinary houses: two unmarried sisters and their series of indoor fountains commemorating a trip to Old Faithful; or a widower who turned the tower of his three-story Victorian into a lighthouse and cast nightly beams across his fields, where the shadows of corn stubble could have been anything. With all my clients I worked on the cheap, I even gave discounts because I didn't want to make too much money, I wanted to work off my father's sins.

I remember him returning home in the evenings, taking off his coat with great deliberation and regarding me and my two younger sisters as if we were carpet stains that Mother hadn't cleaned up yet. He barely had to speak to remind us we were failures for not having been born boys and that Mother was the failure who produced us.

"Hello, Phyl," he said to Phyllis, who nodded.

"Hello, Pat," he said to Patricia, who smiled her guilty smile.

"Hello, Jo," he said, looking at me.

"Josephine," I always corrected him.

My father was a house builder, and his office was a demonstration home where the furniture displayed in all the rooms was three-quarter-sized. The smaller the furniture, he slyly reasoned, the larger the rooms looked, so when potential customers walked casually through his demonstration home they believed they were in much fuller spaces. I thought this was a terrible way to make a living, to insure that a home grew smaller once a family moved in with their full-sized furniture. Think of it, an entire house a subtle, secret lie! Their walls static but always closing in, the family would become increasingly irritable and argue over nothing. Throughout my childhood I wanted my father to be a fireman, someone who *saved* homes.

We moved from place to place before Father's dissatisfied customers could accumulate, and over the years he filled our successive homes with three-quarter-sized cast-offs from his old displays. Each chair and table was a hard example of his special talent for belittling those around him. My mother was already shrunken under his steady contempt, and Phyllis and Patricia, with their carefully imposed silences, were ripe for squeezing themselves into reduced limits. My sisters fit so well that Father soon took them along to work on weekends, where they became part of his devious display and helped his sales. I was never invited to the showroom because, happily, I was too tall for my age.

I grew up frightened by and yet longing for furniture. A simple chair with its inviting cushions was a forbidding object, and when I thought of my mother and sisters forever crimped, I was prepared for the discomfort of fitting nowhere in our home. I remember at dinnertime looking at all the plates and glasses, obscenely huge on the runty table, and I insisted on sitting on a telephone book. "It's for my posture," I explained, though my secret reason was I didn't want to touch that chair, and because I never leaned back—to avoid resting against the tiny wicker backing—I endured those childhood dinners with aching shoulders.

My willful isolation from the contamination of touch also extended to my mother and sisters: I couldn't bear the thought of a stunted embrace. So it was a thrilling release to hear, however cautious and clinical the telling in my school's sex education class, about the grapplings of love. I was proud to discover how girls were much more complicated than boys, that women were born with their ovaries full, an egg waiting decades to be fertilized by a single shrimp of a sperm. My opinion of Father lowered still further for his inability to appreciate us, and then I learned it was the male who determines the sex of the child.

I took no small pleasure in telling my father that *he* was the failure of the family. "I don't need to hear such language from *you,* young lady," he said.

Mother sat across from us, her eyes made dull by patience. Yet there was a minute smile on her face—a smile that I would see at the oddest moments for the rest of my life— and I wondered, was it faint support, or relief that she was momentarily forgotten?

"That's right," I laughed, "I *am* a young lady, not a stupid son."

"Don't you talk to me that way," Father shouted, "you sit down here and . . ."

"In this creepy furniture? Forget it." While Father sputtered, my sisters huddled beside their dollhouse: prisoners playing a game of Warden, poking their dolls into furniture even smaller than ours. And then I remembered something else from biology class, about age and the atrophy of bones. I shouted at Father that like everyone else he was going to shrink with old age and die three-quarter-sized on a full-sized bed. He stood there silent and trembling, with a face so fallen I ran from the room, furious that my father wasn't as untouchable as I had imagined. That night, and for long after, I dreamt *I* was three-quarter-sized: my legs, arms, head, and heart, and I was crammed inside that damned dollhouse. My body was bent and buckled, an arm out a window, a leg down a stairwell, and then I reversed and grew so small I could fit in one of those rooms, sitting comfortably on a tiny couch, staring at the blank screen of the plastic television.

Years later, the hardest part of architecture school for me was making models. Whenever I resisted realizing my vision of a building in minia-ture, I discovered that my professors had their own version of my father's frown and they lectured with his voice. But I had long been adept at defying the local measurements, and anyway I found myself more and more at-tracted to interior design. I devoured every book I could find on any sort of home—nothing could be too exotic—and when I discovered that in Indian longhouses even the placement of the most humble hammock is charged with mystical purpose, I knew that I wouldn't be satisfied with just dry walls and doorways, plumbing and thermal units.

When those first interior design projects of mine landed me a ten-page color spread in *Plains Living,* I received enthusiastic calls from both coasts. I decided to go East—I didn't like the idea of an earthquake leveling my best efforts, since my father was still selling his houses somewhere and I felt I had a lot of catching up to do. Now, lying here stretched out on my bed, I think, What's so bad about earthquakes? and I pound my arms and legs against the mattress to make even the pillows shake.

But at the time I thought I'd hit pay-dirt, since all my new clients could much better afford to reproduce their desires for comfort. There were the sociology professors Jack and Maxine, who were cashing in on the third and final edition of their once popular textbook, *Class Marx.* "We're the last bastion, and we want no false consciousness in our house," Jack said, and Maxine continued, "Jack and I are noted for the theory that walls were the first form of social obfuscation." And so they asked for glass panes on the walls to reveal the electrical wiring and the heating ducts, a porthole in the hallway overlooking their bed, even a stained-glass panel on the bathroom door. They requested Lucite steps for the stairway to the second floor, in order to expose those stairs directly beneath that led to the basement. "Get it?" Jack beamed, looking down, "it's a critique of the myth of social mobility!"

Another client lavished a fortune on redesigning his apartment after the recent deaths of his three dearest friends. A quiet, alarmingly thin man who liked to crumple cellophane wrappers and paper cups while he talked, during our first consultation he said, "I dream that I'm walking along these rained-out gullies and crevices and it's funny, I wake up crying but I feel relieved." He wanted his apartment to resemble erosion: the corners of baseboards split apart, a comforting wall of rubble, bookshelves artfully eaten away as if by termites, lampshades carefully ripped to create disjunct slashes of light. All this static decay both commemorated his losses and hinted at an end to them, just as he hoped his own disease would stop at a certain point and go no further.

Almost every one of my projects became a magazine spread, and I was much in demand. But in all of these homes I was a stranger—I helped my clients find their comfort yet it was never mine. Attempting to save others, I began to suspect, was not the same as saving oneself. Something in me still distrusted furniture, as if my father were a noxious, invisible wallpaper waiting to clash with whatever interior I might choose for myself. So I lived in a studio apartment with the barest of essentials—table, chair, bed—that would even confound my conforming sisters, and I was resigned to this spartan shelter because of my recurring dream.

In this dream I was always floating in a vast and empty darkness, my body flat as if lying on my back. I'd been floating for quite a long time, it seemed, and as I drifted aimlessly through this absence of architecture I wondered what patterns my body made, what involuntary dance I was creating. The longer I levitated, like some buoyant vagabond, the more I began to suspect that this floating endlessly was my own form of oblivion. But whatever my fears, I continued to drift.

That strange, characterless space seemed to accompany me through the day, seeping into my thoughts at any moment. Why not define that emptiness, I asked myself, why not design my own dream? I began a little game of mentally collecting furniture, imagining that each piece patiently anticipated a release inside me, just like eggs in the ovaries. I produced a Louis Quinze chaise voyeuse to sit on as I floated, I materialized a hovering halogen lamp, though its small circle of light couldn't possibly penetrate the vast darkness. I felt like my sisters playing with their dollhouse, trying to do their best with the space given them, though instead of tiny walls I had an infinite layout, and I conjured up arrangements until I had not a room but an entire home spread out in that nothingness.

It was those private designs that led me to the secret history of objects: they're all the products of desire. The first chair didn't just appear like some mushroom rising out of the floor. Instead, long ago someone, somewhere, thought, "I'm tired," and only then was a chair built, its wooden existence fitting the need. In the same way, the thought, "I'm cold," conceived walls and a roof. We actually turn ourselves inside out and find comfort in what we've imagined. If the guitar, the violin, the piano are extensions of us, created to give voice to our longings, then furniture is no less musical, though its song is silent. Lounging on a divan in my dreamy home, I realized that if every object around us is a bit of mind, made material, then my father was guilty of lobotomizing the homes of his clients.

But with that thought my mother suddenly appeared from behind a wardrobe with her ambiguous smile. Then Phyllis and Patricia arrived, their shoulders hunched as they tried out a bar stool, a rocker, which seemed to shrink at their touch. And when I heard my father's thick footsteps—on *what,* in that void?—I let everything vanish and I was back to floating, safe once again.

And then I met Frederick. When I entered his office he was jotting down a note, perched on the edge of his seat: his body cantilevered over the desk and casually defying gravity, the fingers of one hand holding him steady while he wrote with the other. I wanted to see how he'd keep that up—observing my clients' relationships to their furniture was always important to me—so when he glanced up and said, "Sorry, just one moment," I quickly replied, "Please, don't let me disturb you," and I marched over to a chair.

I looked around: the typical investment counselor's office, computer terminals and telephones the dominant features. On the shelf was a photo of him and a beautiful woman who was obviously a wife, and I was oddly pleased to see there were no children. She was short, about three-quarters of his height, I couldn't help thinking. How tall *is* he? I wondered, wishing

I'd let him stand up, but he was still precariously balanced and scribbling away. Here's a man on the edge, I thought, and I didn't mind admitting to myself I was right when he finally put down the phone, sat back, and immediately announced he'd just been divorced. I couldn't help gaping at the photograph—how sweet that he still kept it—and he caught me and glanced over too, a furtive, lingering look. I sympathized, knowing what it was like to be gripped by the insistent past, and I thought he was touchingly hesitant when he said, "I have a new house. It's small, but elegant, and . . . uh, empty. I'm living out of an apartment now. Is it true, from what I've heard of your work, that I'll have to dream up this new home of mine?"

I started in with my usual speech about personal, continuing environments. Frederick nodded, taking a note or two, and he seemed so alone behind his desk, so abandoned. Suddenly I couldn't concentrate: my secret cache of furniture was emptying itself inside me. A Philippe Stark table, a Bank of England swivel chair, octagonal marble tiles, an Alsatian blanket chest and more tumbled out into empty vistas, impeding the responses I made to Frederick's questions, though he didn't seem to notice. Oh god, I thought, what'll I do when my family starts to climb over this jumble? He rose, thankfully, before those apparitions could arrive and he said, "I really think we can work together." We shook hands, and somehow I was able to notice we were the same height, a perfect match.

But we couldn't begin designing his house because his imagination locked up. All day he carried a blank notepad, unable to snatch a stray idea. Each morning he woke with a vision of nothing, and though he tried setting his alarm randomly for different times in the night, he was never able to snare a single dream. In our meetings in his office he recounted these difficulties in a very businesslike manner, almost as if I were taking dictation, while he tried to avoid glancing over at that damn photo on his shelf.

In an effort to unblock him, we agreed on a tour of his new house. We walked through his echoing rooms, all that bare space so fraught with possibility, yet nothing came to him. "What do *you* dream?" he finally asked me in frustration. I stood there, stirred up by the seductive tensility of the empty room, and I told him about that vast, dreamy void I floated in at night, and as he listened I was suddenly certain about the cause of his trouble: in his mind he was still married to his ex-wife. She was haunting his new house, occupying space that just wasn't hers, and I decided right there to become a homewrecker: how else could Frederick's house become his own unless I chased her away?

I leaned a little too close to him. "It's warm in here," I said, and I started taking off my sweater. I could feel it pull my blouse up a bit, exposing my navel, a little circle of darkness to set him off. Frederick reached over for me, and when his hand circled my own I knew he could do whatever he wished.

Afterward, I lay on my back beside him on the hard wooden floor. His hand played with me lazily and I kept dripping: already we were marking our territory. "Tell me that dream again," he whispered. Lying there, I felt as if I *were* floating, and as I spoke I imagined Frederick above me again, my eyes scanning his face and the ceiling, and then I knew what could be done for the lighting in the room: bury the lights in the ceiling and space them to echo the traffic pattern below, so they could be turned on and off by passing feet. I saw us walking through the room, creating a path of light.

We moved into Frederick's empty house, intending to design rooms as we needed them. It was the first time I allowed myself to gather in the hidden signals, and my mind was inflamed with possible order. And although Frederick was still blocked, there was something about his helplessness before an empty space that drove me wild. So *I* began to fill up the house. Every idea I suggested delighted him, and he said, "That's fine, let's try it," as if our intuitions were identical.

I wanted our bedroom to be my dream, or *our* dream, since Frederick had adopted it. I wanted us to feel we were floating in the air. I took out the windows and replaced them with glass bricks, the thick panes filtering in a hazy, self-contained light like no other. All the walls and the ceiling were painted sky blue, though scumbled in places with white powder for a hint of cirrus, and in one corner the blue gradually deepened to navy—acknowledging the possibility of storm, but easily confining it. Above the turquoise carpeting all the furniture was white—the two wardrobes, the night tables, and the bedframe that seemed to hover on its thin legs—and every edge was rounded, like a solid ooze of cloud. Against the white headboard nestled blue pillows over a white quilt, which in turn covered blue sheets, so when we clambered over each other in bed we kicked up a convulsion of sky and cloud. *We* were the moving parts that made the house breathe and change.

So I finally allowed myself to empty my inner warehouse. I purposely cluttered every room with furniture of all varieties and epochs, a style I secretly titled Cornucopia. I gave in to the warmth of wood, the fluted metal edges of high tech, the plush comfort of a velvet seat, and this laying out of plans gave me a sexual pleasure, each arrangement an inducement to a tryst. On the walls I hung up paintings, prints, and photographs of furniture and nothing else, echoing that flood of furniture when I first met Frederick. I matted and framed them at slight, odd angles that only the most acute eye would unambiguously notice. I liked the tension of the pictures firmly on the walls and yet seeming only momentarily suspended, as though they were about to float down and take their places in the rooms.

This sense of expectancy reminded me of the women in India who daily decorate the earth in front of their houses with elaborate designs of rice powder, the interwoven lines being offerings to the gods. I thought colored chalk would do nicely for our house, though a drawing a day was too much. I had no gods to propitiate, I simply wanted to exemplify the shifting moods of our house, and only when one pattern wore off or was rained away would I start another. Once I began an elaborate motif of numbers— large and small, in every possible color—to influence Frederick's fortune into a limitless success. He tried to help and we knelt on the porch together, our hands dirty with colored chalk. Frederick grew annoyed with himself for his awkward sketching, which he couldn't improve despite my helpful hints. Eventually I eased him out of sight of the street and we smeared each other's face with our chalky hands until we were harlequin twins, our improvised masks making us familiar strangers, and we made a ferocious, technicolor love.

Blissfully domestic, all day I transformed the house into a dreamscape we could walk through wide awake, and in the evenings I waited for my man to come home and be amazed. But I worried about Frederick. He had stopped trying to remember his dreams. I couldn't understand it—in certain areas he suffered no lack of invention. I was afraid he might resent my success at filling empty spaces, so I kept trying to goad his imagination.

It was October and I had just sketched a giant stadium on the porch, with baseballs flying out—all of them homers for our team. While we watched the Series, a huge bowl of popcorn between us, I said casually, "Hon, did you know there's a country where hosts polish their chairs incredibly care-fully, so when a visitor sits on one its smoothness will rub off and make him a good guest?"

"Shhh," he said, "a three and two pitch."

I waited until the strikeout before trying again. "Y'know," I said, stretch-ing back a little, hoping he'd glance at me, "I read somewhere there are people in Africa who believe your soul lives in your chair. No one else can sit there. And when you're not sitting on the chair you tip it over, so your soul can't be stolen."

Frederick kept his mouth stuffed with popcorn so he wouldn't have to answer. I knew he was annoyed, but I couldn't help myself, I flicked off the game with the remote control.

"Imagine that," I said, "a chair isn't just a chair, it's what people *think* a chair is."

He grabbed the control away from me and mumbled through his pop-corn, "Well, that's certainly *one* way to look at it."

That stopped me. I always told him there were many ways to see some-thing, but it was true that I wanted him to see it *my* way. He knew the con-tradiction I was caught in. He flipped a kernel in the air and caught it in his mouth, enjoying my discomfort.

All those happy rooms in the house were slowly transformed into traps with invisible springs, waiting to be set off by my reproachful suggestions and Frederick's sullen resentment. He didn't want to be a disappointment, so he was trying to make me one. I thought of my mother, enduring too much contradiction with her slight smile that was impossible to read. I wouldn't let *that* happen to me. I fought back.

So we argued over even the silliest things. And then came that evening when, while washing dishes—though I suspected it wasn't my turn—I told Frederick how my father blamed my mother for having girls. Suddenly, in-credibly, we were disagreeing over what men and women were most like, the letter Y or the letter X! This was somehow connected with the X and Y chromosomes, though at that point we could have argued over the letters G and K.

"C'mon, people are like the Y," he said, sitting restlessly at the kitchen table. "When we're born, we don't know what sex is, and we grow up to-gether through childhood like the base of the Y. But look, at puberty we become different and split off, we move farther apart the older we get." His feet tapped at the floor tiles in a most annoying fashion.

"No, no, no," I said, "you're all wrong, we're like the X. Our sex makes us different right from the start, so we're like the opposite bottom legs of the X. But that difference attracts us, and when we make love, we're joined together in the middle. Then we move apart until we make love again."

He wouldn't agree. I hated that—I wanted us to be the same letter, and though the X and Y are right next to each other in the alphabet it was no consolation. "X, X, X!" I screamed at him, red-faced like a child, and I slapped a sponge and soap bar into the dishwater, just for emphasis. I had come to that. Frederick stood up, and his look of contempt forced me to slam the kitchen cabinets. I thrilled to the sound of the spaghetti and cereal boxes shuddering inside. Frederick almost spoke, but then he turned to leave, tripping over his chair. He gasped and they both tumbled down.

I stood at the sink and watched him lying there beside the overturned chair: I waited for him to give it a good kick, to shout at it, to smash it in anger. But he simply rubbed his shoulder. I kept waiting, until he began to pull himself up. Then I rushed over and we made our usual, insufficient apologies, enough to last us another evening.

Later that night, after a half hour of ineffectual clutching, we turned out the bedroom lights and I felt that the ominous patch of navy blue I'd consigned to one corner had grown into the surrounding dark. I lay there listening to Frederick's satisfied breathing. I tried so hard to imagine his hand rising to strike the chair, but his fist kept dissolving into the air until I finally fell asleep.

The next morning I woke in bed alone—Frederick had already left for the office. Furious at him for sneaking off like that, I kicked away at the clinging sheets, felt the satisfaction of my anger releasing, and then I understood how terribly dead Frederick's world must be. He didn't assume in his deepest self that a chair was somehow alive and could be hurt. Punching it was a childish but endearing form of revenge he was incapable of pursuing, and what I had thought were just contrary arguments were actually his most personal way of seeing. The true essence of our house had escaped him: for Frederick, furniture was just furniture.

Then everything in the room became dead for me as well and shed its invisible skin: the carpet was mere tufted wool, the bedframe only painted pine, the blue walls an ordinary acrylic blend. And though this lasted only a few seconds, it was unbearable. I closed my eyes and when I opened them I was once again surrounded by resonant expanses of blue and white. But I was no longer floating. I was falling, and I didn't know where I'd land.

I couldn't see Frederick again. I was afraid he would infect me with that hidden deadness of objects. Worst of all, I realized I had done something I'd tried to avoid all my life: I had imposed an interior. I had forced Frederick to live with an alien vision and I actually hoped he would eventually tear it all down, though what he tore down would be me. Everything ends, I thought bitterly, even houses collapse. I fingered the white quilt and remembered my teenaged days of sexual discovery in a thick woods, romping on a leafy bed among empty beer cans and old condoms within a scattered stone foundation—all that was left of an abandoned house. In a way, those exuberant scramblings had briefly made it a home again. Would young kids someday find a haven here?

I knew I had to leave, though I was everywhere in that house. I knocked over all the furniture so my soul couldn't be stolen, but I was afraid that when Frederick returned he might simply set it all upright again, merely perplexed and angry. So before I left I crawled about the porch and drew my face again and again: in sorrow, pain, anger, reproach, and fear, each face partially superimposed on the other like a chain of dismaying portraits before his doorstep. I imagined him arriving home and, seeing what I'd drawn, know instantly that I'd left. I wanted him distraught, unaware he was scuffing up my faces as he rushed inside, only later realizing that he'd tracked chalk all over the floor. And when he discovered what he'd done, would he see those smears as my sadness, would they seem more than mere chalk?

I returned to my nearly empty apartment and surveyed its comforting, spartan denial; then I pulled out the phone and slept.

My dream had changed. My body was no longer weightless, airy. I was plunging through that limitless darkness, the air pressing against my back. I fell for so long I grew accustomed to the resistance of the wind and barely noticed it. But somewhere in my descent I worried about where I was falling to. Perhaps the pressure I felt wasn't the wind. What if it was the ground? Perhaps I had already landed and was lying on my crushed back. In the complete darkness, how could I be sure? I could certainly try to move my outstretched arms, but I didn't want to finally know.

I remained still until I woke and saw the gray dullness of early morning light. I recognized across from me the outline of my bedroom window, recognized my heart's staggering beat like my own fleeing footsteps. I *have* landed, I thought, right where I'll always land, in my own room. I closed my eyes again but I still saw those same boundaries: the familiar walls and ceiling that will always face me, the same windows and door forever resisting my exit. How can I possibly escape my home when it's inside me?

And I'm not the only one who lives here: I'm bursting with accommodations for my daily, involuntary family reunion. My sisters, shorn of their current angry husbands and crowd of kids, skulk down a hall. My mother manages to find any unassuming corner, where she keeps to herself behind that maddeningly faint twist in her lips, harboring complexities I can't imagine, and I cannot animate her, I cannot make her speak. My father marches out of his room whenever he wants to command attention, trotting out his repertoire of contempt. "So, you finally inflicted yourself on someone's home," he begins, but I don't have to listen further because I know those terrible words in advance—they're my own, I have them memorized. He's really me, my own harsh and unrelenting critic that I've given my father's face and voice. These phantoms aren't my family—they're familiar faces I've put on my perplexing, hidden impulses.

So I've decided to lie here and design myself a new life, with the freedom of one of those desert nomads who sews the skins of her goat herd to make the family tent. I can feel the thick thread, rough against my dark hands in the dry air, while my children play around me. And I imagine that when my husband and I make our night noises, our thrashing is echoed above by those taut skins skitting in the wind: with my eyes closed and swishing my hands against the bedsheet, I can believe I'm almost there. But first I have to evict my current occupants and empty the rooms, and I'm going to start with Frederick.

He should be the easiest to banish, having spent so short a time here, yet when I try to change his name, his height, his weight and face into someone less Frederick, I never succeed. I can't help returning to the room he occupies inside me. It's empty, with nothing on the walls, not even a window. On the floor is a box of colored chalks I've placed there to force him to imagine his room and sketch a chair against a wall, a sofa in the corner, even draw his own window and fill it in: maybe a city street with a luncheonette and gallery across the street, or a clutch of forest with a path leading into the shadows. But he draws nothing and, as always, he will not speak to me.

Though lately I've noticed Frederick fingering the chalks, and I'm certain that one day he will finally animate his room. When I come to visit there will be a bed drawn on the floor, and a smudgy figure within it left by his body where he slept. On the wall is a shelf, and on the shelf a photograph, though I will not be able to make out the details of the faces. There will also be a window, and a view: a star-filled evening sky, with the dim shadows of mountains on the horizon. His window will look so real he must have tried to force his way through it, because there will be chalk stains on his forehead almost indistinguishable from bruises. I will think that perhaps I misjudged him, perhaps he *had* thought of striking the chair and splintering it in rage and only restrained himself in embarrassment before me. Yet these are thoughts that are not good to think. I won't say one word to him, though he will stand there waiting, and when I leave his room he'll listen to my footsteps down the hall until they can't be heard. He'll wait for the silence to settle and then, if I am very lucky, when he opens the door I will let him make his escape.

▼

Western Russia—Winter 1941–42

The Provider

by Ian MacMillan

A long way from our village we found a building, and next to the building there was a bench with four naked men sitting on it, and their feet were in a horse's drinking trough. Frost covered their hair and faces and hunched shoulders. We walked past. Grandfather Saburov went close. "They're tied to it," he said. "Their feet are tied in the water. I mean ice."

"Why?" I asked.

"In these times the question would be 'why not?'"

He reached out and with his cane lightly hit one of the men on the shoulder. He was as hard as a rock, so that I heard a pinging sound, almost as if Grandfather Saburov had hit something made of metal, or glass.

My sister Anna did not look. Little Maryusa did, with her huge brown eyes, then ran ahead to Grandfather Saburov.

Now we walk across the blank, monotonous plain, so bright that we nearly shut our eyes. A light wind lifts loose snow from the surface like wisps of steam. Grandfather Saburov says that when the sky is blue like this, so huge and blue that it hurts to look at it, the temperature will stay so low that spit will freeze before it hits the snow, that trees in the woods will explode and shatter like glass. He says that snow is a spider and your mind is the fly—it will lure you into its web if you are not careful, and you will end up as cold and hard as those soldiers the partisans killed at the horse trough.

The snow crunches under us with a flat, glassy squeak. The neck of my sweater, where I breathe, is heavy with a block of frost. Anna lags behind. Little Maryusa is ahead, following Grandfather Saburov as a duckling does its mother. We are looking for a place to spend the night, and eat.

Grandfather Saburov stops, adjusts the pack on his back, and motions us to stop. We stand like statues, numb and stupid, staring ahead of us. Anna is moaning behind me, and I turn. Her breath slides to her right, and I can see her eyes in the little hole her hood and sweater make. They are weeping, not because of the usual reason. The brightness is so hard that our eyes run whenever we make the mistake of opening them.

Now I see that Grandfather Saburov is looking at something. I cup my hands around my eyes and make little tubes like binoculars through which I can see without them hurting. In the far distance across the flat, glittering plain is a line of trees and shrubs. In the center there are black shapes. Trucks or tanks or cannon on wheels.

"We must take the chance," Grandfather Saburov says.

"Smoke," I say. My lips feel dead, my mouth slow. "There isn't any smoke."

Little Maryusa says something, but I can't understand. It sounds like a sharp but garbled sentence spoken out of a dream.

"What?" I say.

"Food."

"Yes, Grandfather has food. We'll eat soon."

"Come, children," Grandfather Saburov says.

Anna isn't coming. I turn and trudge back, the snow squeaking under me. "We're going."

"What?"

"We're going."

I turn and walk. Anna stays. "Come on," I say.

"What?"

I repeat it.

"Oh," she says, and stumbles in the path we broke. I know what is wrong. When you stop, you lose your mind. Someone speaks to you, but you don't understand, even the simplest sentences. I think it is the way you'd be if you were a snail, or a plant. I touch my tongue to the block of frost on my sweater. It tastes like wool and spit, so I leave it alone and walk behind Grandfather Saburov and little Maryusa, who look so rich in color that my head swims.

The line of trees is larger. Grandfather Saburov is fifty meters ahead, walking slowly, looking around. I see a long truck with tracks under the box. I see a tank with a white double cross on the side. They are German.

Grandfather Saburov comes back. His breath is shooting out of the hole where his face peeks out. He is winded.

"There are dead soldiers there," he says, waving his cane behind him. "We will rest by the trees. There's a gully. There are horse tracks, too."

"Won't people come?"

"No. I don't know. We must stop and rest."

Anna stares at the trees. She is thinking about our village, a cluster of thatch houses inside a grove of trees like that one. There were only a few families left because of the shootings during the summer. Our parents left to fight with the Soviet army. The Germans came in two tanks and four trucks. They were cold and had no food and took ours. They shot a few people, and then they took sheets from beds and they took curtains and sacks to wrap themselves in. After a day the Soviets found them, and for one day we hid inside an old root cellar while the Ilyushins bombed, and the cannon shells exploded all around. The close explosions sucked the breath from our lungs. Snow and frozen dirt rained on the root-cellar doors. Later there were frozen corpses littered around, creating glittering little drifts in the wind hollows next to them. The Germans left after that, first burning the remaining houses. Grandfather Saburov collected what was left of our food, and for two more days we tried to put our house back together. Grandfather Saburov worked day and night. Then he yelled one afternoon, "Why do you burn a house!" And he turned to us and said, "Because the house is there." He paused and said, "You burn it because you can burn it. We must leave. We are going to the village where I was born." He made us wear so many clothes that we felt like dolls, with arms sticking out that we could hardly bend, and legs the same. We wrapped quilt on our boots; they became so huge that we look like characters from a cartoon, bears or gingerbread men. Grandfather Saburov fixed it so that our blood would move. "You'll need to pee," he said. "That will be most difficult. But you must not get your clothes wet."

Grandfather Saburov tells us that we will build a smokeless fire near one of the tanks. I want to ask what that is, but can't move my lips.

"A smokeless fire," he says, "is one that you keep very small until it is hot. Then you build it up slowly, always keeping it almost white-hot."

Little Maryusa says something in a high squeak. It is another dream-sentence.

"What?" Grandfather Saburov asks.

She doesn't speak. Her eyes are wide and glassy and distant inside her hood, which is wrapped up around her head. Her eyes look like a dog's or a cat's eyes because they show only that she sees, but nothing else.

"Wake up, little doll," Grandfather Saburov says. "The snow is putting you to sleep."

"No," she squeaks, and laughs.

Grandfather Saburov will heat pieces of metal and stones in the smokeless fire, and then we will sleep near them under an oily tarpaulin from the shed. We will sleep where the snow is thin, or not there at all, so the melting will not be enough to get us wet. I see one side of the gully, wheat stubble. There. I sniffle, and my nostrils stay shut.

"I want to look at the tanks," I say.

"Later," Grandfather Saburov says.

Anna looks. "Are there dead men there?"

"Yes," Grandfather Saburov says. "Sitting hard as stone around a field kitchen. The fire went out, and they were caught in the web." He removes the pack from his shoulders and winces with pain, then takes off his gloves and looks at his hands. "Chilblains," he says.

The cracks in the joints of his fingers are scabbed over and oozing little pinpoints of blood. "Dead branches," he says to me. "Dead branches, my boy. Any size, from the bushes or the trees." I walk toward the tanks. Anna walks the other way. She will go any distance for privacy to pee, because she is fourteen. She will go far enough so that the curvature of the earth will hide her. I laugh, thinking how smart that is. I learned about the curvature of the earth in school. Anyway, I saw her yesterday, squatting in a cloud of steam she made.

I break dead branches and twigs from the bushes, seeing the grouping of bombed tanks and trucks. It is like a magnet. I work my way toward them, studying them while I pick twigs, which I put under my fat arm. The twigs snag in my mittens. Now I see the little kitchen on wheels, with the group of men sitting around it shoulder to shoulder, hunched down as if studying something very closely. I can see by the collected snow in the folds of their clothes that they are frozen.

Then I have a strange vision of a man of ice rising from the group and coming to wrap his stone-hard arms around me, his face held in a glittering grin. I am so frightened that I nearly yell out, but stop myself. My heart bangs in my chest.

I see Grandfather Saburov beyond the tank, looking down at something. His presence makes me feel brave, so I walk past the men at the field kitchen, close enough to see exactly the shapes of their backs and shoulders and legs. I see the face of one man, staring at the ground, with ice in the corners of his mouth and in his eyes.

"Look here," Grandfather Saburov says. I look. Another man is lying in a strange posture, on his side in a sitting position, both hands holding a machine pistol nestled against the side of his head, like a pillow. "See? He was sitting with his cheek on it." I look closely. He is wearing no gloves as he grips the frozen metal. "See how the hairs on his fingers are singed?" On the backs of his fingers the hairs are curled up into whitish ash. "The fire was so hot he put his gun next to it and burned his fingers. Then, when it went out, he died just like that. The other men dragged him here." Grandfather Saburov looks down at the man. Now I see the man's face. He is unshaven, and his skin has pockmarks. He has a long nose.

"A gun like that," Grandfather Saburov says. "We could use a gun like that, for protection."

"From what?"

"Bandits, Germans, Kazaks. If the Kazaks found Anna—" He places his quilted boot on the barrel of the gun and pushes. The entire body moves on the snow, a single slab of frozen flesh, seesawing slightly on its hip. Grandfather Saburov raises his boot and brings it down hard on the bluish, bony hand. There is a glassy pinging sound, like an icicle snapped in two. "Mother of mercy," he whispers. The hand snapped off at the wrist, and hovers near the forearm, two centimeters off, almost joined, held by the other hand and the gun on the cheek. The wrist snapped like a carrot. "Mother of God, holy saints protect us," Grandfather Saburov whispers, and crosses himself. Then he brings his foot down on the other fist, snapping it off cleanly, so that I can see the cross section of the soldier's wrist joint, red and white and glittering with tiny points of light. Just like a carrot.

I know what he wants to do. He wants to warm the gun up so that he can get the hands off. "Maybe you can hammer the fingers off."

"I am afraid of damaging the gun," he says. "Mother of God." He leans down and pulls the gun, but it is glued to the soldier's cheek. He reaches under and turns the soldier up, so that he lies on his back with his knees up. Then Grandfather Saburov pulls the gun with the hands gripping it away from the soldier's face, leaving the imprint of the gun on his stubbly cheek. "Merciful Jesus," he says, holding the gun in his hands. It looks like something from a horrible dream, with its four hands. Grandfather Saburov seems to be pulling it from an almost invisible soldier. We leave the soldier with no hands behind. He seems to be protecting himself from a blow.

"We must not let the girls see this," he says. "I will wait until they sleep, and later I will get the hands off and see what valuables these fellows left around."

"How will you get into their pockets?"

"A tool of some sort. But I will do this later, while you sleep. The girls must not see."

Grandfather Saburov leaves the gun near the trailer with no wheels and goes to start a fire. Anna and little Maryusa are sitting on the thin, stone-hard sheet of snow wrapped in themselves, their breaths curling up from their scarves like white fire.

Grandfather Saburov is right. There is almost no smoke. The little fire of twigs burns almost white-hot, boiling the air above it. The radiation feels so strange that we all stare at the fire, concentrating on the sensation of heat.

"And now," Grandfather Saburov says, "we will eat more of the Fat Princess of the Donetz." The Fat Princess is a sow we raised. Grandfather Saburov is an expert at drying and curing meat. The Fat Princess was so huge she continues to last, in dark, salty strips that he keeps in his sack, buried inside the tarpaulin with the other food he brought for the trip— hard bread, cheese, which is now gone, and for him, vodka. Grandfather Saburov is so strong he can carry his own weight without stooping, and now he will add to his loot the beautiful machine pistol, if he can warm the hands off it.

Little Maryusa and Anna now show an alertness that they haven't shown since we ate this morning. Grandfather Saburov adds sticks to the fire, building it slowly without smoke. One of the sticks hisses and puffs smoke. "Ah," he says, looking at me, "a saboteur."

"I thought it was dead."

"It might as well be," he says. "I don't believe there is a soul within half a day's walk. Tonight we shall let the fire snap and spit sap and smoke. The Germans bury their dead. Here"—and he sweeps his arm around him— "the situation has been left as it is without even the appropriate burial of the dead. We are alone, except for their poor spirits."

Little Maryusa gasps and slides closer to Anna. "Are these frozen men like the frozen men at home?" Her eyes are huge. "Can they walk?"

"No, no," Grandfather Saburov says. "The ones at home can't really walk."

"But you said they could," she says.

"No, no, " he says, and laughs at her. "Poor child. No, winter is merely God stopping things. In spring those poor souls will melt into the earth, and the war will go on. But for now—" he pulls his pack to his side. "No more talk about walking men who are frozen. We have bread and dried meat. As for the fire, let it burn. Then you children will sleep near it under the tarpaulin."

"Will we get to the village tomorrow?" Anna asks.

"No. Maybe the day after. We must be careful. Why? What's the matter?"

"Nothing," she says.

"Is it your time of the month?"

I snicker softly and look away. Anna kicks me as hard as as she can, but I feel almost nothing because of the clothes.

"No, it isn't," she says.

"We must be careful," Grandfather Saburov says. "Horse tracks means cavalry. Cavalry may mean Kazaks, Mongol soldiers."

Anna's face is still, her eyes wide.

"Yes," Grandfather Saburov says. "Even though they fight for the Soviet army, they'll take you according to their warlike traditions. It it's ten men, then all ten, and if it's a hundred, then—"

"Stop it," Anna says.

"I am only explaining something."

"I understand," she says.

The satisfaction of eating makes us stupid and glassy-eyed again. Grandfather Saburov, smoking his pipe and taking little sips from his vodka jug, tells us about his war while we get comfortable under the tarpaulin. The breeze blows the smoke away from us, but the radiation from our odd-shaped stones keeps us warm. Grandfather Saburov fought with the Whites against the Reds. If we thought this war was terrible, we should have been around for his war. Then, in twenty-one, the famine. That was just as bad. There were bodies everywhere, and everyone was eating grass, bark, roots from the earth. We drift off to the sound of his voice.

The ice men walk in the silver darkness. They walk with a rigid, jerky step, their faces locked in petrified expressions of lust and hunger for the living, to flood their hot flesh with frost just by the touch of a finger. The ice men want to possess the living. Kazaks on horseback circle our fire, looking at Anna. They dismount, and go to drag her from the fire and fight among themselves to get between her legs. She does not protest. The cold makes her stupid and willing, and I see them hunched over her and moving roughly in a cloud of steam. I cannot move. The ice men hover nearby wanting to breathe death into my lungs and make me one of them. Then I sit with them, petrified, bluish flesh, at the field kitchen. Behind me, Anna sings, and whispers my name.

I awaken sweating. I can feel it trickling on my skin inside the oily shell of my clothing. I feel the presence of Anna and little Maryusa, and lift the edge of the tarpaulin to let air in.

Grandfather Saburov sits hunched over the fire with his back to us, so that the light from the flames creates a bright orange halo around his black form. Smoke slides away from us on the snow. He is doing something. Then I see the muzzle of the machine pistol just emerging from his silhouette on the right. I want to go and see, but I am too tired.

In the morning we eat bread. Then Grandfather Saburov folds the tarpaulin around his vodka jug and puts it into his pack. I walk off toward the tanks to pee. I open the flys of three pairs of pants, and then shudder as I watch the urine bore a yellow, steaming hole in the snow. By the field kitchen, the soldiers are now lying down in their strange, rigid postures. I wonder if Grandfather Saburov found anything of value.

Walking back, I smell vomit. Anna is standing by the fire crying. "The poor girl got sick," Grandfather Saburov says. "Is it the grippe? My lord, you must try to keep it down."

"I'll be all right," she says.

"Very well, but don't exert yourself. Do you have a fever?"

"No."

Little Maryusa walks to Anna and puts her arms around her hips. "I will walk with you," she says. Anna pats her on the head.

"All right," she says. "I'm all right."

Inside of twenty minutes we are stupid and half-asleep again, crunching through snow so cold that it is as dry as dust. The dome of the blue sky sits on the absolutely flat, bluish white plain. That is all there is. Except for Grandfather Saburov, Anna, and little Maryusa, ants, or lost mice. Grandfather Saburov says we see little of the war because soldiers fight at rivers, cities, forests. Out here they would be lost. They would have nothing real to fight for. There is no east, west, south. We are tiny specks inching from nowhere to nowhere.

Anna lags behind. I turn and go back to her. "They're way ahead," I say.

"Who?"

"Come, I'll help."

"No. I can't."

"You have to."

"No," she says. "I'm too cold. I can't."

She looks dizzy and stunned. I call for Grandfather Saburov. The sound of his name dies quickly without echo. He waves us forward. I take Anna by the arm and walk her in the glittering path. When we reach Grandfather Saburov and little Maryusa I say, "She's tired and cold."

"We're nearing a river of some sort," he says. "Trees, shrubs, maybe a village."

"Where are we?" I ask.

"Orel is that way and Bryansk is that way."

"How far?"

Grandfather Saburov holds his arms out in a long shrug. "We will rest ahead."

But ahead is hours. We stumble, fight the deeper snow, barely aware. Finally I see the odd picture of Grandfather Saburov, his cane in his pack and the machine pistol in his gloved hands. We are approaching a village, but there are no roofs on the houses.

Grandfather Saburov approaches the first house carefully and, after a few moments, rises up from his crouch to wave us forward. We stagger toward him. Anna's expression is so vacant that she knows where to go only by the tracks in the snow. When she moves, keeping her moving is easy. When she stands, it is hard to get her to move because she wants to stand. I know the feeling.

We end up in the still, icy hollow of a house foundation. It is littered with charred furniture, broken crockery. There are no corpses. The wind blows snow over the ground like steam. Grandfather Saburov looks worried. "Listen."

We listen. Then I hear it, the sound of artillery, way off over the plain. "That's to the north," he says. I am not sure, but I may hear the sound of engines.

"Tanks?" I ask.

"I don't know, but we can't start a fire."

Little Maryusa begins to cry. "I'm freezing," she wails.

"Get down here under the wind," Grandfather Saburov says. "We'll get the tarpaulin out, and you can keep each other warm."

The broken furniture and burned thatch and the still, perfect little waves of hard snow formed in tiny drifts all around make me colder than when we were outside. It is because we are in a house. Because it should be warmer, it is colder. We sit against a rock and mud wall, and Grandfather Saburov puts the tarpaulin over us. "Stay here," he says. "I'll explore and then we'll eat."

The warmth begins to wake us up. Anna stirs and says, in a quaking voice, "I don't know. If we can—oh, I don't know anymore. I don't know."

Grandfather Saburov returns in a few minutes. "Wrapped up German corpses all in a line, with crosses on them. That's all. I still hear the booms. I will start a fire, at least to heat stones." Using furniture pieces and twigs and thatch, he begins a smokeless fire. Something about the wind sucks the heat from it, and then puts it out. He tries again, and this time it works. But I can't feel the heat. It is stolen by the wind. "This pork'll be as hard as a rock," Grandfather Saburov says. "The bread, too. We may not have time to heat it up if that artillery gets any closer. It'll be dark soon. But chew it anyway."

The three of us sit up. We are hungry. We have been hungry for weeks. The idea of food makes us alert. We begin to chew the dry, brittle meat. Anna chews and looks awake now, staring at Grandfather Saburov's hands as he warms them over the little fire. Her eyes aren't focused on anything. Then she stands up quickly, her face ashen, as if someone has slapped her.

"It is because I *knew* it," she whispers, and begins to cough and retch, as if to vomit. She doesn't. She moves past the burned chair and stumbles over a milk pail, and then goes to her knees and begins praying.

"What's wrong?" I ask.

"Anna?" little Maryusa says.

Grandfather Saburov looks away, thinking inside himself, and muttering softly.

Anna begins to sob hoarsely, her hands on her face.

"Then do you want to die?" Grandfather Saburov asks. "Is that what you want?"

"Yes," she says.

"No, you don't," he says. "We would all be dead if—" He looks away.

Then I understand it. I see the soldiers spread away from the field kitchen, lying in their odd postures in the snow. I see Grandfather Saburov hunched over the fire, with the smoke sweeping away across the brittle ground. I see him preparing for our trip back to our village. The Fat Princess of the Donetz. We finished her a long time ago. He was always somewhere else.

Anna returns and burrows under the tarpaulin. Little Maryusa watches her, chewing slowly. "Don't cry," she says, "they won't get you."

"God in heaven!" Grandfather Saburov says. "None of you would be alive," and he walks out of the house.

I feel it in my stomach. I leave the other part of the dark, now-sticky meat on the littered dirt floor. I eat the bread. Then I think, no, I don't want to die.

Near dark I sit across the fire from Grandfather Saburov. Anna and little Maryusa are under the tarpaulin with their warm stones. "None of you would live," he says. "We do what we must do. We must do it. We can't eat dirt."

"I know."

"We don't kill, or burn houses. We eat to stay alive."

"I don't want to die," I say.

"The sureness of death opens up all sorts of possibilities, do you see? There was a point where I decided we would do this. We are free to do this, if we want to live. Even a man who loves God as I do may be pushed to it. I don't like it, but I like death less. I prefer this to seeing each of you lying frozen stiff on the ground."

"I see."

"In twenty-one this happened all over. It's nothing new. God understands." The fire makes his face look savage, with devil's eyebrows on his forehead.

"Why does it taste like pork?" I ask.

Grandfather Saburov looks shocked. He thinks, as if I have asked a difficult question. "The salt," he whispers.

Under the tarpaulin I can't sleep. The fire is out, the stones are cold. Little Maryusa is between me and Anna, rolled up into a little ball against my knees and forearms. Grandfather Saburov, under his little tent, is near our heads, blocking us from the cold.

I digest part of a German soldier. I see his fiber moving through my stomach and intestines. I don't know what to think of that. I am alive. Maybe Grandfather Saburov is right—we would be dead otherwise. It is absolutely quiet. The ground is so brittle that I think I can hear it squeak and groan from its own coldness.

In hot weather and then in rain and then over ice we wander, seeing nothing. Grandfather Saburov is always a hunched speck on the horizon just at the beginning of the curvature of the earth, waving us forward, and like cattle we follow, sometimes in hot weather, sometimes, not even feeling it, in cold weather so intense that branches shatter, even explode, as I touch them, and fall into the snow in a tinkling sound. I don't wear gloves, or even shoes. A boy I know walks across our path, stops. He opens his shirt. I laugh. He has no insides. Thick strips of muscle run from his hips to his ribs, and I can see the red backbone from the inside. He is gutted like a pig, hollowed out inside, red and glistening. You should have this done, he says. Grandfather Saburov orders him on his way. You should do this, he calls back to me.

At dawn, I feel little Maryusa latched to my middle like a hot leech. Then all at once I know that Anna is not there. Her form is there but she is not. I bolt from the tarpaulin and reach for her.

"The poor child," Grandfather Saburov whispers. I look. Her face is still, hard as stone. Frost is in her eyes and mouth. "She threw the tarpaulin off in the night, " he says. "The poor child. The Lord protects her in heaven now. She sleeps with the angels."

"Why?" I feel light and hollow, and the ground is not level under my feet.

"A little sickness, the loss of will. That is all it takes," Grandfather Saburov says. "She is at that age, I suppose. She takes things too—"

"What age?"

"You are eleven. When you are fourteen you will know."

"What will I know?" I don't know why I say it. It is breathless chatter. "Maryusa!" I say, reaching for her. But she is all right. Still asleep. I rise and look out the broken wall at the plain. In the early morning the snow is blue. The universe is frozen.

Maryusa can't stop talking as we walk. Ahead Grandfather Saburov struggles in the snow, his pack dancing on his back.

"Did she go to heaven?" she asks in a high, quaking voice.

"Yes."

"Was she frozen solid?"

"Yes. It didn't take long."

"When we see her in heaven, will she be old? Or will she be fourteen?"

"I believe angels don't age. She will be fourteen."

"Even if we're old?"

"Yes, I think so."

"Are Mama and Papa frozen, too?"

"No. They're with the army."

"Where is the army?"

In the distance we hear artillery. I almost fell down into the snow when we left her. It was the most horrible feeling of my life. Grandfather Saburov made a charred cross from the chair and wedged it into her folded arms so that it stuck up in front of her face. When we walked away, my legs had no feeling. My hands had no feeling either. My voice was up in the top of my throat, behind my tongue, and when I talked it choked me.

Grandfather Saburov is higher now, ahead of us. The land rises. He is looking at something ahead. Then he looks back at us. Is it the village? I suddenly feel myself shaking with fright and shame.

With a secret look on her face little Maryusa whispers, "Maybe we'll stop and eat more German soldiers."

"What?"

"We're too far away for the ice men to come for us."

"Where did you hear that?"

"Grandfather. I saw him cutting one's leg with the ax, back home. He made me promise not to tell, or he'd leave me for the ice men to eat." Her face is innocent, even happy. "Don't tell," she says.

"I won't."

Grandfather Saburov waits on the rise, looking back.

I walk ahead and then stop. Little Maryusa stands looking at me, and I feel a flash of fright. She is so small. I don't understand how she can make it. I take her hand. "Come," I say.

Grandfather Saburov turns to us when we reach him. He looks shocked by something. His face is pale. I look ahead. The plain sweeps away, flat and blue-white, toward a line of thin, brilliant clouds. There might be a road halfway. Something ripples the flatness. But otherwise, it is so flat and huge that I am numb.

"We are lost," he says.

I pick little Maryusa up, and she throws her fat arms around my neck in one jerky, frightened motion. Her eyes are huge.

"Let's keep walking," I say. "Let's walk."

I look at little Maryusa's eyes. "Do you want me to carry you?" She buries her face in the hollow of my shoulder.

We are lost. It is strange, but I feel comfortable walking, balanced on the petrified ground under me. Little Maryusa is light, wrapped like a crab around my neck. The sky is huge and blue, darker blue straight up, like space, and in the far distance, under the line of bright clouds, I think I can see the gentle, perfect curvature of the earth.

▼

The Big Ear

by Robin Hemley

The Big Ear, nearly as large as Peter, and brightly colored, stands out wherever he takes it, but no one really knows what it is, unless they ask. Peter
practices withering looks on the people who ask, especially if they're kids.
With the seriousness of purpose and steadiness of a Civil War photographer, he stands beside his Big Ear on its black tripod. He pretends to make
fine calibrations on the plastic orange cone, bending into it and tapping it
with a finger. Most people never get close enough to bother him with questions. That is one of the wonderful things about the Big Ear: it is a powerful
device. You can set it up almost as far away from people as you like, two
hundred yards, and it still picks up what they're doing. It can listen through
windows. It can penetrate plaster walls.

A golf course surrounds the lake; the groundskeepers supposedly use
mercury to treat the greens. The mercury leaks down the hill to the lake,
where the fish ingest it, so you're not supposed to eat fish anymore from
here. Before he found out about the mercury poisoning, fishing was Peter's
favorite activity. A few weeks before, he caught fifteen catfish off the dock,
and gave them to a girl he met. He hasn't seen her since, but that, probably,
is just coincidence.

A couple lies by an inlet on the water's edge. They're positioned behind
a nearly rotten log. Peter stands on a hill overlooking them. He feels like
a general observing a sleeping enemy camp. He swivels the cone toward
the couple. From this distance, he can't make out their features. In fact,
he has not seen the woman at all. The man's face bobs above the log, and
sometimes he reaches out and grabs at a slender branch rising from the top
of the log. Dry rattle, then a crumbling sound as he strips the branch of its
dead leaves.

"You've got to call Catherine," the man says.

A duck calls, the water laps steadily, there is a smacking noise like
chewing gum. From somewhere, Peter picks up the sounds of Magic 98.

"Back-to-back good-time oldies," a cheerful man says, then drowns. Something metal-sounding snaps.

"Her dog's dying," says a woman's voice.

The couple bursts out laughing. There's a scrabbling sound, twigs breaking, bodies repositioning themselves. "Oh, God," says the woman, breathless. "That's not what I meant."

"What did you mean?" says the man.

A match flares up and then a long in-suck of breath.

"Now come here. I didn't mean that."

"No, wait. Later."

"What later?'

"Are you going to salad control tonight?" That's what it sounds like. Salad control. Sometimes, Peter can't make out words too clearly. Maybe the man meant salad control. Maybe he didn't. If there's one thing Peter's learned since his mother bought him the Big Ear for his birthday, it's that people speak in code. You could have all the Big Ears in the world lined up, and still you wouldn't be able to make sense of what people tell each other. He figures there's something people aren't telling *him*, the clue to the code. Not his teachers, not his mother, not his friends. Whatever it is, he needs to find out soon, before he's too old. It just seems so strange to him, life, the whole nine yards. That's his mom's favorite phrase. She uses it most often on the phone when she talks to Guido. At two in the morning, three, when she thinks Peter's asleep. But he always listens. He thinks she calls Guido so late not only because she wants privacy, but because she wants to wake Guido up. She wants to aggravate him the way he aggravates her. That's love.

She's not hard to hear. Her voice bounces through the whole house. "What do I want, Guido? I'll tell you what. The whole nine yards!"

"Hey, look at that kid up there," the man says, startling Peter.

"What?" The woman sits up, arms folded across her chest. "Where?"

"Up there." The man points at Peter.

Peter pretends he hasn't heard them. If the man starts toward him, he can run off with his Big Ear before the man's halfway up the hill. Peter goes to the front of the cone, leans inside, and makes a fine calibration. Then he swivels the cone straight up toward the sun as though this was his intended target all along. An experiment: sunspots and their means of communication. When he looks next, the couple is gone, or maybe hiding behind the fallen log.

"Did you catch anything?" his mother asks, coming around to the trunk of her Taurus so Peter can stash his gear. Obviously, he's not carrying a fishing pole. Clearly, he's not carrying fish. But his mother seems to see conversation as useful even when it makes no sense. The obvious can never be overstated. Fishing poles, Big Ears, they're all the same to her. What matters is that she's talking. He heard the word for it last year in sixth grade when he was studying government. *Filibuster.* His mother filibusters life. She filibusters words the way Peter's father used to filibuster beer—to fill up the silence in the pit of his stomach.

"No, I didn't catch anything, Mom."

"Oh well. Maybe next time. We've got to hustle. My class is coming over in two hours, and I haven't even bought the booze. How do I look?"

Over the last couple of months, she's been dressing more and more strangely, and it's a little embarrassing bringing friends over. Today, she's wearing too-tight black jeans and a white T-shirt that reads BUTTON YOUR FLY in bold black letters. Over that, she's got a thousand tons of Mexican silver bangles.

"Shouldn't you wear something a little more conservative to teach in?" Peter says.

His mother smiles as though Peter's given her a compliment and says, "They hate me here anyway. So just answer the question. Do I look all right? By the way, I've got to go to Atlanta next week."

Peter doesn't say anything, but gets into the car beside her. She gives him a fleeting look of guilt, tears at a fingernail. "Oh damn," she says when she sees it's bleeding. "I've got to," she says. "This is the last time, I promise. We're going to try to figure out a way to patch things up. If not, that's it. Finis. *À bientôt.*"

His mom is always trying to patch things up with her boyfriend—if you want to call him that—Guido. Eunuch, is how she refers to him when things aren't working between them—which is always.

"You're going to need a pretty big patch, Mom," Peter tells her.

She laughs and shakes her head. "Don't I know it, kiddo."

"Who's the lucky gal this time, Mom?" Every time she goes, she leaves him with a different student.

"Oh, you mean the babysitter?" Peter cringes at the word. "You'll meet her tonight. Just your type."

That evening, twelve women sit in the living room, nodding like dashboard figurines to the choppy rhythms of one another's poetry. Peter's mom likes him to sit in on her classes so "you won't grow up to be another prick." She doesn't say it, but she could just as well add "like your father." She says her classes are political with a small *p*, never a large *P*. Usually, Peter reads "X-Men" or "Spiderman" during his mom's classes, but she never seems to notice. Just as long as he "absorbs the ambience." She says the word *ambience* with a slight French accent.

Instead of a comic book, Peter flips through his mail-order gag catalogue tonight. This is where he found the Big Ear. While he half listens to the student poetry, he checks off the items he'd like to own: joy buzzers, itching powder, fake vomit. There's also a large group of things that squirt—Peter already owns a squirting toilet seat, but would like to add to his repertoire. Of course, the famous squirting flower is in the catalogue, but who wants something as obvious as a fake flower? There are plenty of other squirting things: a transistor radio, a diamond ring, a chocolate bar. The pictures of the squirting products all show someone innocently bending down to take a peek at a friend's diamond ring, or about to bite a generously offered chocolate bar, or to listen to the latest song on a top-forty station. The results are similar. A jet of water from the diamond ring blows out the offending eye. A flood shoots through the ears of the rock fan. A geyser chokes the chocolate lover. And in each picture, at a safe distance from the mayhem, stands a little cartoon guy with a big head and electrocuted hair, grasping himself around the waist, bent over with his knees locked together. "HA HA HA!" is written in bold black letters all around the ad, and in smaller letters are the words, "Thousands of gags for incredibly low prices!" To own all those gags—that would be the whole nine yards.

Tonight, one woman reads a poem about shopping for boyfriends at the Winn-Dixie. She describes some of her boyfriends as canned vegetables, condensed Green Giants who give her botulism. Her old boyfriends are stretched out in the frozen-food case, lewd smiles on their faces. The guy she's dating now is in the fresh-meat section, a butt steak. Everyone laughs at this part except for Peter. How did they get in the frozen-food section in the first place? he wants to know. Were they murdered?

The next woman speaks so softly everyone has to bend close to hear her poem. She has a lilt to her voice and a Southern accent.

Strikebreaker

Your body,
tied to routine like a turbine,
your private Industrial Age
a cotton gin rakes seed.
Blind workers strive
for a world the bosses would never
know or approve of, a new light, lighter
than air machine,
engineering nearly bloodless revolutions.
Still, I'm lucky knowing,
at least, the factory in which I work.
I agitate, pass out
leaflets, never knowing the real conditions
or understanding your demands.

Peter listens quietly throughout the poem, and looks around to see the others' reactions. Almost everyone looks bewildered, except for his mother. She has her hands in front of her face as though she's praying. The rest of the class looks down at their laps or up at the ceiling. A woman next to Peter picks the shag carpet. He glares at her until she looks up and stops.

Peter looks at the woman who read the poem. She has her head tilted slightly.

No one speaks for a second when the poem is finished, but then there's a yelp from the bathroom.

Peter looks around to see if anyone else has noticed, but they're still thinking about the poem. The bathroom door opens and the woman who yelped sits down on the living-room floor again. She looks a little pale, but other than that, acts like nothing unusual has happened to her.

As everyone starts talking about the poem, Peter gets up quietly and goes to the bathroom to check on his gag. When he lifts the toilet seat, the little red bulb with an eyedropper attached isn't there anymore. He checks around and finds it at the bottom of the wastebasket. Peter picks up the bulb and dries it off with some toilet paper. He unscrews the eyedropper from the bulb and runs some water. When the water gets cold enough, he places the bulb under the tap. Then he screws the top on again and places it under the toilet seat with the eyedropper pointing up.

Peter has nothing against his mother's students. In fact, he likes most of them. He would like to talk to them but he's shy.

He presses the toilet seat gently and a thin stream of water shoots up. Good. Hair-trigger action. The illustration in the catalogue for this device shows a man with his pants around his knees tumbling through the air on top of a fountain that shoots up from the toilet.

The next poem is about cutting off some guy's dick and wearing it around the poet's neck. The woman reading this poem is the woman who got squirted with Peter's gag toilet seat. The woman whispers the poem and her hands shake as she reads. She glares at Peter. She fingers her collar as though the dick is dangling there. She looks like a nun working a rosary.

Peter's mother is staring down at the carpet, shaking her head, rolling her eyes. Peter wants to cover his ears because the poem is so stupid. He sits in a corner against the wall, hugging his knees.

The poet mentions God, sort of. The poem ends with her stamping a foot three times like a horse, slowly, and saying the word *Goddess*.

When it's over, half the students clap, and Peter's mother exhales. "Whew," she says after a moment's silence, "I need a cigarette."

At break, they all go out on the porch. This is where his mother has set up a pony keg for her students and a mountain of Dixie Cups. Peter joins his mother out there. He could have a beer if he wanted. His mother doesn't want him to think drinking's a big deal. But he doesn't want to drink tonight. He wants to watch his mother smoke. His mother always steps out on the porch for her smoke. Even though it's her house, she's considerate of other people's feelings about smoking—and so she smokes outside when people visit.

"Consideration," she's told Peter, "means that you want what's best for other people, not only yourself." Peter wonders why then she doesn't quit smoking, knowing that he hates it.

She's talking to the student who read the poem about the strike-breaker, and Peter stands around listening as though he's interested, but he's really waiting for her to light up.

They start talking and giggling about the poem with the dangling dick. Peter's mother is almost breathless with laughter. "Oh no, not circumcision!" she yells in a stage whisper, clutching her side and holding onto her student for balance.

Peter doesn't understand everything they're talking about. He never does when his mother talks in this language. This is the language she uses with her favorite students. It is a language of raised eyebrows and short laughter, of people and places that Peter doesn't know. It is a language she speaks with confidence. It is the language of absorbing the ambience. Then there is the language of Guido, full of sighs and complaints and accusations. Peter understands neither language; they seem spoken by two completely different people. Sometimes, he thinks his mother is two people—and that neither would like the other if they ever met.

"Don't you want a cigarette, Mom?" Peter says, interrupting them. "Break's almost over."

The student and his mother turn to him at the same time. His mother smiles and says, "Is it? Well, we can take a few extra minutes. This is Nan, Peter. She's going to be babysitting for you when I go to Atlanta."

"I wouldn't call him a baby," Nan says.

"He'll always be *my* baby," says his mom, trying to give him a squeeze, but he squirms out of her reach.

"Cool poem," Peter tells Nan, bobbing his head and not looking at her. "You liked it?"

Peter has exhausted his ability to discuss literature. He *said* it was cool, but she seems to want him to say more.

"I raised him to be sensitive," says his mother, brushing back some hair from his eyes before he can duck.

"Mom, break's almost up," Peter says.

Nan looks at him and then at his mother. "Is he always this conscientious?"

"Always," says his mother, smiling.

Nan shakes her head wistfully. "I wish you were ten years older," she tells Peter. "I can't wait to see what you'll be like when you're thirty. I'll wait for you."

He wonders if she's kidding. She looks serious.

"I'm too fickle," he says. His mother uses that word when she talks about Guido.

Nan and his mother crack up, then Nan says, "Me, too. We were made for each other." But he thinks she's just kidding.

His mother finally takes out her pack of cigarettes. Peter's not sure if the cigarette she's chosen contains the load, but he made sure that one was sticking up farther than the rest when he replaced it in the pack.

"Mind if I mooch one from you?" Nan asks.

"It's not good for you," Peter says.

"What?" his mother says. "It's not good for her, but it's fine for me?"

"You're hopeless," Peter says.

"Thanks," says his mom.

"Me, too," says Nan, reaching for a cigarette. "I'm hopeless and I'm fickle. I sure am learning a lot about myself tonight. I can't wait to house-sit. This should be an enlightening experience. And you're out in the country, too. I love the country." Nan blows out smoke from her nose and then inhales fresh air.

"I wouldn't call it the country," says Peter's mom. "It used to be the country, back when Joel and I first moved here. All that's left from those days is the well out back."

She launches into an extended history of the subdivision, gesturing over the rail into the dark. Peter listens to everything else around him: the trickle and murmur of conversation from the dozen people crowding the porch. The slopping of drinks. The clean sound of the glass door as it slides open. The pumping of the keg, which seems to pump sounds from the night as well: crickets and a breeze and the rush of the highway a mile off.

The pop seems to come from Nan's finger, and all three of them startle. Nan's sleeve is on fire. He just stares at it. This wasn't supposed to happen. Nan stares at her burning sleeve, too, as though it's something she's imagined. One of his mother's other students stumbles over from the keg and douses Nan's sleeve with beer. Then, without a word, she works her way back to the keg and stands in line for more.

"I'm sorry," Peter says, and he is. He meant to blow up his mother, not Nan.

"I'm so embarrassed," his mother says.

"That's all right, really," says Nan, but he can tell she's upset. This has probably ruined his chances with her.

"Why can't I keep violence out of the picture? Where does he get this from? TV? His genes?" She seems not to be talking to Nan, or anyone else in particular. She's gesturing over the railing, as though filibustering the entire subdivision or a multitude, like the pope in St. Peter's Square.

Peter's mother has been gone nearly all week, and she's only called him once, to tell him she arrived safely. She must be having fun, but Peter doesn't care. He's having fun, too. Nan hasn't held a grudge against him like some of the students his mother's left him with before. He stayed away from these students, skulking in the background, blowing up plastic soldiers with Black Cat firecrackers in the backyard. Nan's different. For one thing, she's funny. She's taught him the word *indubitably.* He has no idea what it means, but he loves the sound of it. "Indubitably," she says in a British accent and he cracks up.

With Nan, he listens to sounds closer to home.

One night, Peter sets up the Big Ear outside her bedroom and listens to her breathe. The phone rings and Peter freezes.

Nan emerges from the bedroom, rubbing her eyes. She jumps when she sees the big orange cone in front of the door. "My God," she says, hand over her heart. "What the hell is that?"

"My Big Ear."

"Your *what?*"

"Sometimes, I can pick up radio stations late at night," Peter says, looking at the floor.

"Kind of like a satellite dish?" she says.

Peter runs for the phone so he won't have to explain any more.

"Peter," his mother says, breathless. "I'm in love. I met someone in the airport. His name is Antoine."

"What about Guido?"

"Look, I'm staying another week. Antoine has got to go back to France, and I just can't bear the thought of being separated from him before then."

What about me? he wants to say, but instead says, "What about Guido?"

"Look, are you getting along with Nan? Do you like each other?"

"A lot. She says she's going to marry me when I'm thirty."

"See, I told you she was your type."

"What about Guido?"

"Why this sudden interest in Guido? I thought you hated Guido. Anyway,

Guido's not giving me what I need, you know, the whole nine yards. With Antoine, at least I get nine yards for two weeks."

"I don't get it," he says. It's true, he hates Guido, but his mother can be awfully tricky. He wants to be sure she's finally gotten over him this time.

"You'll get it when you're older. I know it doesn't make sense, honey, but one thing you've got to understand sooner or later is that no one knows anyone else's thoughts. If we knew each other's thoughts, there would be no need for secrets. There'd be nothing to hide, and people always have something to hide. Guido had his thoughts and I had mine, and that's why I've been messed up for so long. That's over. I promise, honey. No more traveling. I have no idea at all what I want now and I don't expect anything from anyone and I've never been happier. It's crazy, but the world's crazy. It's harmless, so don't worry about me."

Peter hasn't thought about worrying until that moment, but he *is* worried about her. When she gets in a mood like this, she can convince herself to do anything. When she returns, he knows, she'll be so down he'll have to scrape her off the floor. She's met Antoine before, though his name was Robert last time and Clark before that. She'll come back to Guido, and she'll laugh and cry at the same time and say, "God, how could I be so stupid? How could I fall for Antoine's tricks?"

Most afternoons, Peter sets up his Big Ear in the front yard of his house. He points the device down the road, though he doesn't always know what he's listening for.

Nan spends half her days out back, practicing her tae kwon do, the house between them.

At night, they sit up in his mother's room, where Nan is sleeping while Peter's mother is away. They sit cross-legged on the bed, and she sings for him, ancient folk songs about lonesome murderers. For someone who's so small, her voice is deep and rich, and suited to songs of backwoods hollows and hangings. He never asked Nan to sing. It just happened the first night after dinner. After that first night, they were friends. She doesn't only sing, but she talks to him, too. She tells him things about her life that no one has ever told him. Not even his mother. She tells him about a trip last year to Europe with a man named Phil, and how they argued, and how he left her in the middle of this bridge with no money and no way to get home.

"What did you do?"

"I managed."

"How could he do that?" Peter asks. He imagines Nan standing in the middle of a giant white bridge with pillars topped by lions' heads, and a bent figure in a trench coat hurrying away.

Peter remembers the day his father left them. They were in the kitchen. Peter's mother said he was threatened by women, and his father laughed.

"You know it goes both ways," he said.

"Yes it does," she answered calmly. "I'm not denying that. It's natural to feel threatened. Why shouldn't we feel threatened? That's the only thing we're experts at, inspiring fear and weathering it."

"I'm not afraid of you," he'd said.

"You're not listening," she said calmly, her arms folded, but Peter could see she was trembling.

Peter takes out a pack of Wrigley's gum from his pocket, but if you look closely at the wrapping, you notice that it doesn't really say Wrigley's but Wriggles. So Peter always feels justified when he offers people this gum. If they're paying attention, they'll notice the fake name and won't fall for the trick, a mousetrap that snaps on your finger when you pull the stick of gum from the pack.

He thinks of the last person he offered the gum to, a girl named Susan MacNamara. Susan wanted to go steady with him a few months back, and he agreed, but he didn't know what he was getting into. One day, she led him down to a gully near her house, to a hollowed-out log where she said she used to sit and think. She told him she had a surprise for him and then kissed him.

"Ow," Peter said.

Susan pulled back. "Ow? Why'd you say 'ow'?"

"I don't know," he said, feeling ashamed. "I thought you were going to do something to me."

"Peter Costello. You're not supposed to say 'ow' when a woman kisses you."

"Okay," he said, and closed his eyes and puckered his lips. But she didn't feel like kissing him now. That's when he offered her the gum.

"Phil sounds mean," Peter tells Nan.

Nan looks up at the ceiling and says, "I never thought of Phil as mean when I was with him. He didn't do anything outwardly cruel. But it was inside of him all the time. To this day, he probably gets a kick out of the thought of abandoning me like that, thinks it made him a man. If I ever see him again . . . All my life I've been involved with murderers. Part of the attraction of the relationship was the pain, but I really think that's the last time I'm going to let that happen. That's why I'm taking tae kwon do, not so much for the self-defense, but for the confidence. I *was* taking judo. Judo teaches you to use the attacker's own force against him, but you know what? It doesn't work. We've been going that route much too long. I'm never going to put myself in that position again. You know that Billie Holiday song, 'God Bless the Child That's Got Its Own'?"

Peter shakes his head, entranced.

"Do you want to hear it?" She starts to sing, but stops and looks at him seriously. "You're not going to be that way, are you? You wouldn't ever leave anyone stranded in the middle of a bridge."

"Not you," Peter answers.

She narrows her eyes and says, "Not anyone."

"Okay," Peter says.

"Promise?"

Peter nods.

Nan bends over and kisses Peter's forehead, strands of her hair tickling his face. He doesn't understand how someone could hate her as much as Phil must have. He imagines himself and Nan together when he's thirty, watching TV, picking up conversations on the Big Ear.

"I like this," Nan says.

"Me, too."

"Men should stay twelve, don't you think?"

"Indubitably," Peter says.

"Come to think of it," she says, but doesn't finish the thought. "Oh, you have gum?" she says, reaching for it.

"It's my last piece," he says. "I'm saving it." Peter puts the gum back in his pocket. He knows how selfish that sounds. He'd like Nan to read his mind, to know she doesn't really want this fake gum. She smiles and touches his leg and says, miraculously, "That's fine. I don't need it."

Peter hears the telephone ringing. It's his mother. He knows her ring, and he knows what she's going to say before she says it, that things with

Antoine didn't work out, that she misses Guido, that she's returning home early. Peter looks at Nan and she looks at him, and for some reason, they both burst out laughing. He wishes that it could always be like this, that he could relay and receive telepathic messages, speak different languages, that distance didn't matter, that every nerve in his body was attuned to the slightest sounds.

ABOUT THE AUTHOR

▼

ROBIN HEMLEY is the author of eight books of fiction and nonfiction. His work has won such awards as the Nelson Algren Award for Fiction from the *Chicago Tribune,* the George Garrett Award for Fiction, *Story Magazine*'s Humor Award, The Governor's Award for Nonfiction from the State of Washington, the Independent Press Book Award for Nonfiction, *Foreword Magazine*'s Award for Nonfiction, the Walter Rumsey Marvin Award from the Ohioana Library Association, and two Pushcart Prizes. His work has been widely anthologized and published in Great Britain, Germany, the Philippines, Sweden, and Japan. His short fiction has been heard on NPR's "Selected Shorts," performed onstage, and adapted into a short film. Hemley's most recent book, *Invented Eden: The Elusive, Disputed History of the Tasaday* (Farrar, Straus, and Giroux, 2003; Nebraska 2006) was named an Editor's Choice Book of 2003 by the American Library Association. An anthology of nontraditional stories, *Extreme Fiction: Formalists and Fabulists,* co-edited with Michael Martone, was published in 2004 by Longman. He is Director of the Nonfiction Writing Program at the University of Iowa.

Turning Life into Fiction has been typeset in Minion Pro, a typeface designed by Robert Slimbach and issued by Adobe in 1989.

Book design by Wendy Holdman. Composition at BookMobile Design and Publisher Services. Manufactured by Versa Press on acid-free 30 percent postconsumer wastepaper.